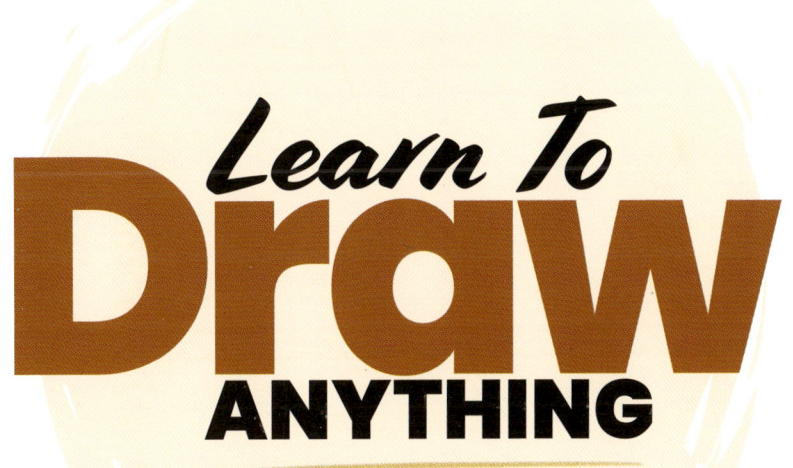

Zoé Leber & Jérémy Hollants

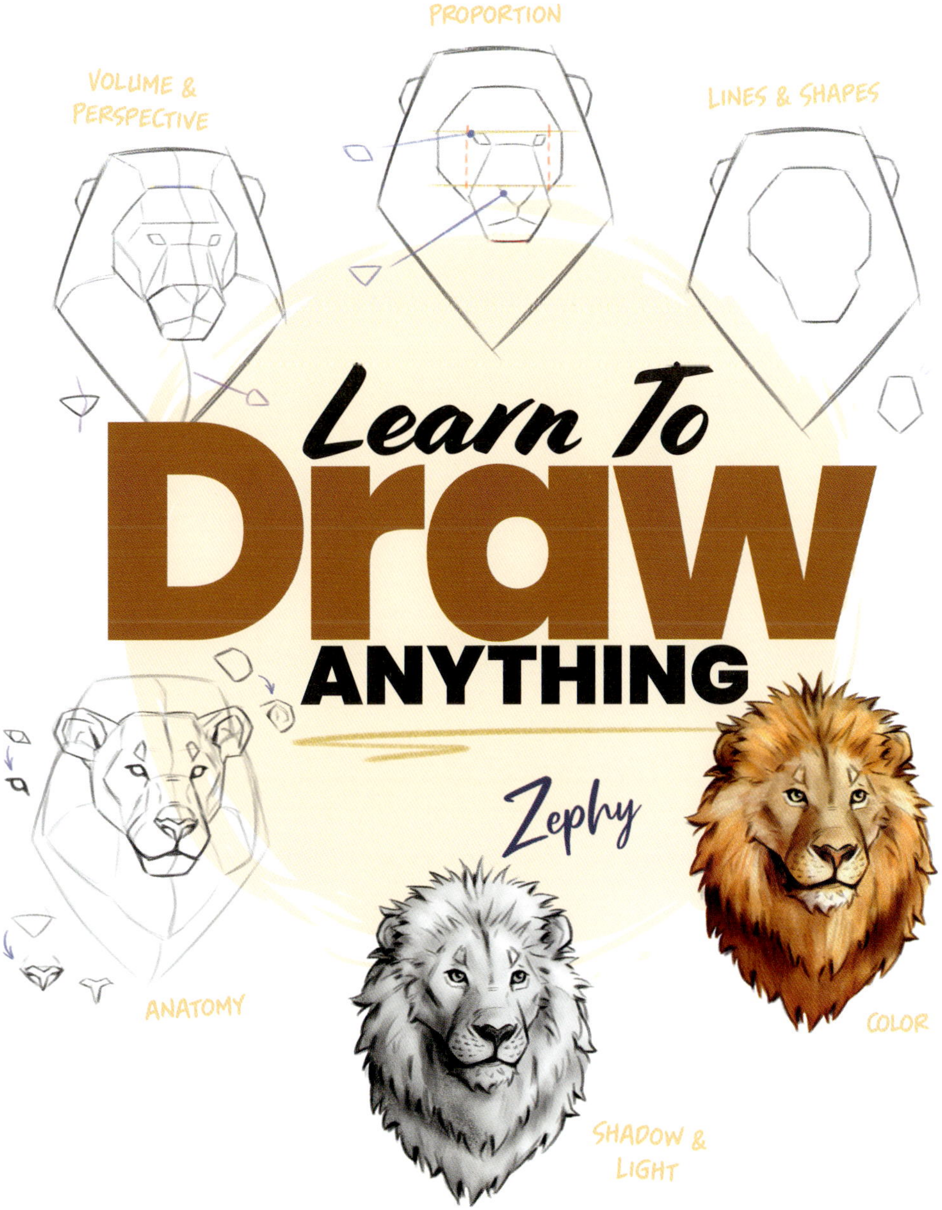

PROPORTION

VOLUME & PERSPECTIVE

LINES & SHAPES

Learn To Draw ANYTHING

Zephy

ANATOMY

SHADOW & LIGHT

COLOR

A SIMPLE METHOD TO START DRAWING IN
15 Minutes a Day

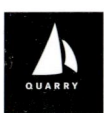

CONTENTS

INTRODUCTION

Drawing is a wonderful tool to express emotions, give life to imaginary worlds, or represent the world that surrounds us. However, jumping into this learning process alone may make the journey seem like a long and difficult one: we don't know where to begin or may even feel lost or discouraged.

After spending years exploring the mechanics of drawing, I realized that the difficulty was often because of the way it was taught to us. I became convinced that beginners would feel more at ease and progress much more quickly by applying simpler methods. Since then, I've accompanied thousands of students online, together in communities of more than 100,000 artists, with great success!

This book is the culmination of many years of exploration of both teaching and drawing. With the help of my companion, Jérémy, who is an illustrator, we've developed clear and efficient tools, giving you all the keys you need to provide a solid foundation. By the end of this book, you will know exactly how to achieve a masterful drawing, no matter what you wish to draw!

Zephy

DRAWING INSTRUCTOR

THE LEARNING METHOD

This book is organized into twelve categories, letting you study each category individually. To keep the lessons simple, imagine that each drawing is a stack of layers. As you approach these categories one by one, you can progressively add them to your drawing.

The Twelve Categories

This book explores the twelve aspects of drawing, from observation to creativity, to get you started on the path to your drawing journey.

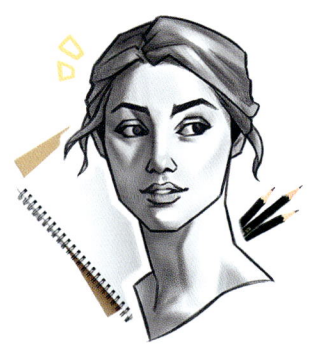

 OBSERVATION

 VOLUME

 ANATOMY

 LINES

 PERSPECTIVE

 SHADOWS AND LIGHTS

 SHAPES

 CONSTRUCTION

 COLORS

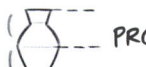 PROPORTIONS

 DETAILS

 CREATIVITY

Transforming Your Approach to Drawing

The goal of this book is to modify and enhance your approach to drawing. Rather than spending hours on one finalized drawing, you'll learn to sketch quick practice drawings. When developing your drawing skills, your progress will depend on repetition and quantity rather than the quality of any one single drawing. By dedicating just five minutes to each practice drawing, imagine the number of drawings that you'll be able to do in one week! In order to draw faster and with more ease, consider drawing on a small scale, 2 to 4 inches (5 to 10 centimeters) maximum, so you can create even more—and thus progress faster.

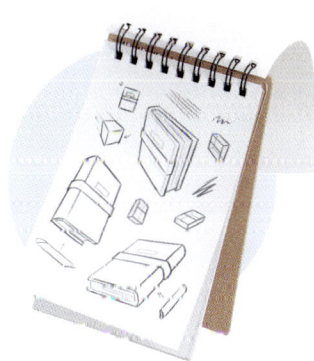

Your drawings don't need to be perfect! Mistakes are opportunities for progress. Have fun with quick sketches rather than looking for perfection.

🖐 THREE GOLDEN RULES

1 **Don't look for perfection.**

Free yourself from the limitations of a hyperrealist style. Of course, drawing from a model is useful for improving your sense of observation, but it's important to liberate yourself to have fun, explore forms, and stimulate your creativity.

2 **Take your time to analyze your models.**

When you create a drawing from a photo, begin by tracing over the model. This approach will help you dissect the image and focus on the aspect that you wish to work on. Utilize the photo as a guide to outline the contours of the model as much as possible, by using tracing paper placed over an image, lightbox, or screen.

3 **Practice the techniques until they become instinct.**

The techniques presented in this book are designed to help you begin drawing and progressing in each category. With practice, they'll become instinctive. Instead of needing to follow each step, it'll come naturally, with almost no effort!

MATERIALS

Beginning to draw does not require costly materials. All you need is some basic provisions to help you achieve satisfactory results. Brand names matter very little. It is your competency, not high-end materials, that will transform your drawings!

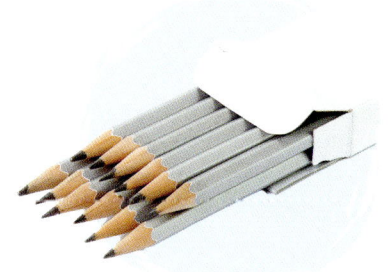

Drawing Pencils

Pencils are an essential tool for drawing. A humble pencil is sufficient to begin, but the goal is to utilize a complete set of pencils with different grades in order to obtain richer renderings with wonderful depth. In this book, you'll need five different types of drawing pencils, mostly for shading, to maximize the contrast of your drawings.

The Five Most Useful Pencils

Pencils are classified according to different grades. The hardest lead pencils, labeled *H*, are ideal for fine lines, while the darkest lead pencils, labeled *B*, are designed for thicker lines and shading.

2H: This pencil is perfect for preparatory sketches and detail work. Its hard lead offers fine and light lines.

HB: You'll use this pencil to revisit your sketches and give a variety of thickness to your lines.

2B: This softer lead is perfect to create contrast. You'll use this pencil for shading and deep tones.

4B: This dark-toned pencil accentuates the contrast of your drawings. It's useful for intensifying certain shadows.

6B: This grade is ideal for polishing your shading and giving that finishing touch to create depth.

Colored Pencils

Colored pencils have many uses. They are used to apply color, of course, but also as training tools. In this book, we'll use colored pencils to distinguish each step of a drawing, helping you understand the various techniques and solidify them in your memory. You can also use them to put the techniques into practice to have a clear vision of the different stages of drawing.

Erasers

* **Classic eraser:** This is the rectangular eraser, gum or rubber, that we all know. It lets us erase lines in a clean way so that we can make corrections.

* **Kneaded eraser:** Soft and moldable, like modeling clay, this eraser is more delicate, picking up the pigment from the paper without abrasion, and it can be shaped to a point unlike the classic eraser. It's ideal for removing your preliminary lines.

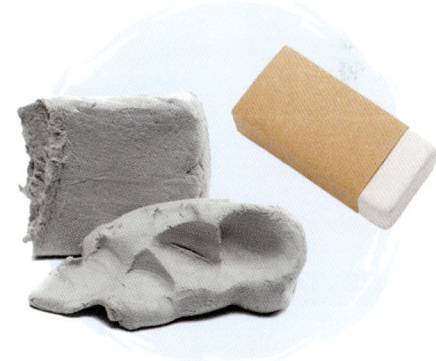

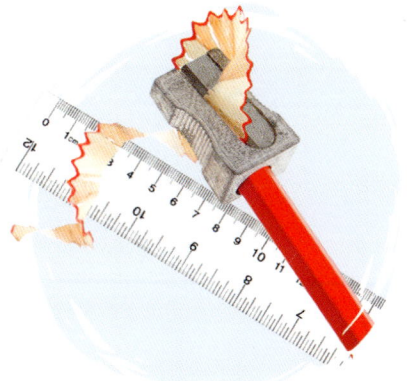

Accessories

For effective drawing sessions, certain accessories are indispensable. A pencil sharpener guarantees that the lead is always pointed, which ensures clean and precise lines. Also, a ruler can be helpful in mastering the principles of perspective if you find that you feel intimidated drawing with a raised hand. You don't need to invest in high-end materials: basic, affordable supplies will do the job perfectly!

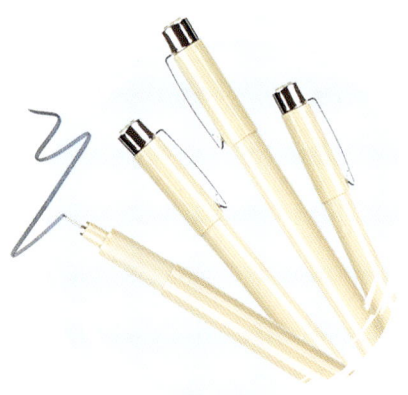

Pens

Pens are interesting tools for drawing because unlike pencil lead, the ink is permanent. They provide an excellent way to enhance and solidify the quality of lines at the final stage of drawing, letting you leave your preparatory pencil sketches behind. While they *do* require a certain mastery and are considered optional during the process of learning how to draw, do not hesitate to try them if interested!

Types of Paper

You don't need to worry about the specific weight of paper when beginning to draw. The most crucial element is to work on smooth paper, such as ordinary printing paper, to obtain clearer lines.

* **White paper:** This is a classic choice that offers complete freedom to draw, thus prioritizing creativity.

* **Graph paper:** This paper can be reassuring for perfectionists who fear the blank page. The squares assist in drawing straight lines.

* **Tracing paper:** This is practical for analyzing models you wish to draw. We recommend using it to examine forms, perspective, and even shadows on the model before you draw it.

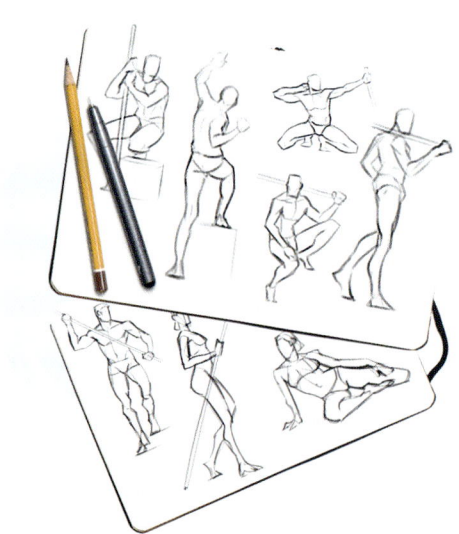

 Use a sketch notebook to keep your drawings in the same place.

HOW TO USE THIS BOOK

The goal of this book is to accompany you step by step as you master the building blocks of drawing, from the initial sketch to the final drawing. To guarantee the best progress and a steady increase in difficulty, we organized this book into three types of page designs.

This book is not meant to be read in one full swoop. It is recommended to concentrate on one concept per day and practice it several times to understand it well.

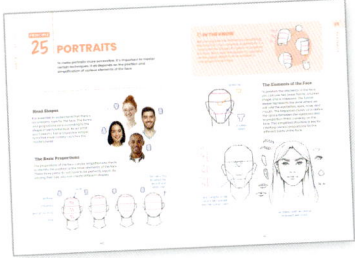

Principles

Each fundamental principle is condensed into one to two (double) pages in a simple format that is easy to understand. Each double page provides one simplified lesson.

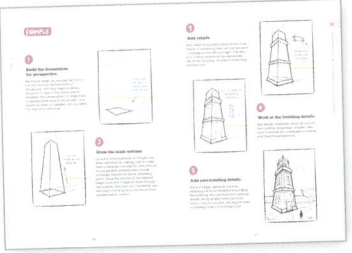

Examples

For more complex principles, additional pages are provided, with examples, to illustrate the full process of executing more difficult drawings, with plenty of tips and advice.

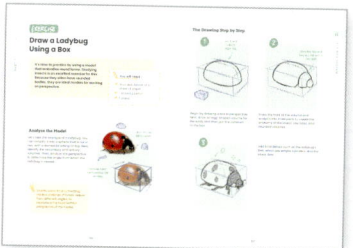

Exercises

Most lessons include an exercise to ensure you understand the principle. Practice them in your drawing notebook.

1

OBSERVATION

01 | OBSERVE LIKE AN ARTIST

The first important step on the path to learning how to draw calls upon your observation. Before picking up a pencil, it's crucial that you take time to thoroughly observe and analyze the chosen model.

Analyzing a Model

To become an artist, you will need to learn to break down what you see into categories. In this way, observation consists not only of looking at a model but also of analyzing the form, proportions, volumes, shadows, colors, and so on.

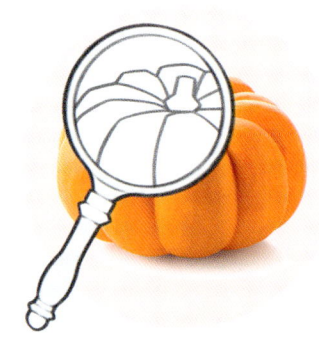

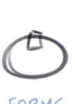

FORMS

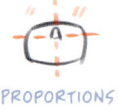

PROPORTIONS

VOLUMES

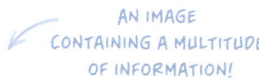

AN IMAGE CONTAINING A MULTITUDE OF INFORMATION!

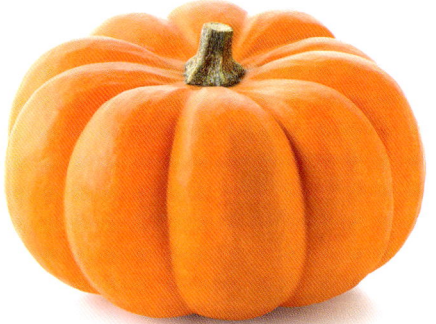

SHADOWS

Learn to observe. This strengthens your ability to sort and prioritize what you see in an object, a photo, a landscape, and the like.

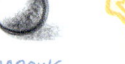

COLORS

Selecting One Characteristic

Before you begin, you'll need to examine your model and divide it into categories. Your goal is to focus your attention on only one category! But how? In your mind, isolate just one characteristic of the model. Let's begin with the simplest of categories: shapes.

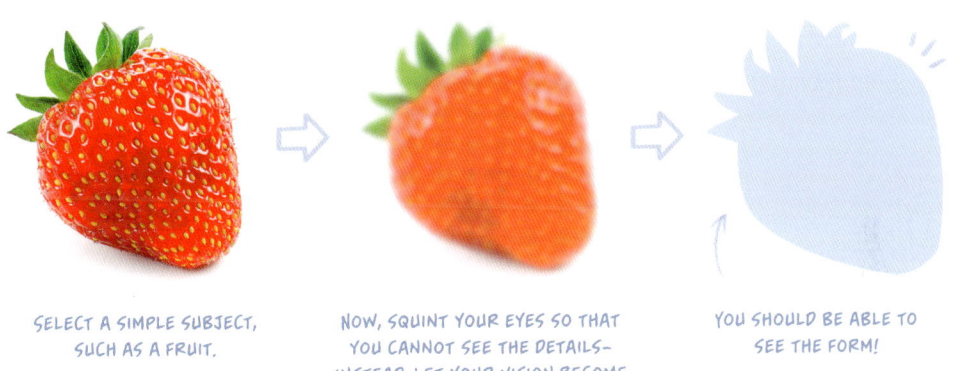

SELECT A SIMPLE SUBJECT, SUCH AS A FRUIT.

NOW, SQUINT YOUR EYES SO THAT YOU CANNOT SEE THE DETAILS— INSTEAD, LET YOUR VISION BECOME BLURRED.

YOU SHOULD BE ABLE TO SEE THE FORM!

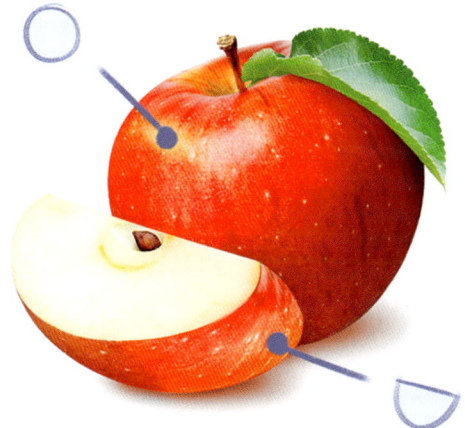

Seeing the World in 2D

To see in 2D, you need to exercise your ability to simplify everything you see into flat, abstract forms. Instead of observing the volumes and details, find the overall shape of the model. This method is perfect for developing your observation skills, gently preparing you to draw.

In 2D, an apple is nothing more than a simple circle, and a quarter of an apple becomes a semicircle.

02 SILHOUETTE

The silhouette is the overall, simplified shape of a chosen model. To achieve a solid base for your sketch, first draw the silhouette. This is a great way for beginners to start, yet experienced artists also use this approach, as it helps to grasp the proportions.

Simplifying Contours

When you begin a drawing, you might have the tendency to focus on the contours of the model and be tempted to reproduce them identically. To improve the quality of your drawings, you'll need to ignore all of the reliefs, or projected details—for example, the fur of the cat here—and focus on the overall shape.

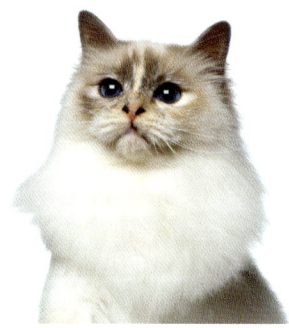 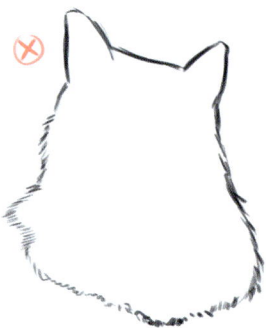 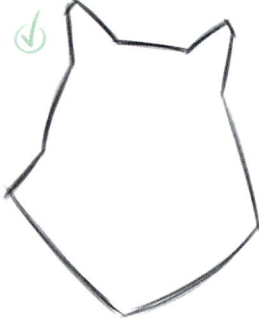

OBSERVE THE MODEL TO REVEAL ITS OVERALL FORM.

IGNORE DETAILS THAT DETRACT FROM YOUR ABILITY TO GRASP THE PROPORTIONS.

BY FOCUSING YOUR ATTENTION ON THE SILHOUETTE, THE PROPORTIONS BECOME EASIER AND FASTER TO DEFINE.

🐾 IN THE KNOW

To visualize the silhouette and better draw it, you can print the image. Tracing over the image will simplify the contours and help you better understand the overall shape of the model. You'll then be able to draw the silhouette by hand—without tracing this time.

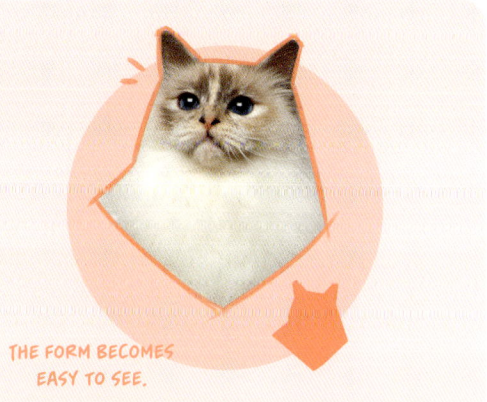

THE FORM BECOMES EASY TO SEE.

Drawing on a Small Scale

For your first sketches, do not go too big! Choose a smaller model instead—it'll be easier for you to define the correct proportions. This way, you can practice with ease: begin with drawings of a smaller scale in your sketchbook. Consider selecting a model that is similar in size to the images in this book.

THE SMALLER THE IMAGE, THE MORE YOU WILL PERCEIVE THE OVERALL SHAPE.

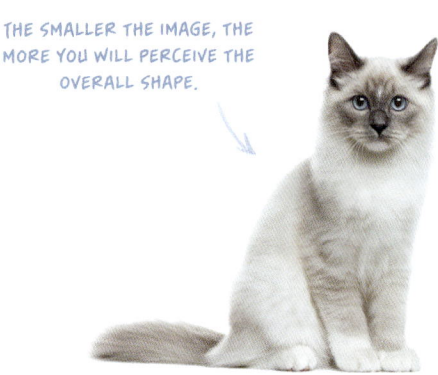

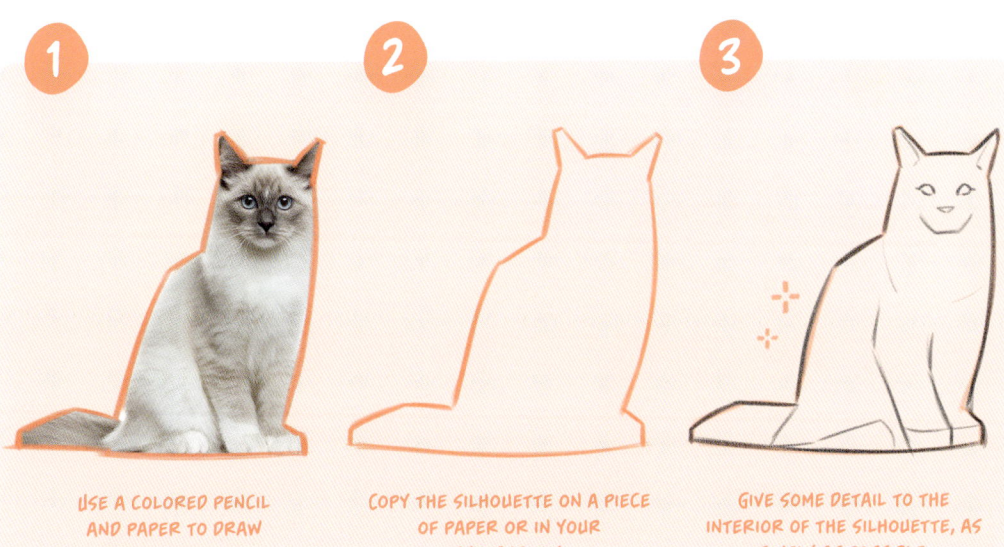

1 USE A COLORED PENCIL AND PAPER TO DRAW THE SILHOUETTE.

2 COPY THE SILHOUETTE ON A PIECE OF PAPER OR IN YOUR SKETCHBOOK.

3 GIVE SOME DETAIL TO THE INTERIOR OF THE SILHOUETTE, AS SIMPLY AS POSSIBLE.

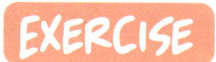

Draw the Silhouette of an Animal

It's your turn to draw! With this first exercise, you have the chance to practice what you just learned.

You will need :

* Your sketchbook or a sheet of paper
* 1 colored pencil
* 1 drawing pencil
* 1 eraser

Analyze the Model

Let's take the example of a fox. The ideal is to print a photo of a fox and then trace the contours of the silhouette over the printed image. Or you can simply observe the image of the model and perceive the global shape of the animal.

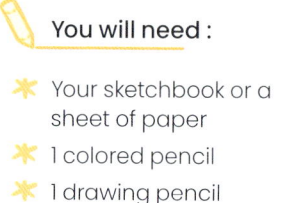

INSTEAD OF DRAWING THE DETAILS OF THE FUR, DRAW THE STRAIGHT LINES.

You can either draw a fox or choose another model. The principle can be applied to any figure.

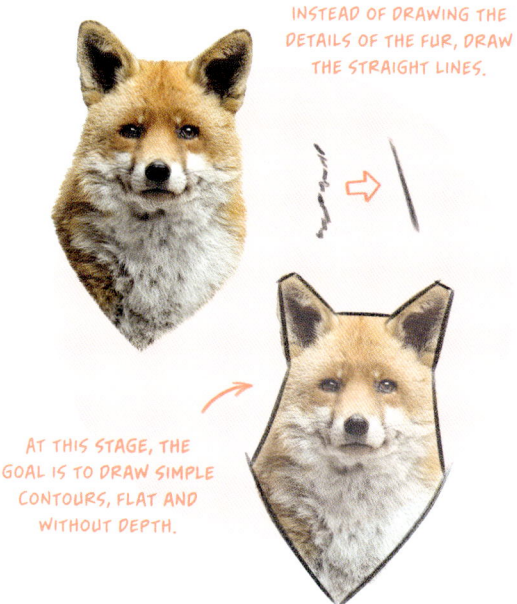

AT THIS STAGE, THE GOAL IS TO DRAW SIMPLE CONTOURS, FLAT AND WITHOUT DEPTH.

The Drawing Step by Step

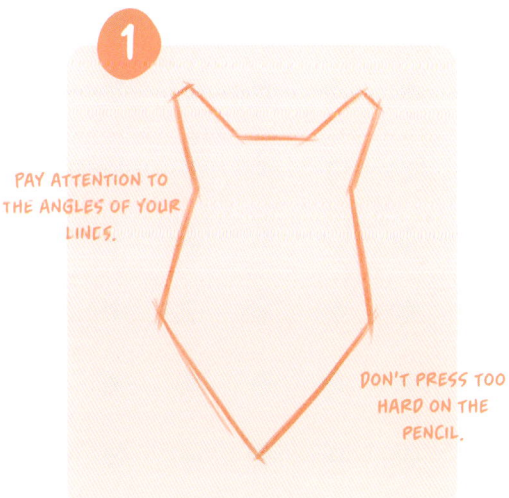

1

PAY ATTENTION TO
THE ANGLES OF YOUR
LINES.

DON'T PRESS TOO
HARD ON THE
PENCIL.

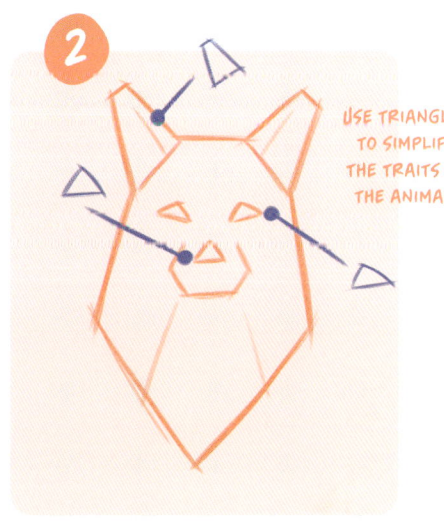

2

USE TRIANGLES
TO SIMPLIFY
THE TRAITS OF
THE ANIMAL.

With the colored pencil, sketch the contours of the silhouette. You can start over several times. You don't have to succeed on the first try!

Lightly erase your sketch and go over the contours with a drawing pencil.

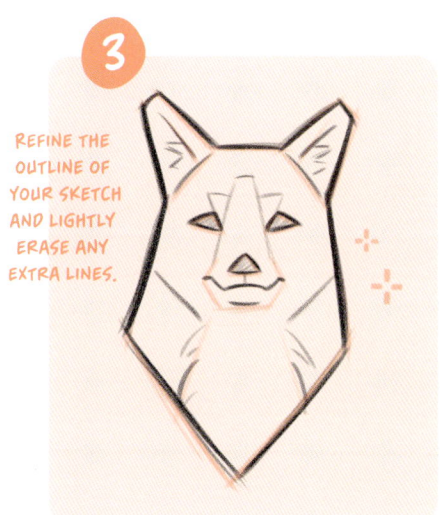

3

REFINE THE
OUTLINE OF
YOUR SKETCH
AND LIGHTLY
ERASE ANY
EXTRA LINES.

For the final sketch, use the pencil to thicken the contours and draw some details. Rest assured that you will further develop all of these techniques as we move along!

2

LINES

03
THE MAJOR TYPES OF LINES

After observing and drawing the silhouette, it's time to learn how to simplify your lines. Three types of lines will suffice: straight, curved, and wavy.

I Lines

Straight lines, or I lines, give a lot of solidity to a drawing.

C Lines

Curved lines, or C lines, are the most utilized lines and help create volume.

S Lines

Wavy lines, or S lines, evoke fluidity and should be used in moderation.

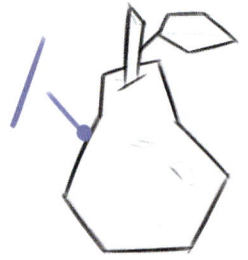
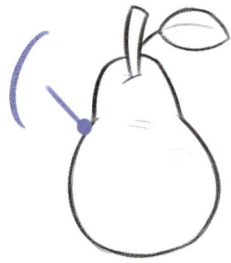
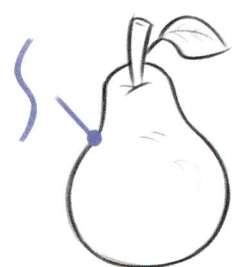

Begin with Straight Lines

Straight lines allow you to get your first sketch of shapes or silhouettes down on paper. These lines are much easier to draw than curved or wavy lines, as straight lines lend better control over the slant.

The lines do not need to be perfectly straight. A light curve makes them more spontaneous and natural.

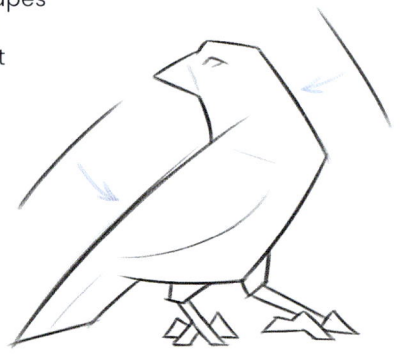

Adding Roundness

When you are comfortable with straight lines, you can add rounded ones. Imagine your drawing as a layered stack. You can begin by sketching the shape using straight lines. Next, go back over the drawing with curved lines to soften the angles. Now, you just need to add some wavy lines, the most delicate of all, to complete your drawing. With each additional layer, the difficulty increases!

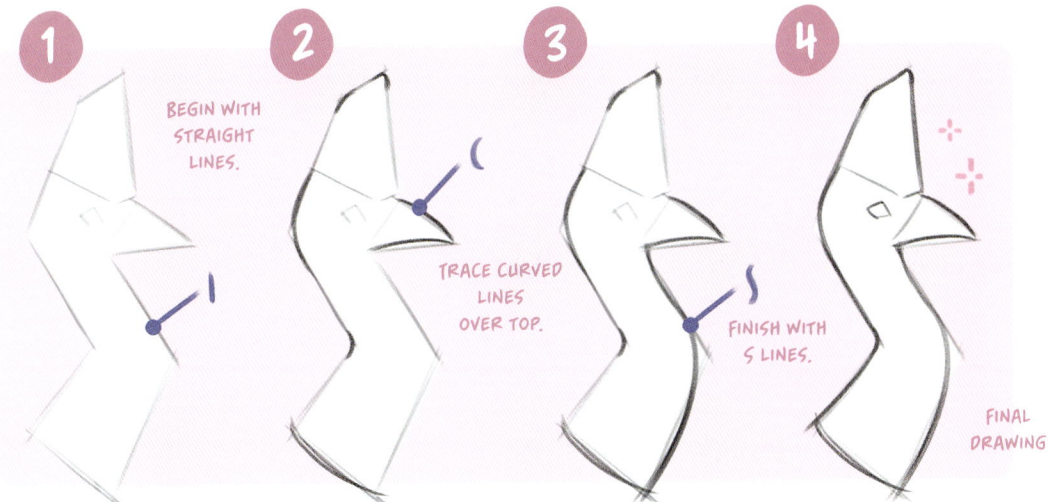

1 BEGIN WITH STRAIGHT LINES.

2

3 TRACE CURVED LINES OVER TOP.

4 FINISH WITH S LINES.

FINAL DRAWING

Combining the Three Types of Lines

In time, you will be able to smoothly combine the three types of lines in the same drawing, making it all the more balanced. The portrait here illustrates this combination: I lines for the salient elements like the jaw; C lines for the rounded features like the neck and mouth; and S lines for the more fluid elements like the hair.

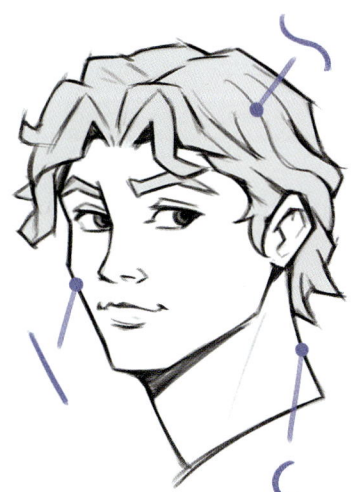

04 LINE QUALITY

Lines are the skeleton of the drawing. Often, beginners draw shaky or hesitant lines. The quality of the drawing automatically suffers from this because the lines are the first element that we see. If your lines are inconsistent, don't despair; it's totally possible to correct this!

Beginner Lines

(X) When the pencil moves too slowly, shaky lines can result.

(X) Hatched lines are the result of a lack of confidence and precision.

(X) One single line, overworked while trying to obtain a "perfect" line, results in excessive detail.

Expert Lines

(✓) Fluid lines are obtained by quick movements of the pencil.

(✓) Uninterrupted, fluid lines are the result of strokes executed in one movement.

(✓) Spontaneous, light lines can be passed over again several times with the pencil.

One Line = One Direction

The first principle to incorporate the quality of lines into your drawing practice is to draw a line in each direction. Instead of using just one line to draw a shape, break the line at each change of direction. This is about the I, C, and S lines. Raise the pencil at each change of direction.

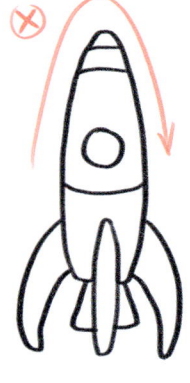

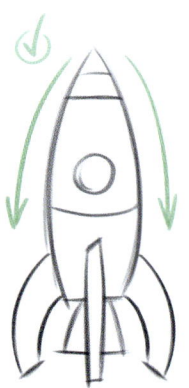

ONE SOLE LINE
ONE LINE PER DIRECTION

Adopt the Ghost-Tracing Technique

To gain in quality, you will need to work equally on precision. How? By adopting the *ghost-tracing technique*, which consists of simulating the line in the air several times before tracing it on the paper. Use this technique before each trace, until it becomes automatic.

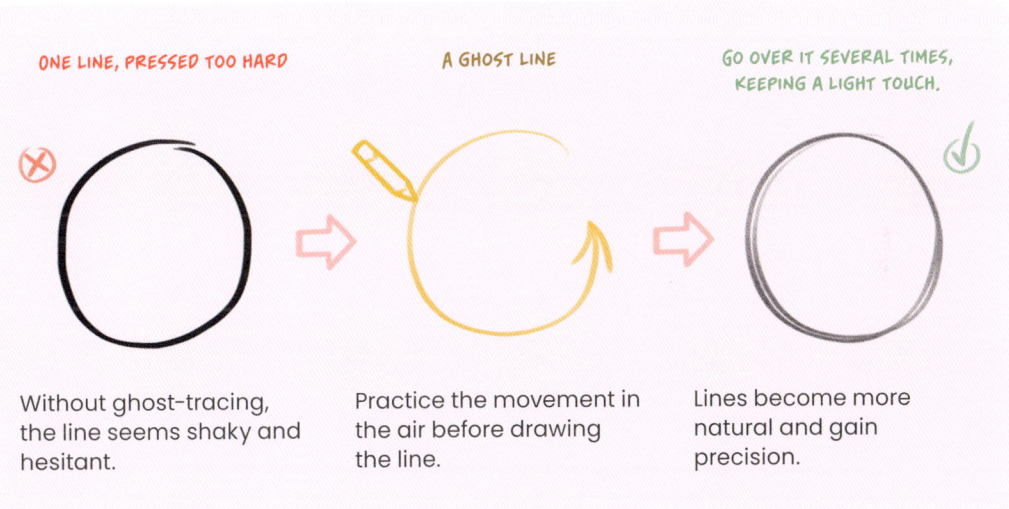

ONE LINE, PRESSED TOO HARD

A GHOST LINE

GO OVER IT SEVERAL TIMES, KEEPING A LIGHT TOUCH.

Without ghost-tracing, the line seems shaky and hesitant.

Practice the movement in the air before drawing the line.

Lines become more natural and gain precision.

The Importance of Warming Up

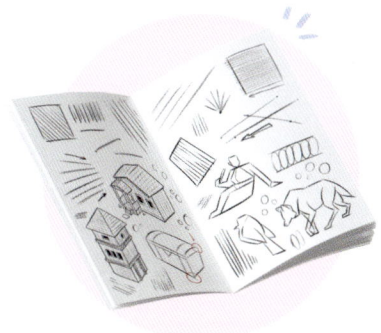

In order to make good progress, it's just as essential to establish a warm-up routine. This helps you gently prepare for the drawing session while limbering up your arm.

Waking Up Your Hand

Warming up lessens the involuntary shaking of the hand and encourages more precise and fluid movement. It relaxes your hand and improves your mastery of the pencil.

Preparing Your Mind

Warming up is like a creative meditation. You'll gain focus as you concentrate on your drawing session, immersing yourself in the present moment and clearing your mind of distractions.

Four Warm-Ups to Improve Line Quality

These exercises are perfect for preparing your drawing session. Take about ten minutes and practice these exercises regularly until you obtain fluid, clear, and confident lines.

Joining Points

One of the most efficient exercises to improve line precision is to draw two points and practice connecting them with a line. For the line, the movement should be fast to obtain a clean line, with no trembling! Vary the angles without moving the paper to strengthen your dexterity and emerge from your comfort zone.

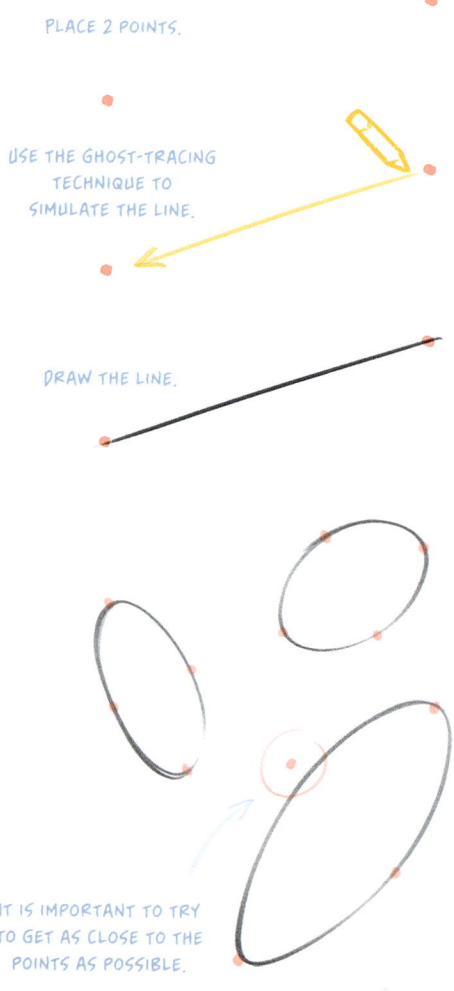

PLACE 2 POINTS.

USE THE GHOST-TRACING TECHNIQUE TO SIMULATE THE LINE.

DRAW THE LINE.

Ellipses

To practice drawing rounder shapes, this time draw four dots. The farther apart the dots are, the harder the exercise. The goal is to draw an ellipse that passes through all four dots. You will not succeed in the first try, and this is normal! Your lines will become more precise by simply repeating this exercise.

IT IS IMPORTANT TO TRY TO GET AS CLOSE TO THE POINTS AS POSSIBLE.

3

Fans

This fun and simple exercise involves drawing a reference line, then placing a dot farther away to serve as a reference point. The goal is to draw several lines from this point to the reference line. Try to avoid going beyond the reference line by controlling the end point.

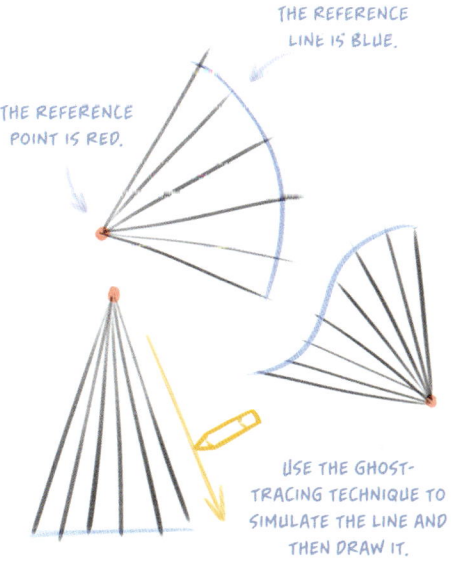

THE REFERENCE LINE IS BLUE.

THE REFERENCE POINT IS RED.

USE THE GHOST-TRACING TECHNIQUE TO SIMULATE THE LINE AND THEN DRAW IT.

4

Parallels

In this last exercise, you'll draw rectangles using parallel lines. Be careful to maintain similar spacing between each trace to work on your consistency. Opt for light lines, drawn with a fast movement. The quicker you go, the less shaky your lines will be.

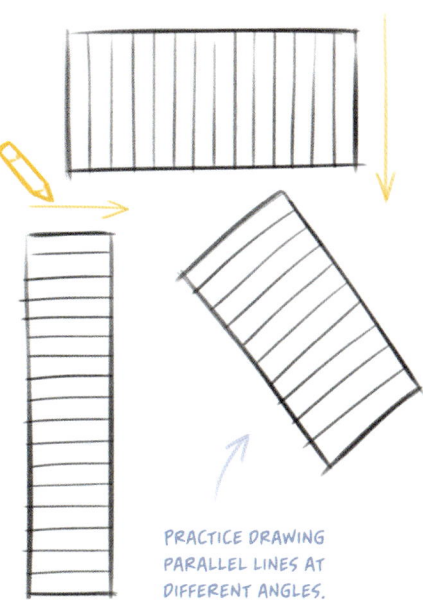

PRACTICE DRAWING PARALLEL LINES AT DIFFERENT ANGLES.

3

SHAPES

PRINCIPLE

05 | BASIC SHAPES

In drawing, we call the most rudimentary of shapes *basic*. This helps simplify the subject by breaking it down into only several lines. There are two types of shapes: geometric and organic.

Two Types of Basic Shapes

Geometrical Shapes

Recognizable, these precise, symmetrical shapes can be associated with several objects. For example, the sail of a boat can be represented with two triangles while a square can evoke the shape of a pillow.

Organic Shapes

Contrary to geometrical shapes, organic shapes are marked by their asymmetry and their irregular aspect. You can utilize these to bring more life and a natural quality to your drawings.

SYMMETRICAL SHAPES: FIXED AND RIGID

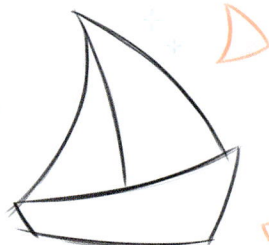

ASYMMETRICAL SHAPES: DYNAMIC, WITH MOVEMENT

To begin, it's interesting to simplify a model into geometric shapes to understand it better. A boat can be broken down into two triangles for the sail and a trapezoid for the boat's hull. By energizing these shapes, the boat becomes all the more lifelike!

Breaking Down a Model into Basic Shapes

Do you recall the principle of the silhouette, discussed on page 18? It's time to go further into the details and work on the interior of the shape. After identifying the contour, you will be able to break it down into several shapes. Each shape will represent a specific part of the model.

1

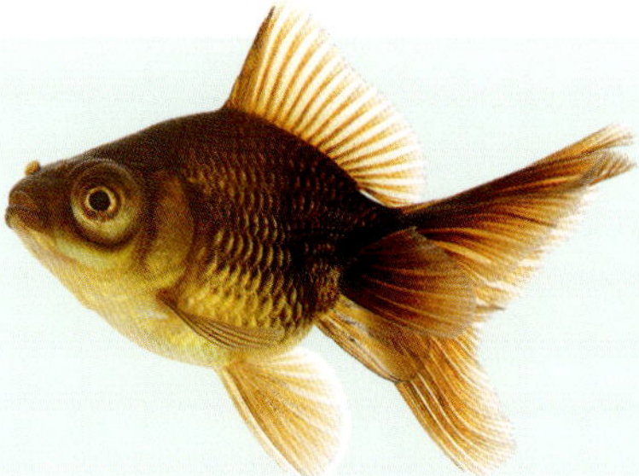

OBSERVE THE FISH.

2

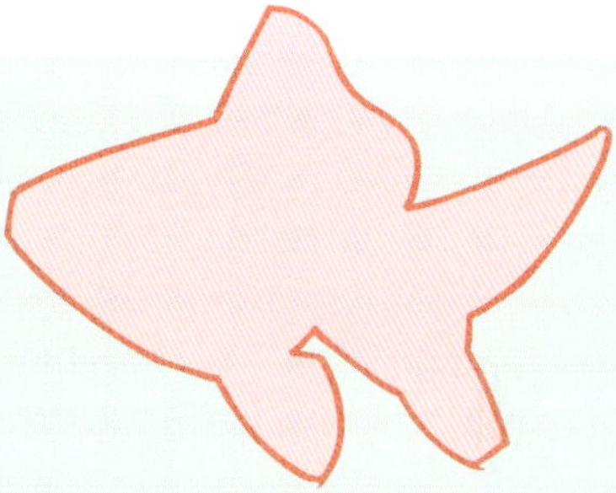

AT FIRST, VISUALIZE THE SHAPE.

3

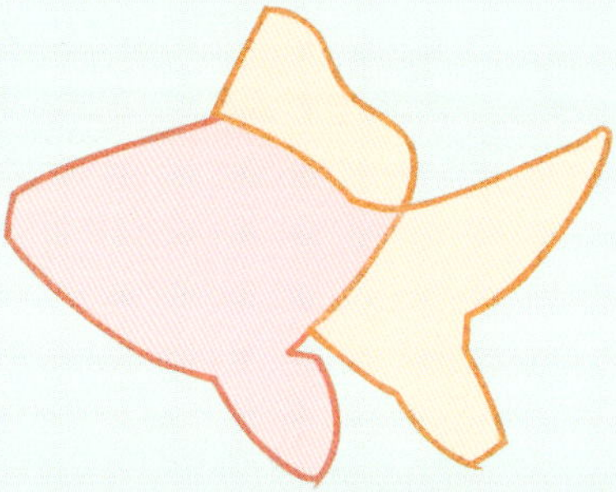

DEEPEN YOUR OBSERVATION BY ADDING MAJOR SHAPES.

4

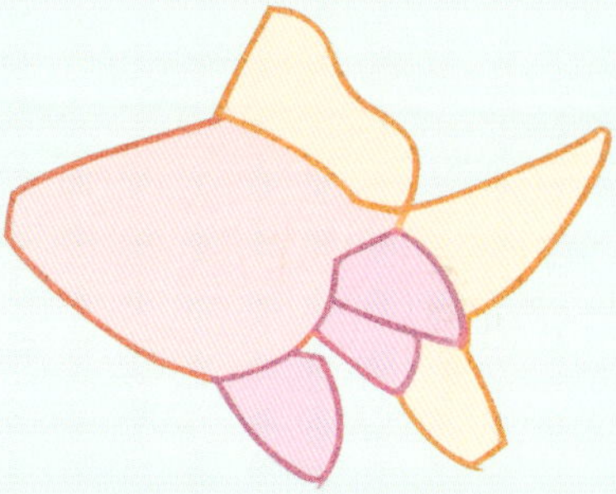

FINISH THE OBSERVATION PHASE WITH THE SMALLEST SHAPES, SUCH AS THE FINS.

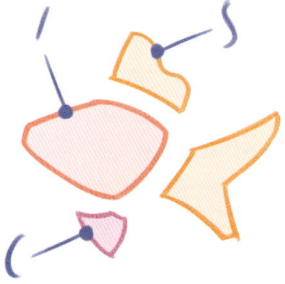

 Here, we combine what we have learned: observe the model and determine its silhouette, break it down into basic shapes, and then draw it with three types of lines: I, C, and S.

Drawing an Object with the Basic Shapes

The moment has come to practice connecting and drawing the basic shapes that compose an object.

You will need :

* Your sketchbook or a sheet of paper
* Colored pencils of your choice
* 1 drawing pencil
* 1 eraser
* 1 pen (optional)

Analyze the Model

Let's examine a lamp. The most important part is to take the time to observe it attentively. Always begin by identifying the silhouette, then locating the different shapes that compose it.

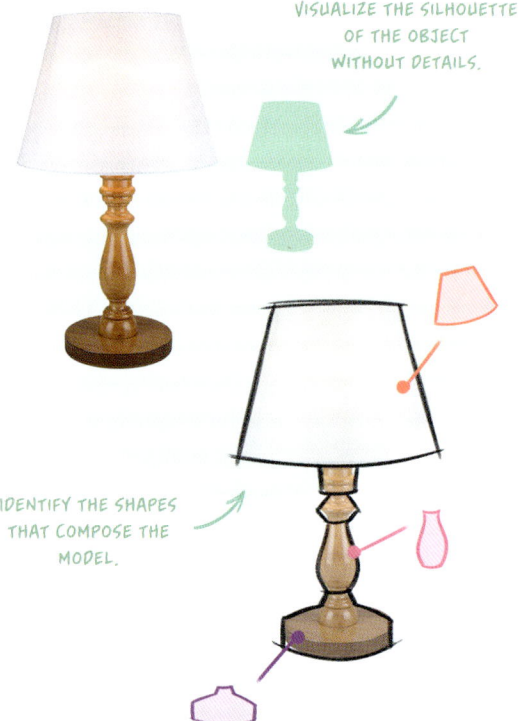

VISUALIZE THE SILHOUETTE OF THE OBJECT WITHOUT DETAILS.

IDENTIFY THE SHAPES THAT COMPOSE THE MODEL.

The Drawing Step by Step

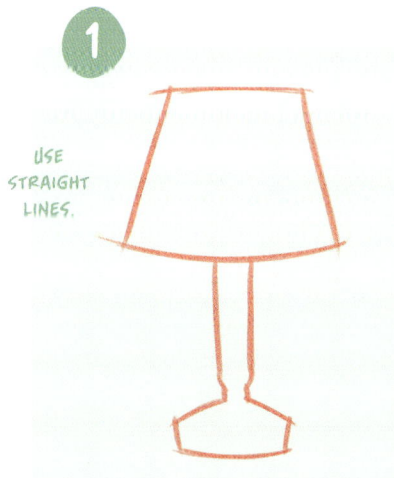

①

USE STRAIGHT LINES.

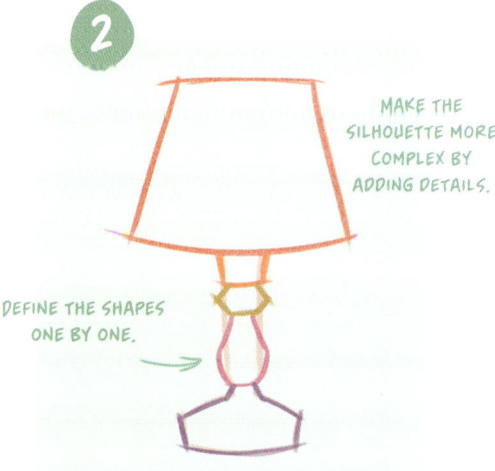

②

MAKE THE SILHOUETTE MORE COMPLEX BY ADDING DETAILS.

DEFINE THE SHAPES ONE BY ONE.

With a colored pencil, trace the silhouette of the lamp. Keep a light touch and simplify the contours while avoiding the details.

Erase the preliminary sketch but keep a light trace of it to draw over. You can use different colored pencils to distinguish the various parts of the lamp.

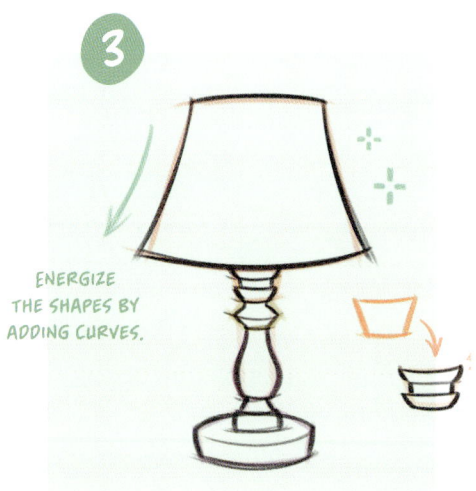

③

ENERGIZE THE SHAPES BY ADDING CURVES.

Lightly erase the sketch lines and use a drawing pencil or pen to produce the final drawing. Give detail to the most important shapes by adding even smaller shapes.

06 PRIORITIZING SHAPES

You've learned to break a silhouette down into shapes. Now, it's essential to learn how to prioritize these shapes, which are organized into three levels: major shapes, secondary shapes, and tertiary shapes.

From the Biggest to the Smallest

The drawing process is progressive: we always work from the general to the particular, from the biggest to the smallest, from the most schematic to the most detailed. This is why we first draw the silhouette, which is the dominant form of the model. Next, we identify and draw the big shapes, then the middle-size shapes. We finish with the smallest shapes, which are often the details.

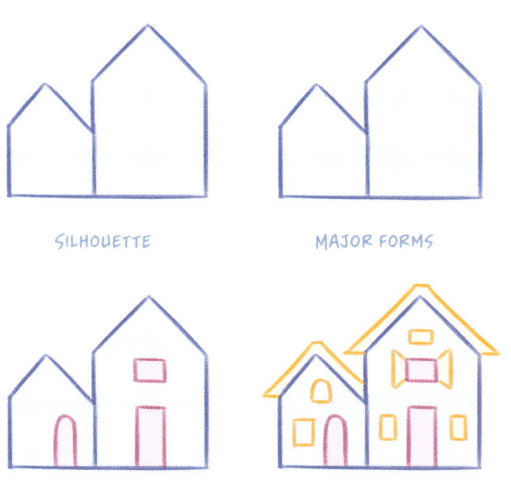

SILHOUETTE

MAJOR FORMS

SECONDARY FORMS

TERTIARY FORMS

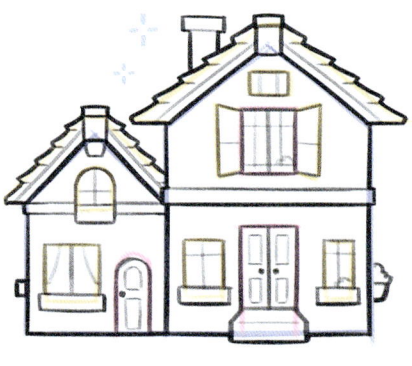

THE SKETCHING OF SHAPES ALLOWS US TO REFLECT ON THEIR PLACEMENT AND TO ACHIEVE MORE SUCCESSFUL DRAWINGS!

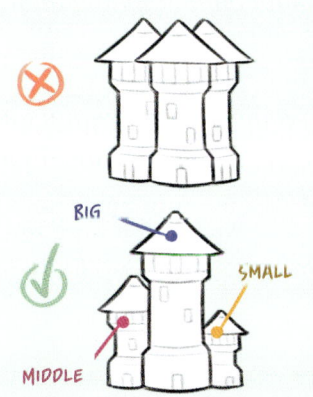

🖐 IN THE KNOW

It's crucial to vary the size of subjects and the shapes that compose them. Take these three towers, for example: If they are all the same size, the drawing can seem monotone and repetitive. Conversely, by varying their sizes, we can prioritize them. Our attention is guided toward the middle tower, which is the largest of all and thus becomes the main subject of the drawing.

First, Second, and Third Planes

Working on superimpositions refines the hierarchy of elements composing the drawing (here, a house, a tree, and a plant). The notion of *planes*—the placement of elements one over the other—plays an important role. Positioning the central element (the house) on the second plane emphasizes it. Placing a detail (the plant) on the first plane brings more life to the drawing.

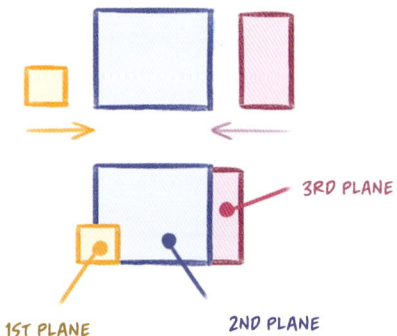

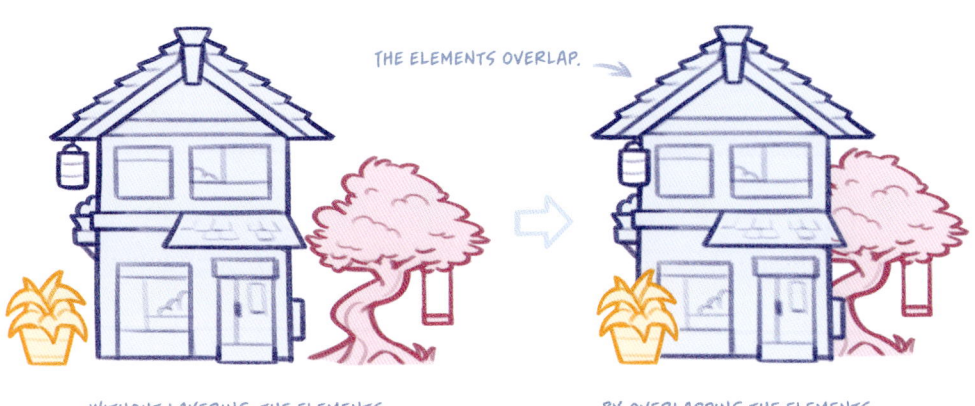

WITHOUT LAYERING, THE ELEMENTS APPEAR TO BE STATIC AND UNNATURAL.

BY OVERLAPPING THE ELEMENTS, THE IMAGE IS MUCH MORE AUTHENTIC.

EXERCISE

Drawing a House with Basic Shapes

Now let's dive into how to create a drawing by prioritizing shapes. The goal is to draw a house step by step, from the biggest shape to the smallest shape.

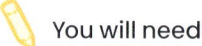

You will need :

✳ Your sketchbook or a piece of paper

✳ 3 colored pencils (1 per shape size)

Analyze the Model

As always, observe the silhouette. Next, identify the basic shapes and classify them by order of importance, into three categories of size: big, average, and small. For example, the roof is much larger than the windows.

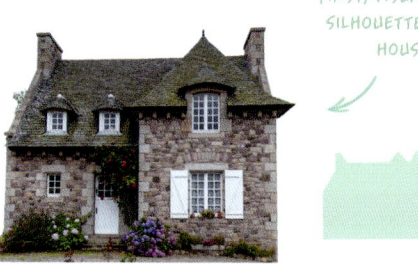

FIRST, VISUALIZE THE SILHOUETTE OF THE HOUSE.

Houses are particularly helpful for this exercise. Use a photo of your choice or follow the step-by-step example of the adjacent figure.

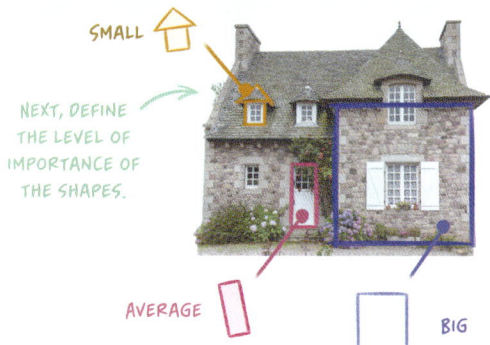

SMALL

NEXT, DEFINE THE LEVEL OF IMPORTANCE OF THE SHAPES.

AVERAGE

BIG

The Drawing, Step by Step

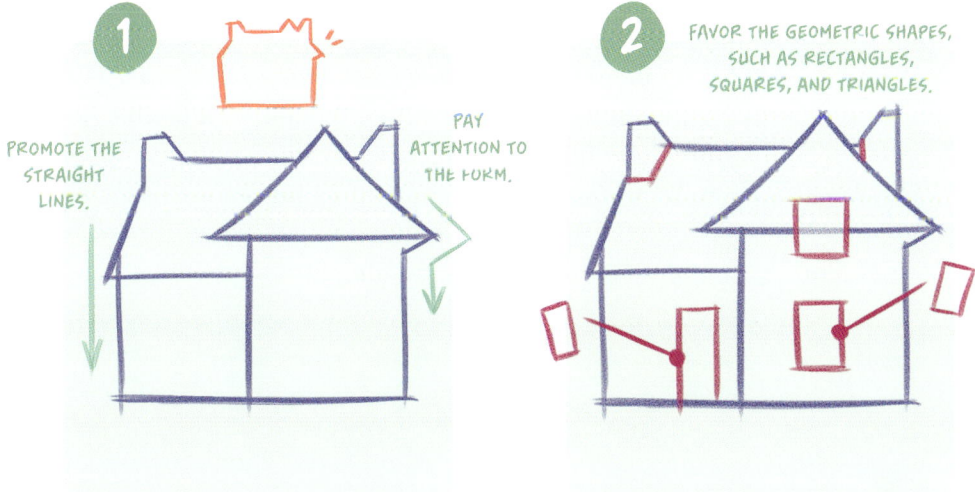

PROMOTE THE STRAIGHT LINES.

PAY ATTENTION TO THE FORM.

FAVOR THE GEOMETRIC SHAPES, SUCH AS RECTANGLES, SQUARES, AND TRIANGLES.

Draw the simplified silhouette of the house (here, in red). Then, work on the inside by defining the largest forms: the roof and structure of the house.

Deepen the sketch by adding the medium forms. Think about all the secondary elements, such as windows and doors.

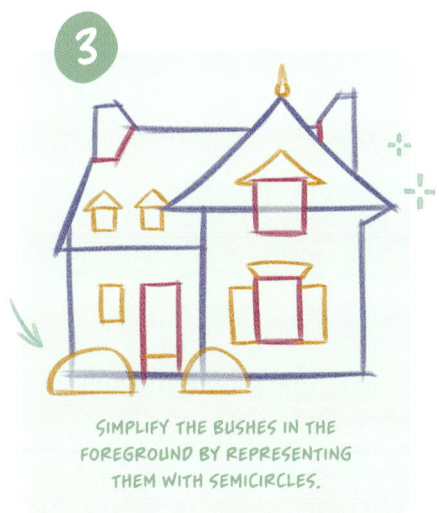

SIMPLIFY THE BUSHES IN THE FOREGROUND BY REPRESENTING THEM WITH SEMICIRCLES.

Add the small shapes using basic shapes, such as triangles or trapezoids. You can even place elements in the foreground!

4

PROPORTION

07 | **PROPORTION**

Proportion determines the way you position different parts of the subject in the composition and give them dimension. It's all about establishing a balance between different elements within the drawing to achieve a harmonious and realistic result.

The Three Aspects of Proportion

Drawing with good proportions requires not only careful observation of the silhouette and the basic forms, but also measuring, by eye, the dimensions of each element. The proportions are correct when these three aspects are faithfully rendered: distance, size, and position.

Size

Giving careful attention to the size differences of the various elements allows you to draw the model in the most authentic way.

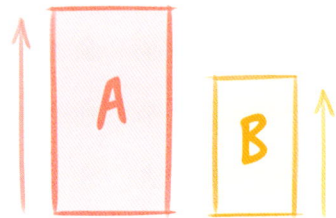

Distance

Respecting the proportions of the subject in your drawing means respecting the distance between each element. This step will be something to carry forward in your drawings.

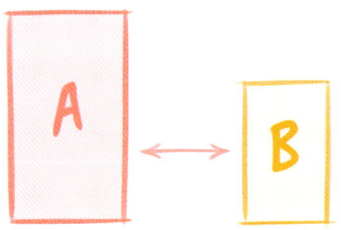

Position

This last criteria involves the position of the elements in relation to one another. You'll need to carefully observe the location of each element in the space.

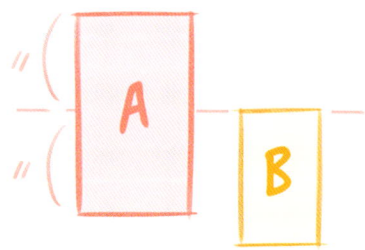

Marking the Height and Width

Now you know the three criteria for respecting proportions, but how do you apply these steps to your drawings? In our experience, the simplest and most efficient technique is to establish correct proportions, which can be done by marking the width and height of the subjects. Mark these points on the photo with two colored pencils, one color for the height and the other color for the width, to best replicate the size of the elements, their distance, and their position.

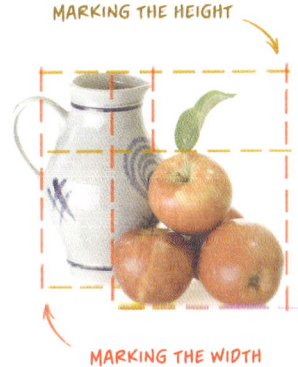

MARKING THE HEIGHT

MARKING THE WIDTH

1 **2** **3**

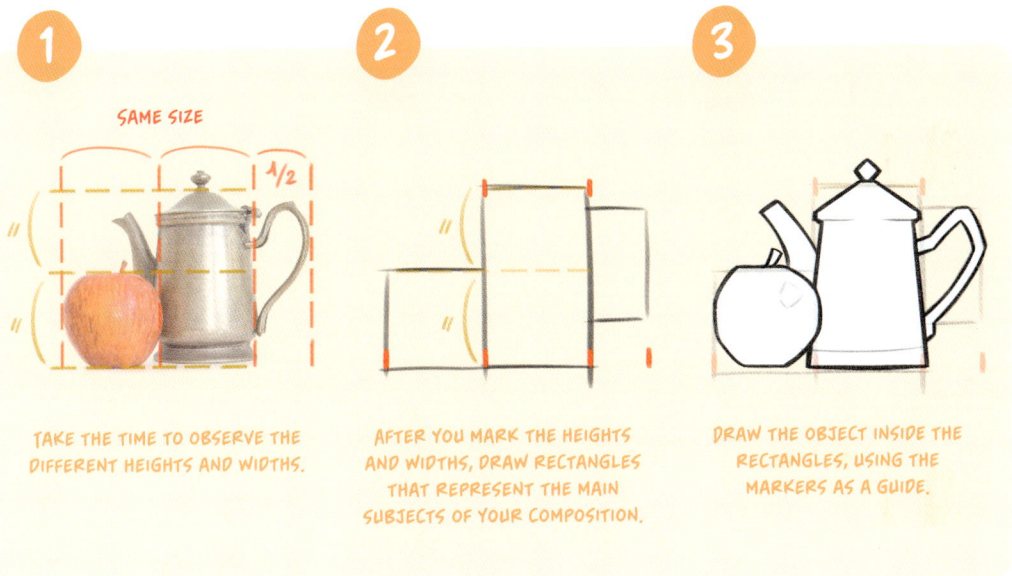

SAME SIZE

1/2

TAKE THE TIME TO OBSERVE THE DIFFERENT HEIGHTS AND WIDTHS.

AFTER YOU MARK THE HEIGHTS AND WIDTHS, DRAW RECTANGLES THAT REPRESENT THE MAIN SUBJECTS OF YOUR COMPOSITION.

DRAW THE OBJECT INSIDE THE RECTANGLES, USING THE MARKERS AS A GUIDE.

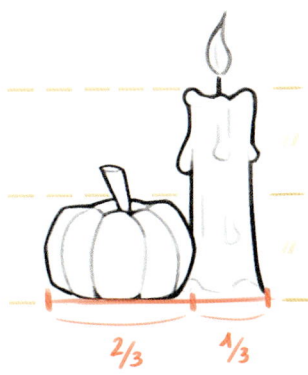

2/3   1/3

Working with Ratios

To correctly place the points, always keep ratios in mind. Instead of measuring the size of the elements in inches or centimeters, you can get an understanding of the scale of the elements by comparing them to one another. For example, in the drawing on the left, the pumpkin is twice the width of the candle—and the candle is twice the height of the pumpkin!

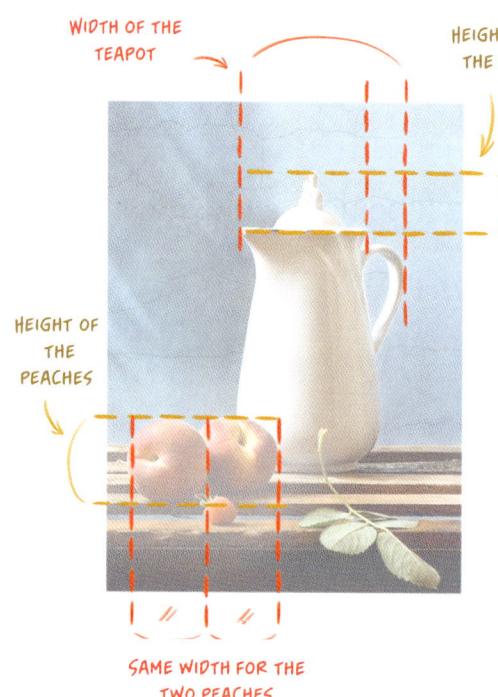

WIDTH OF THE TEAPOT

HEIGHT OF THE LID

HEIGHT OF THE PEACHES

SAME WIDTH FOR THE TWO PEACHES

Using a Frame

As you have seen, it's essential to use points as markers of height and width to get the most correct proportions. To make this step easier, you can use a frame—a simple rectangle—in which to draw the object.

This technique works best when you are drawing from a photo, which is an excellent way to train yourself in the beginning. First, draw the frame using the same ratios in the photo—the relation between height and width should be similar. Next, add the points along the borders of the frame. If these points are positioned well, your drawing will automatically be well-proportioned!

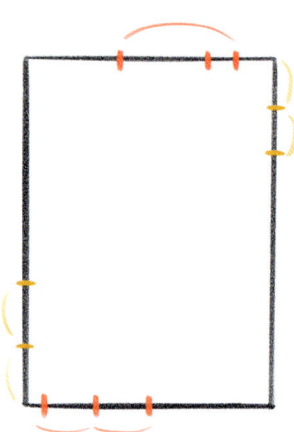

DRAW A FRAME, THEN MARK THE POINTS ON THE BORDER.

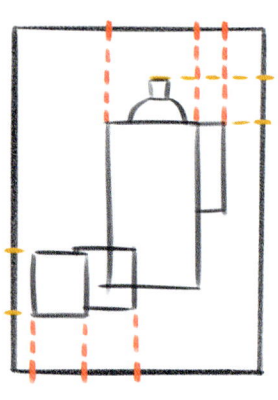

EXTEND LINES OUT FROM THE POINTS, DRAWING GEOMETRICAL SHAPES.

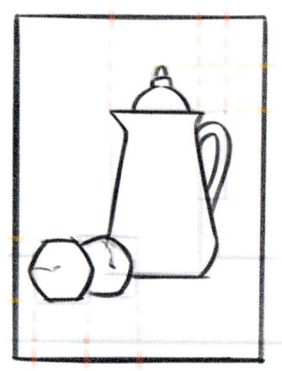

LIGHTLY ERASE THE SKETCH. THEN, DRAW OVER TOP OF IT TO CREATE YOUR FINAL DESIGN WITH MORE PRECISE AND ROUNDED SHAPES.

🔥 IN THE KNOW

Adding a frame makes it easier to respect proportions and also allows you to choose the size of your drawing. Whatever the dimensions of the model may be, the ratios will always be constant! You are therefore free to draw either in a small format or a large one.

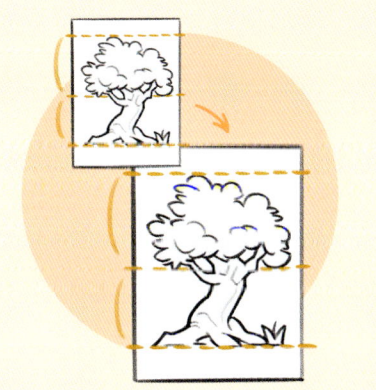

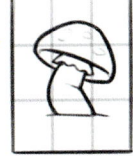

❌ Using Grid Lines

Some people recommend using grid lines to recreate the proportions. Here, you would create geometric grid lines before drawing in each square. We don't recommend this method, however, because it encourages simple copying rather than developing your own sense of proportions.

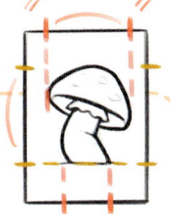

✅ Using Points

Using a frame and points invites you to truly understand the model's proportions. Instead of replicating what you see, you observe and analyze the size of the elements, their respective distances, and their position. Thanks to this technique, you'll be able to draw anything while respecting the proportions!

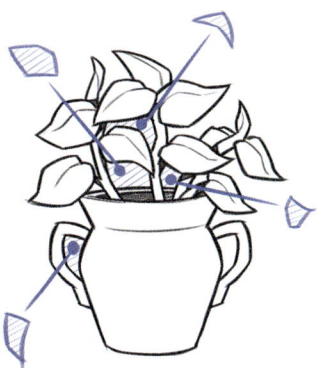

Negative Spaces

One last tool that's useful for creating good proportions is the use of negative spaces. This term refers to the empty spaces between the forms in the composition or the various parts of the model, such as the hole in between the handle and the teapot or the spaces between the leaves of a plant. Negative spaces are helpful when you want to adjust the proportions once the drawing is complete because they also have a shape and a size. Pay attention to the dimension of negatives spaces on the model of your drawing to ensure that the shapes are as accurate as possible.

SIMPLE EXAMPLE

Choose your model.

Let's choose simple models to begin our practice. In this photo, the whale stands out from the background, making its form easy to follow.

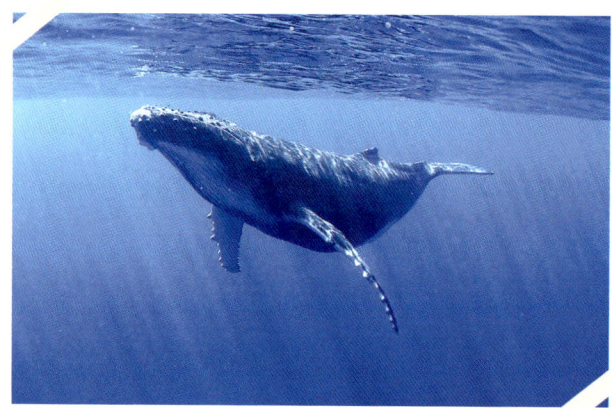

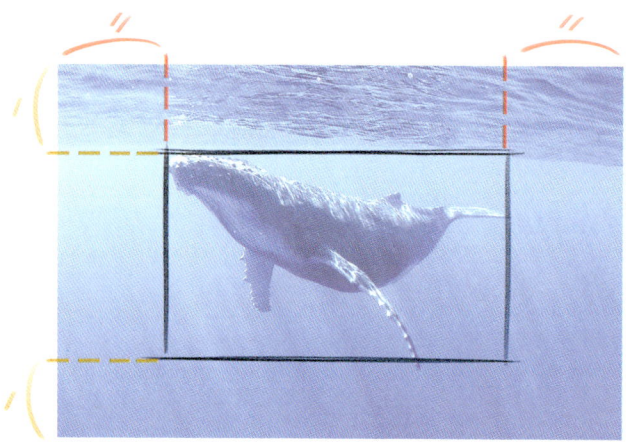

Identify where to place the points.

Paying careful attention to the photo allows you to establish the points. Taking into account the height and width of the whale, mark the points along the borders of the photo.

3

Draw the frame and the points.

Once you have analyzed the proportions in the photo, draw a frame on a piece of paper that corresponds to the dimensions you observe in the photo. Then, add the marks of height and width, extending them out to then create your drawing space—which, in this example, is a rectangle.

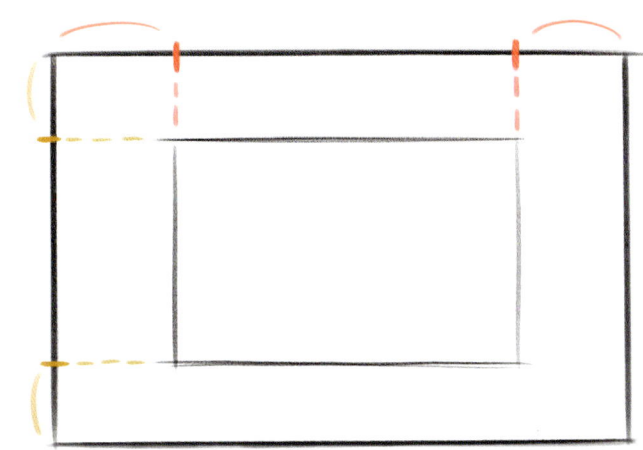

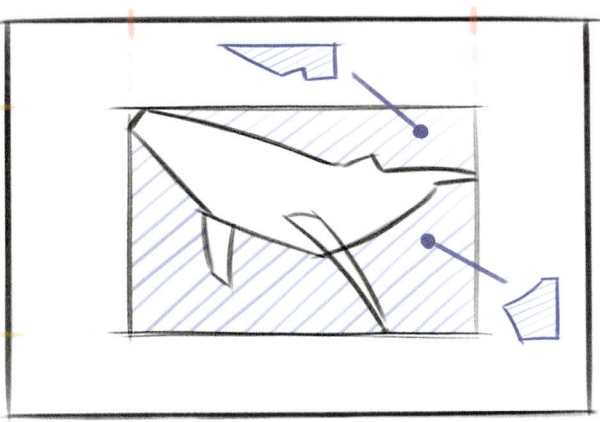

4

Use negative spaces.

Draw the whale with basic forms (see p. 33) and straight lines (see p. 24). You can rely on the negative spaces to give you the best sense of the spacing between the subject and the rectangle (or frame) that you drew. Imagine carving the whale out of a piece of paper.

5

Add the final details.

Now that you have sketched the proportions, you have complete freedom to have fun with the final version by adding curves and details, which we will cover later in this book!

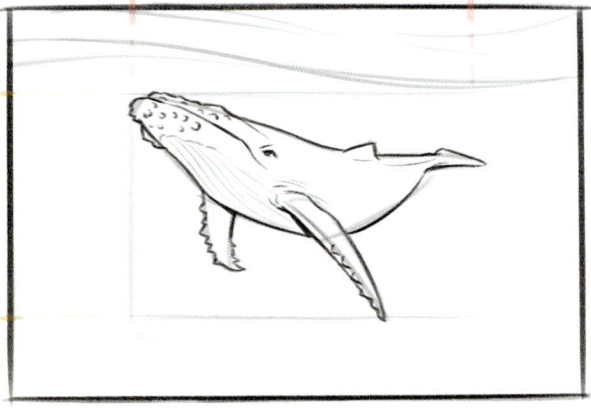

COMPLEX EXAMPLE

Choose the model.

Choosing the correct model is essential for working on drawing proportions. This image, which includes several elements of different sizes, is ideal for practicing placement.

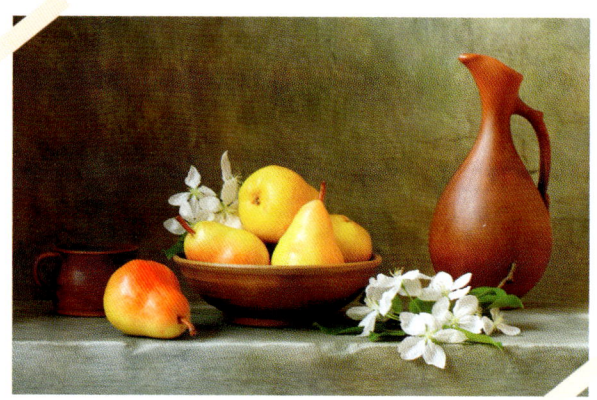

THE OBJECTS OVERLAP!

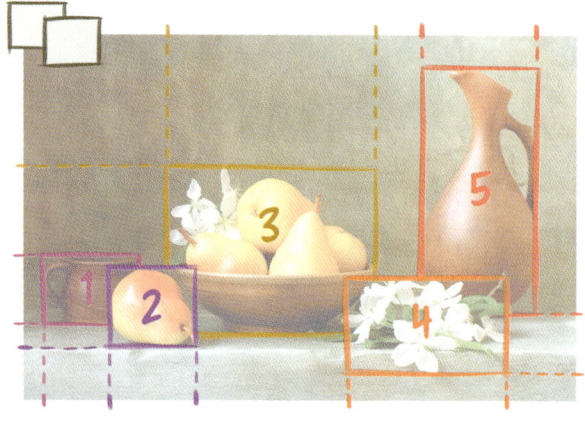

Identify the markers.

Before drawing, always take the time to analyze the image to identify the main forms. Next, mark the height and width on the borders of the photo.

Simplifying the object using a rectangle makes its placement in the composition much easier.

Draw the frame and the points.

Begin this phase of the drawing with the frame. Next, place the points as we did in the second step of analysis. This helps mark the zones where you'll draw each element, all while respecting their proportions.

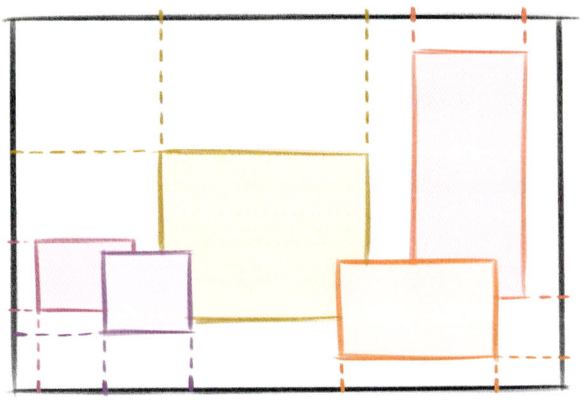

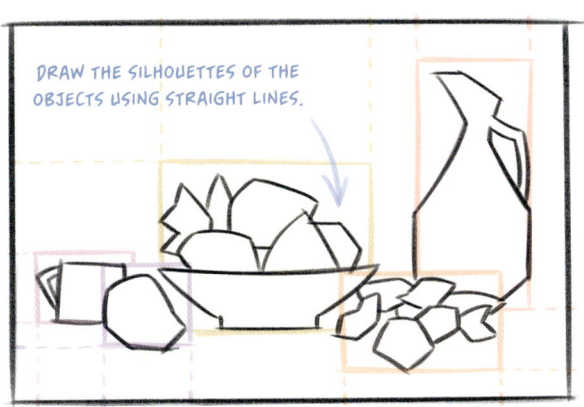

DRAW THE SILHOUETTES OF THE OBJECTS USING STRAIGHT LINES.

Use negative spaces.

It's easiest to draw the elements of the composition by using rectangles: simply draw inside them! Ideally, you'll let the negative spaces help you to sculpt the forms and maintain realistic proportions.

Add the final details.

The last step is to focus on the curves and details. Lightly erase the sketch, then draw over top of it using a pencil or pen, giving more finesse to the lines.

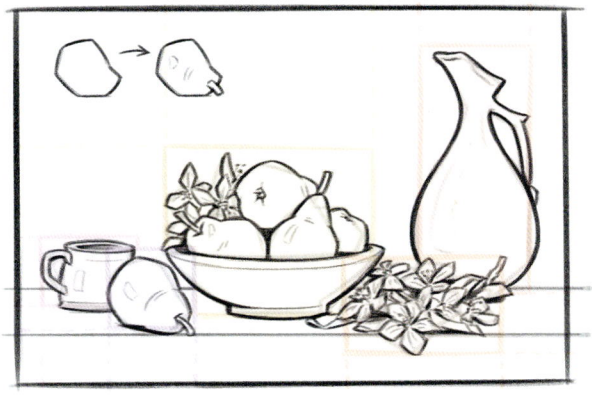

Draw a Still Life to Practice Proportion

To practice proportion, a composition with at least two elements of different sizes is ideal. Still lifes, especially fruits or everyday objects, lend themselves wonderfully to this exercise.

You will need :

* Your sketchbook or a piece of paper
* 2 colored pencils
* 1 drawing pencil
* 1 eraser

Analyze the Model

As in the two preceding examples, we always begin by observing the model. Mark the points of height and width. Keep in mind the principles of the silhouette and basic shapes. The work of proportions can be thought of as an additional tool: adding this to our skill set enhances our proficiency.

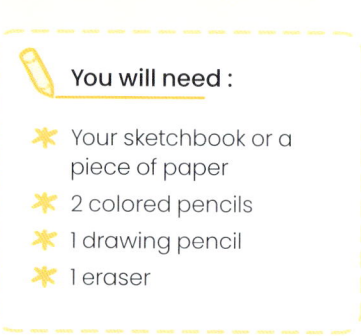

KEEP IN MIND THE PRINCIPLE OF BASIC SHAPES.

You are free to draw (or not) a frame for this exercise. When we draw anything based on an image, a frame provides a helpful guide, although it's not necessary.

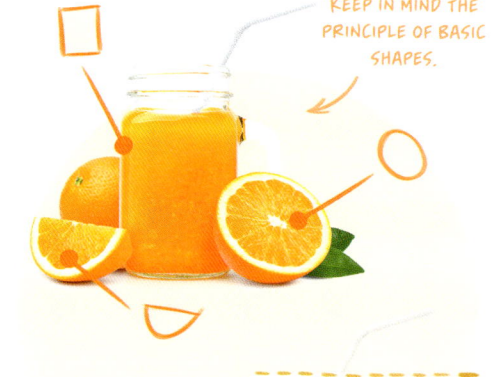

ANALYZE THE SIZE AND POSITION OF EACH ELEMENT.

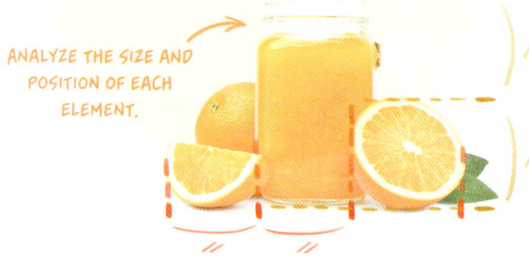

The Drawing Step by Step

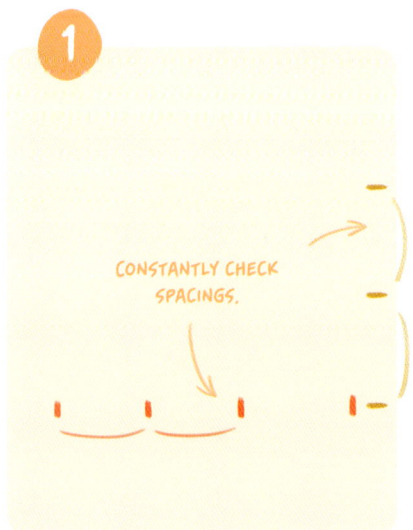

CONSTANTLY CHECK SPACINGS.

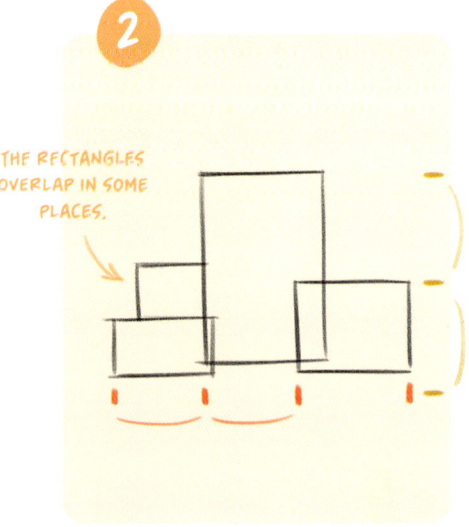

THE RECTANGLES OVERLAP IN SOME PLACES.

Mark the points with colored pencils. The goal is to estimate the height and width of each element in the composition.

Draw rectangles for each element, correcting their dimensions as needed.

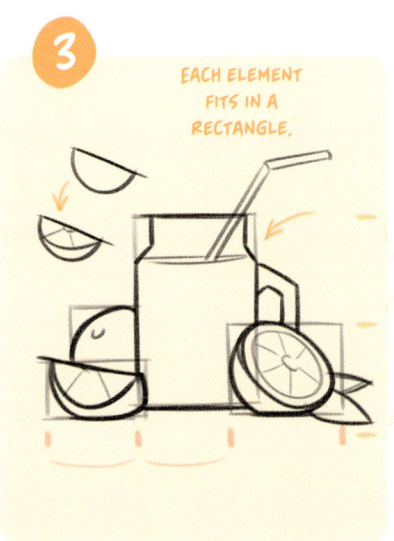

EACH ELEMENT FITS IN A RECTANGLE.

The only thing left to do is use a pencil to fine-tune the sketches you made in the rectangles. Use simple shapes and take care to simplify the lines (I, C, and S).

5

VOLUME

PRINCIPLE

08 | GRID

To draw a grid, we visualize imaginary lines that follow an object's surface and draw them in to help us portray volume. This is an important technique for focusing on volume and working in 3D (three dimensions). The grids you draw will not be visible in your final drawings, but they'll help you to enhance your understanding of dimension.

Moving from 2D to 3D

So far, we've explored silhouettes, simple forms, and proportions. To summarize, you learned to draw in a simple way—in two dimensions. It's time to add a new dimension to your drawings using the grid. A grid will allow you to give relief, or dimension, to your sketches, bringing them from 2D to 3D!

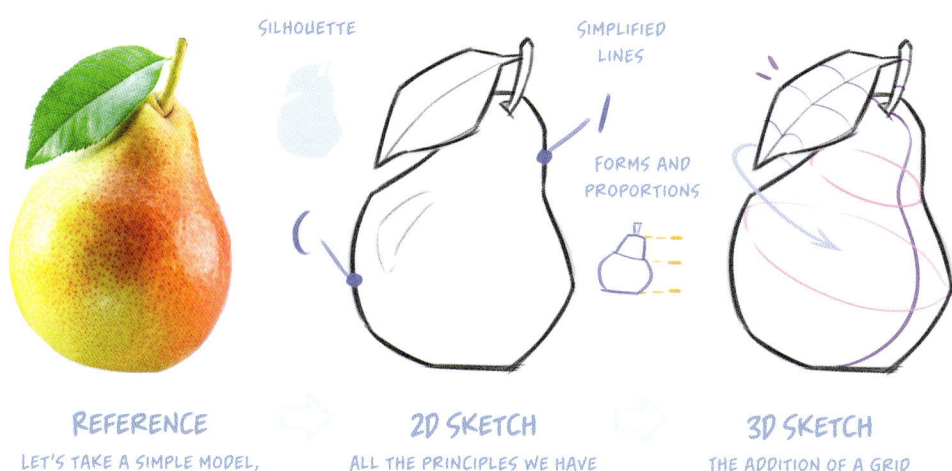

SILHOUETTE

SIMPLIFIED LINES

FORMS AND PROPORTIONS

REFERENCE

LET'S TAKE A SIMPLE MODEL, LIKE A PEAR.

2D SKETCH

ALL THE PRINCIPLES WE HAVE EXPLORED SO FAR WERE USED FOR THIS SKETCH.

3D SKETCH

THE ADDITION OF A GRID IMMEDIATELY GIVES VOLUME TO THE PEAR.

Two Types of Grid Lines

The grid is a preparatory step that will help you to gain familiarity with volume. Think of the grid like a wired okoloton! To draw the grid, two lines are used: vertical lines and horizontal lines. Together, these lines will give relief to your sketch.

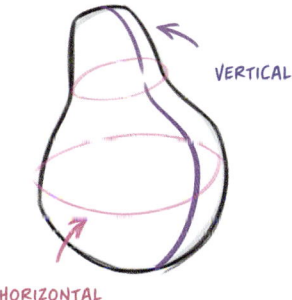

VERTICAL

HORIZONTAL

Vertical Lines

These lines follow the object's relief from the top to the bottom. Imagine cutting the model into pieces.

THESE LINES FOLLOW THE SAME DIRECTION AS THE CONTOURS OF THE OBJECT.

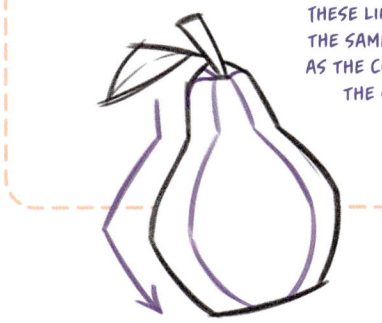

Horizontal Lines

These lines go around the object horizontally. You can draw as many of these lines as you like to follow all the variations of the object's thickness.

THESE LINES PORTRAY CIRCLES AROUND THE OBJECT.

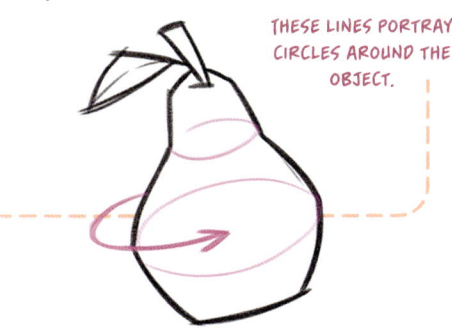

🖐 IN THE KNOW

To better draw the grid of an object, imagine that strings are tied around it. Envisioning how these strings curve around the object will help you discover the direction your lines should follow. For rounded objects, the grid should be made of curved lines, while squared objects will require straighter lines.

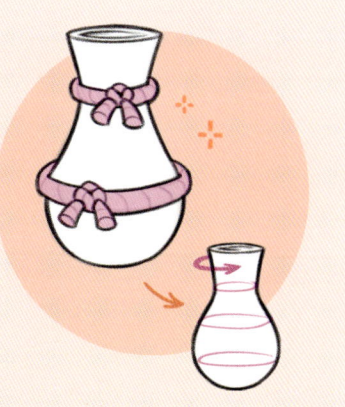

Use the Visible Grid Lines

Some objects offer a grid that's already visible. By identifying the lines that follow the object's volume, drawing the grid will become easier and more intuitive. Desserts are a great example!

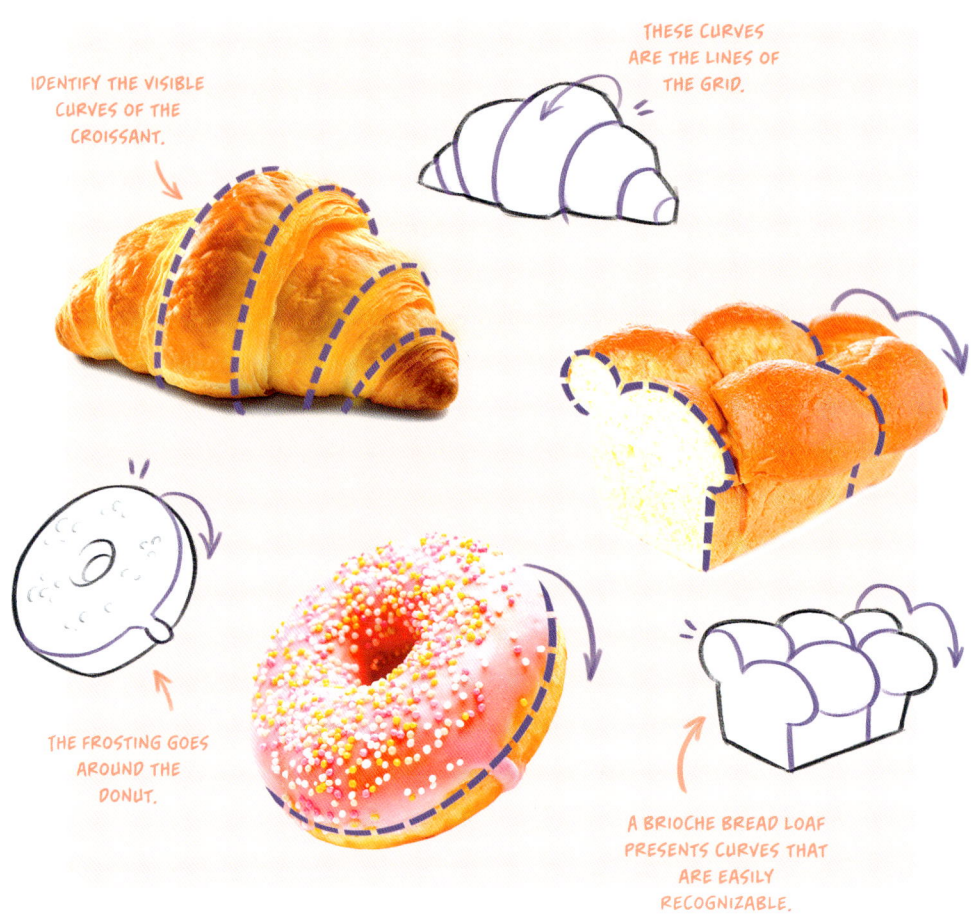

IDENTIFY THE VISIBLE CURVES OF THE CROISSANT.

THESE CURVES ARE THE LINES OF THE GRID.

THE FROSTING GOES AROUND THE DONUT.

A BRIOCHE BREAD LOAF PRESENTS CURVES THAT ARE EASILY RECOGNIZABLE.

Draw the Invisible Lines Too

To perfect your use of the grid, it's important to draw it through the volumes, as if they were transparent. This way, the grid will be more precise. Before tracing the grid, imagine that the object has become translucent. Focus on this technique until it becomes automatic.

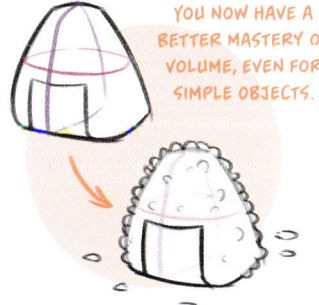

YOU NOW HAVE A BETTER MASTERY OF VOLUME, EVEN FOR SIMPLE OBJECTS.

By drawing an object as if it was cut in half, you can achieve the shape that follows the surface line of the grid. The drawing becomes that much easier!

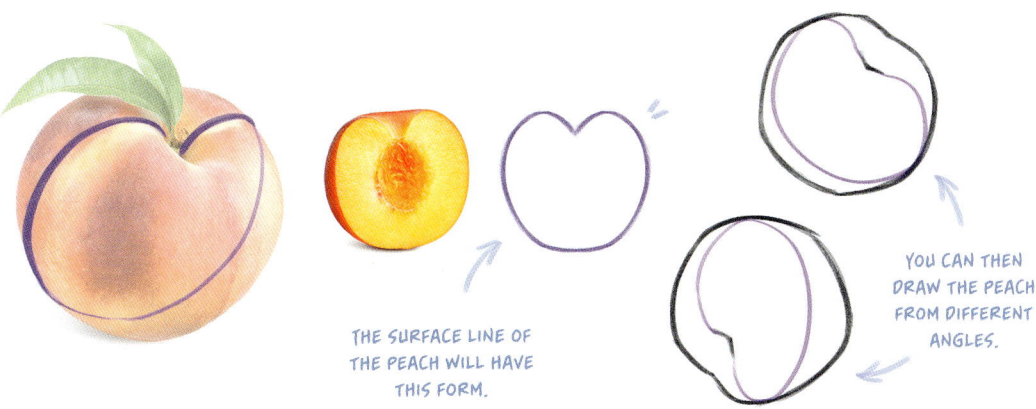

THE SURFACE LINE OF THE PEACH WILL HAVE THIS FORM.

YOU CAN THEN DRAW THE PEACH FROM DIFFERENT ANGLES.

👋 IN THE KNOW

The grid also plays a crucial role when used to add details to a voluminous object. It serves as a guide. The details themselves also must follow the curves of the object to make it more realistic! Creating the impression of dimension gives a truly lifelike quality to your drawings!

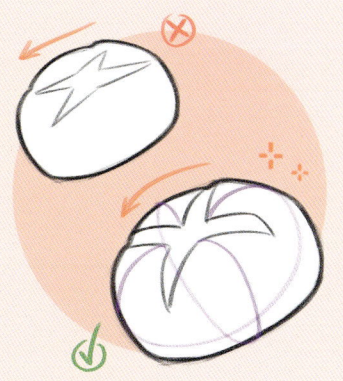

Create a Grid for a Piece of Fruit

In this exercise, you will apply the principles we have studied so far, now including volume, to create a complete sketch. The goal is to practice by drawing the grid for a simple subject.

You will need :

* Your sketchbook or a sheet of paper
* 2 colored pencils
* 1 pencil
* 1 eraser

Analyze the Model

Cherries offer interesting, spherical volumes to study. We see a light-colored hole near the stem. The grid will help you create different variations of relief for this and other details.

To help, don't forget to imagine strings tied around the shape of the cherries—follow each detail of their surfaces.

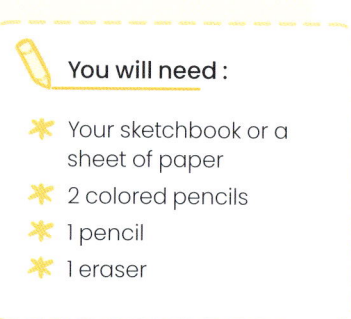

IMAGINE THE CHERRIES CUT IN HALF TO IDENTIFY THE SHAPE OF THE GRID LINES.

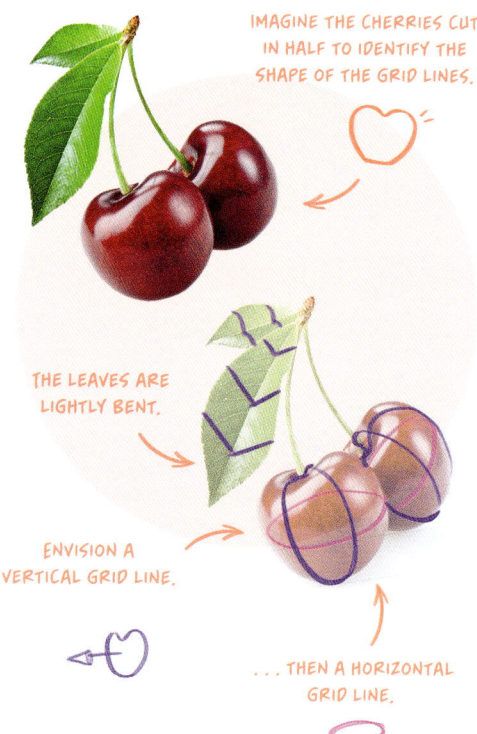

THE LEAVES ARE LIGHTLY BENT.

ENVISION A VERTICAL GRID LINE.

... THEN A HORIZONTAL GRID LINE.

The Drawing Step by Step

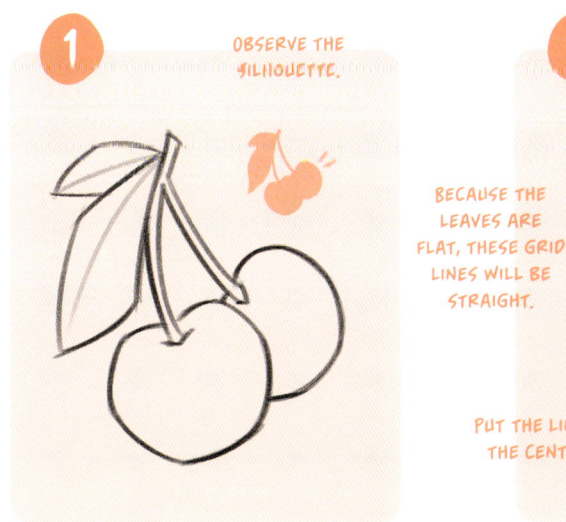

1 OBSERVE THE SILHOUETTE.

Make a first quick sketch with pencil using the techniques we have studied so far: silhouette, simplified lines, shapes, and proportions.

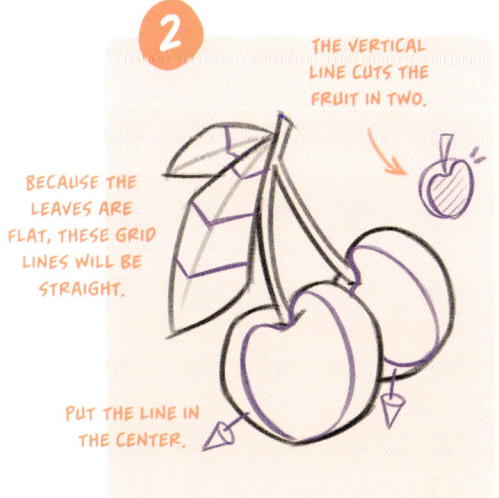

2 THE VERTICAL LINE CUTS THE FRUIT IN TWO.

BECAUSE THE LEAVES ARE FLAT, THESE GRID LINES WILL BE STRAIGHT.

PUT THE LINE IN THE CENTER.

To draw the vertical grid lines, imagine a string tied around the fruits. Really exaggerate the curves and use volumes to maximize the relief.

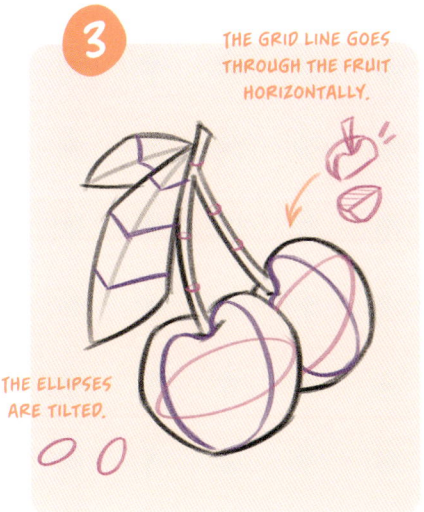

3 THE GRID LINE GOES THROUGH THE FRUIT HORIZONTALLY.

THE ELLIPSES ARE TILTED.

Finish the sketch with horizontal grid lines, tilting the ellipses to better illustrate the angle of the cherries.

PRINCIPLE

09 | BASIC VOLUMES

The grid lets us transition from drawing in 2D to drawing in 3D. However, we must go further to understand volumes and learn to incorporate them in our drawing.

The Three Basic Volumes

Each object can be simplified into one of three basic volumes: cube, sphere, or cylinder. Look around you. You will see that volumes make up the fundamental structure of many objects: a mug becomes a hollow cylinder, a ball becomes a sphere, and so on.

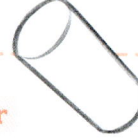

The Cube

The cube is one of the most important volumes. It'll help you to solidify your sketch, especially in terms of perspective (see p. 68).

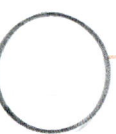

The Sphere

The sphere is ideal for drawing round or organic objects. It brings softness and realism to your sketches.

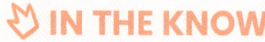

The Cylinder

The cylinder is midway between a cube and a sphere, as it is both solid and round. It will be helpful for simplifying long elements.

🔥 IN THE KNOW

Using only these three geometric volumes will quickly limit your options. To create more natural drawings, it's essential to adapt the volumes according to your subjects. You can contort the volumes, bend them, lengthen them, and so on to get more precise variants.

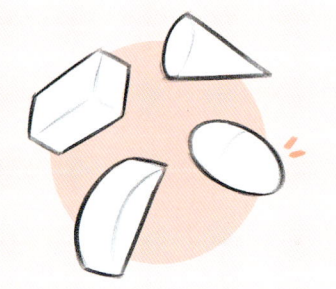

Choosing the Volume to Draw

When you begin to work with volumes, it can be hard to know which one to choose to represent a given element of your sketch. When should you draw a sphere rather than a cube? Which is the best choice? In reality, there's not one single solution. Countless options are possible because one subject can be interpreted in many ways.

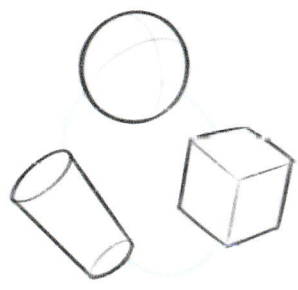

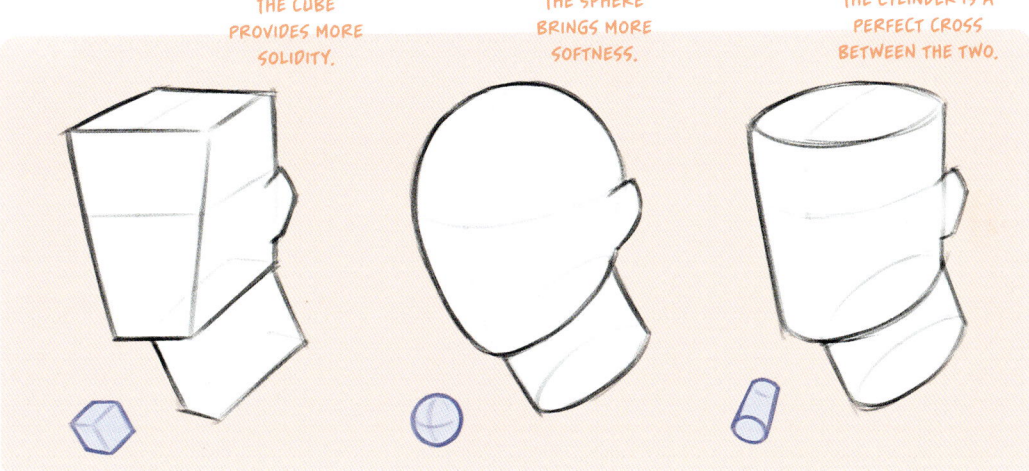

THE CUBE PROVIDES MORE SOLIDITY.

THE SPHERE BRINGS MORE SOFTNESS.

THE CYLINDER IS A PERFECT CROSS BETWEEN THE TWO.

Your choice of volumes is a question of style and feeling!

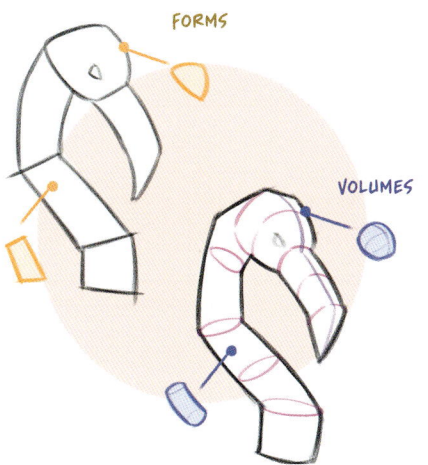

FORMS

VOLUMES

From Shapes to Volumes

To go from a flat drawing to a voluminous one, you will visualize 2D forms (see p. 54) as their corresponding 3D volumes. Thus, a square becomes a cube, a circle becomes a sphere, and so on. Begin by breaking your drawing down into several elements. This gives your drawing distinct volumes. Finally, apply the grid principle (see p. 54) to give more relief to the sketch.

Breaking the Subject Down

The basic volumes we have discussed can be found in a great variety of subjects, such as the bodies of humans or animals, trees and plants, or everyday objects. Taking the time to observe what you want to draw in an attentive away and carefully analyzing it is crucial. Breaking down what you see into extremely simple volumes will help you draw complex subjects with greater ease. Drawing in volume is not about copying an image—rather, it's about reinterpreting the image to give the illusion of dimension on the paper.

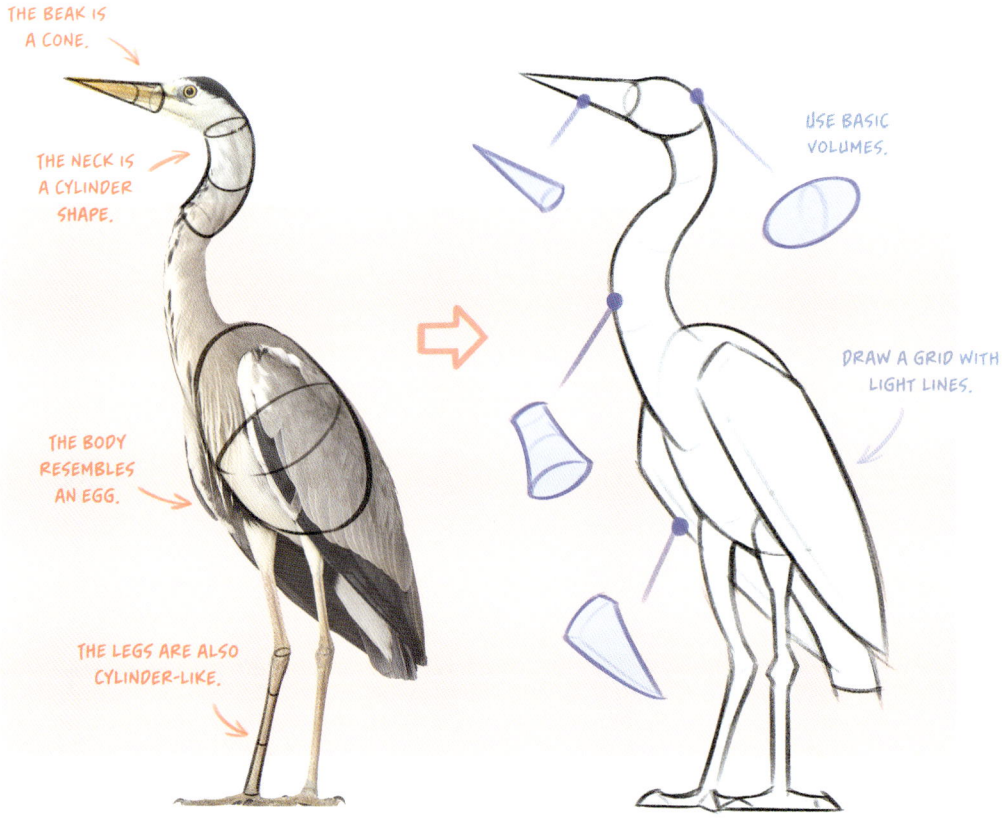

THE BEAK IS
A CONE.

THE NECK IS
A CYLINDER
SHAPE.

THE BODY
RESEMBLES
AN EGG.

THE LEGS ARE ALSO
CYLINDER-LIKE.

USE BASIC
VOLUMES.

DRAW A GRID WITH
LIGHT LINES.

🔥 IN THE KNOW

To better understand how to break down a subject, try to see how different volumes combine within it. The volumes interconnect at various cross sections to form one coherent whole. By drawing through volumes as if they were transparent, you'll be able to better position them. Your drawings will be more realistic.

THE CYLINDERS OF THE FINGERS INTERCONNECT WITH THE CUBE OF THE PALM!

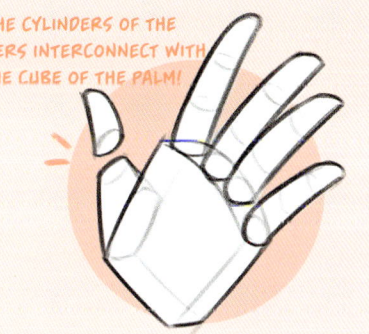

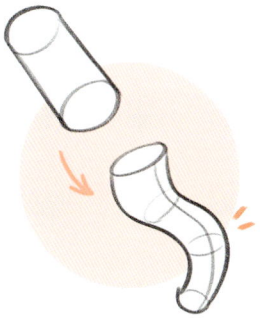

Giving Life to Volumes Little by Little

Practice first with the three basic volumes of cubes, spheres, and cylinders. Then, go to the next level of difficulty and practice using a more complex array of volumes. For example, the neck of a bird (below) can first be simplified into a cylinder, then enlivened with a curved cylinder, which gives it a more natural feel.

BASIC VOLUMES

SIMPLIFY BY USING THE MOST BASIC VOLUMES POSSIBLE.

DYNAMIC VOLUMES

EXPERIMENT WITH DIFFERENT VOLUMES TO RENDER COMPLEXITY.

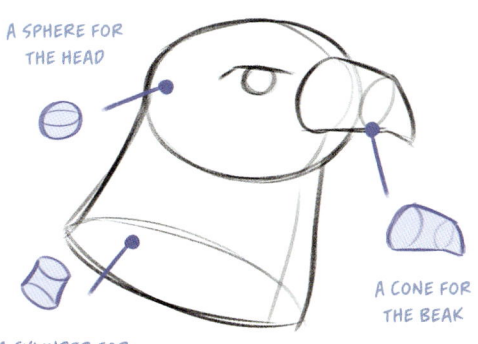

A SPHERE FOR THE HEAD

A CONE FOR THE BEAK

A CYLINDER FOR THE NECK

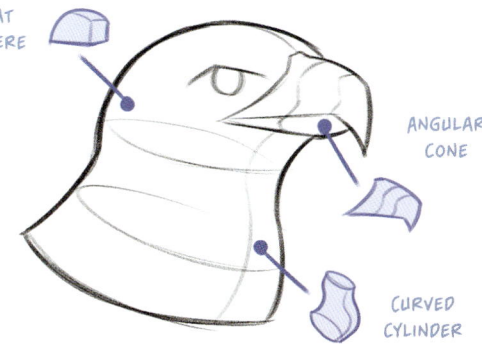

FLAT SPHERE

ANGULAR CONE

CURVED CYLINDER

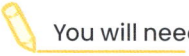

Draw a Bird Using Basic Volumes

Let's focus now on breaking a model down into basic volumes. Our goal is to identify which volumes best represent each part of the animal. Several solutions exist, so don't hesitate to explore them all!

You will need :

* Your sketchbook or a sheet of paper
* 1 drawing pencil
* 1 eraser

Analyze the Model

Let's take the example of a bird, which is composed of several parts: the head, body, wings, tail, and feet. The head looks like a flattened sphere on top of the body. Analyze the cross sections interconnecting the various volumes to see how each piece is inserted into the whole.

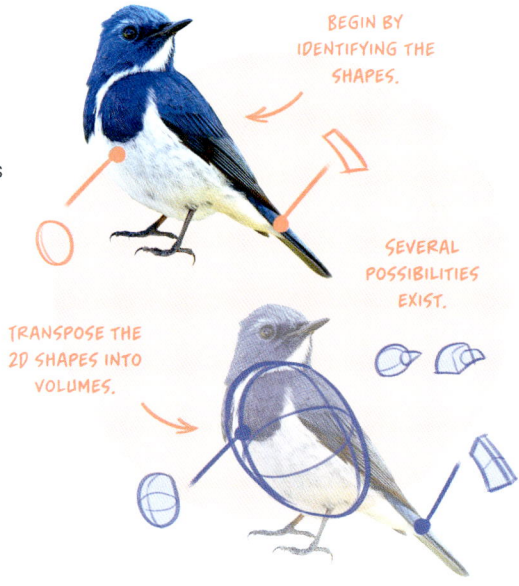

BEGIN BY IDENTIFYING THE SHAPES.

SEVERAL POSSIBILITIES EXIST.

TRANSPOSE THE 2D SHAPES INTO VOLUMES.

The Drawing Step by Step

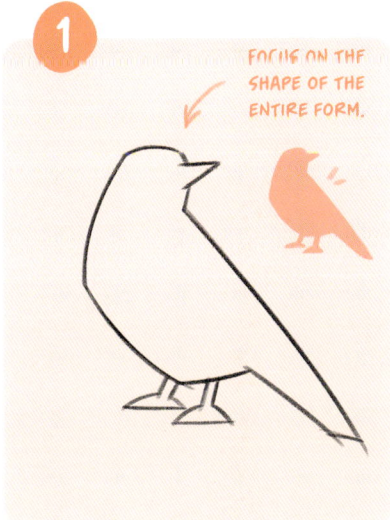

1 FOCUS ON THE SHAPE OF THE ENTIRE FORM.

Do a first sketch, concentrating on the silhouette and definition of the proportions. Work with straight lines—start over however many times is necessary!

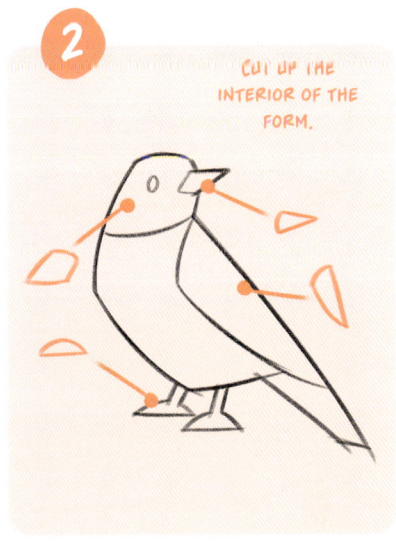

2 CUT UP THE INTERIOR OF THE FORM.

Give more detail to the interior of the form by using basic shapes. Draw the head, beak, body, and feet of the bird.

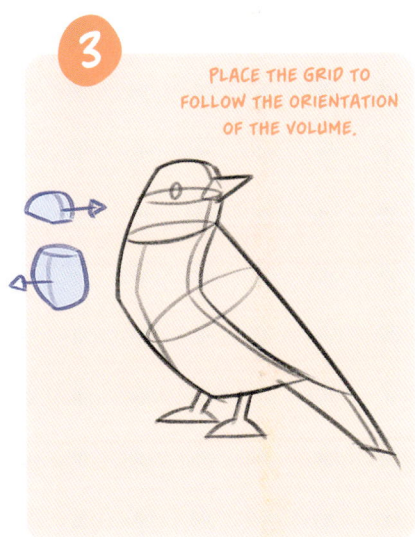

3 PLACE THE GRID TO FOLLOW THE ORIENTATION OF THE VOLUME.

Finish by applying volume to the bird. Transform the 2D forms you drew into 3D basic forms, then add grid lines.

6

PERSPECTIVE

10 REPRESENTING PERSPECTIVE

Mastering perspective allows you to create the illusion of depth on a flat surface, that is, the sheet of paper. In the last section, you learned to draw volumes. Now, you will develop your ability to position the objects in space with more precision.

Two-Dimensional (2D) Forms

These are the basic forms you learned to draw at the beginning of this book. They are limited to two dimensions: height and width.

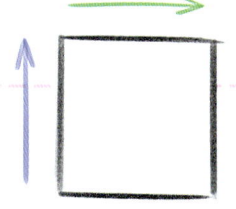

HEIGHT
WIDTH

Three-Dimensional (3D) Forms

These forms of volume offer an extra dimension: depth. Perspective allows us to represent depth in an accurate way.

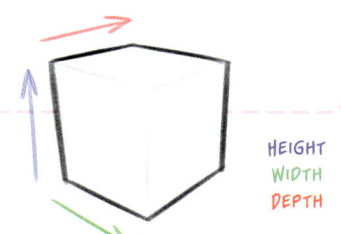

HEIGHT
WIDTH
DEPTH

🔥 IN THE KNOW

A drawing always represents the artist's point of view. To draw with perspective, it's essential to determine your position. Think of yourself as a photographer on the hunt for the best angle to capture a scene.

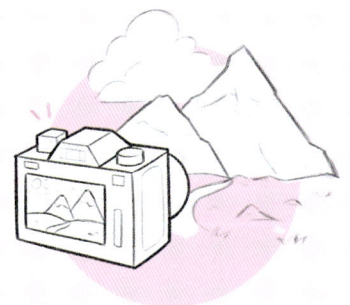

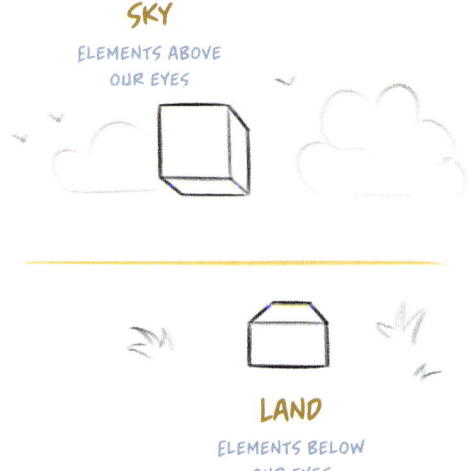

SKY

ELEMENTS ABOVE
OUR EYES

LAND

ELEMENTS BELOW
OUR EYES

The Horizon Line

Whether it's visible or invisible, the horizon line is essential to drawing with perspective. This imaginary line corresponds to the artist's gaze. If they look straight ahead, it is positioned exactly in the middle of their field of vision.

Choosing the Angle of Vision

The placement of the horizon line depends on the viewer's point of view. It's not always in the middle, as the viewer does not always look straight ahead! By modifying the height of the horizon line, you get different angles of vision.

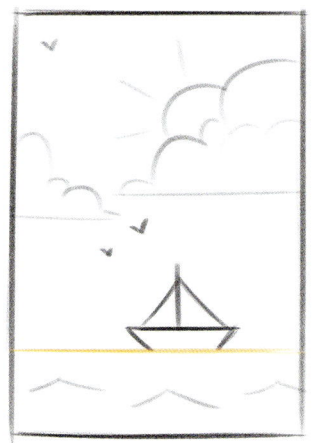

LOWER HORIZON LINE: LOOKING
TOWARD THE SKY

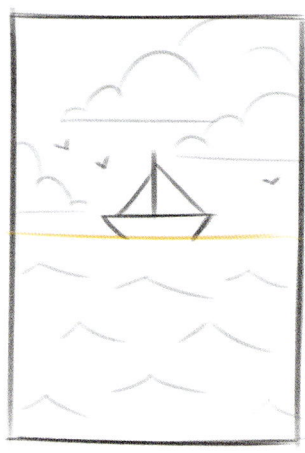

MIDDLE HORIZON LINE: LOOKING
STRAIGHT AHEAD

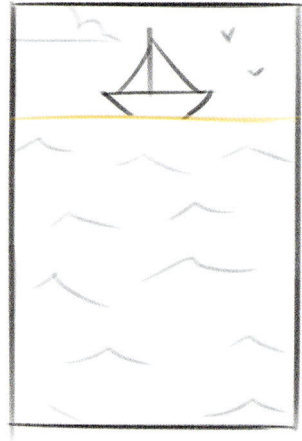

HIGHER HORIZON LINE: LOOKING
TOWARD THE GROUND

11 | POINTS AND VANISHING LINES

Beyond the horizon line, two other tools are essential for creating perspective: vanishing points and vanishing lines. Vanishing points are imaginary points that are usually placed on the horizon line. Vanishing lines are lines that converge toward the vanishing point(s).

The Convergence of Vanishing Lines

To the human eye, objects that are distant seem to converge at a far-off point on the horizon line, which is called the vanishing point. Rather than using parallel lines to draw a road, for example, it is best to draw lines that go toward one same point: these are vanishing lines. Most of the time, the vanishing points are too far off to be drawn on the sheet of paper. You will thus need to trace vanishing lines by imagining the points that are far away.

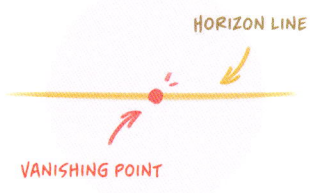

HORIZON LINE

VANISHING POINT

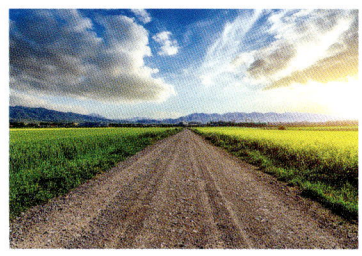

LET'S TAKE THE EXAMPLE OF A PATH.

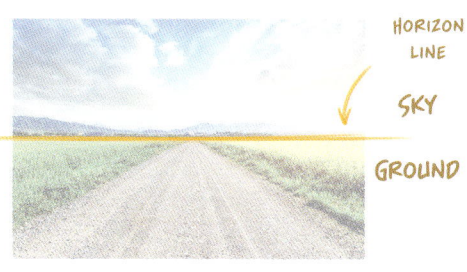

HORIZON LINE

SKY

GROUND

THE FIRST STEP IS TO ESTIMATE THE HEIGHT OF THE HORIZON LINE.

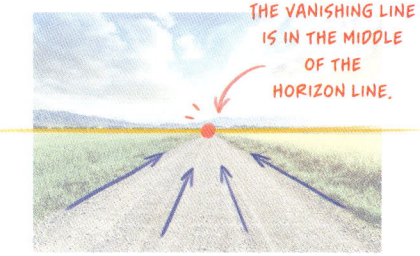

THE VANISHING LINE IS IN THE MIDDLE OF THE HORIZON LINE.

OBSERVE THE DIRECTION THAT THE ROAD TAKES (REPRESENTED BY THE ARROWS) TO PLACE THE SCENE.

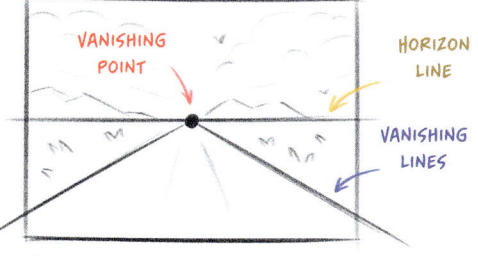

VANISHING POINT

HORIZON LINE

VANISHING LINES

YOU CAN TRACE A SQUARE TO BETTER REPRESENT THE VANISHING POINT.

🔥 THREE KEY ELEMENTS

To draw perspective, only three elements are required:

1. A horizon line
2. One or more vanishing points
3. Vanishing lines

We begin by drawing the horizon line, then placing a point on it. To finish, we trace lines that converge at this point.

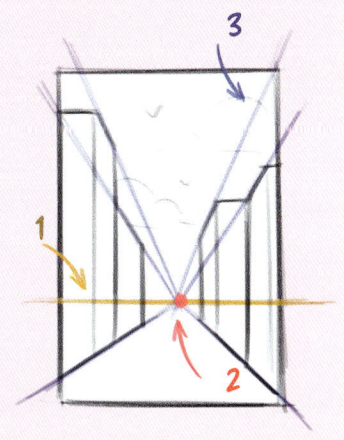

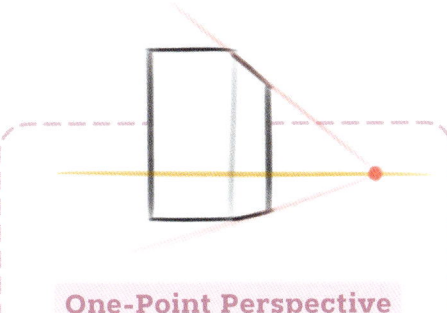

One-Point Perspective (One Vanishing Point)

This is the easiest to create. It allows a frontal view of the subject.

Different Types of Perspective

There's no limit to vanishing points. The more there are, the more complex the effect of perspective becomes. The three most used perspectives in drawing are as shown:

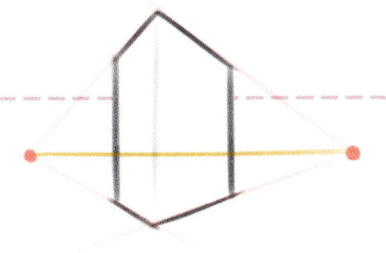

Two-Point Perspective (Two Vanishing Points)

More dynamic and natural, this lets you create three-quarter views or obliques of the subject.

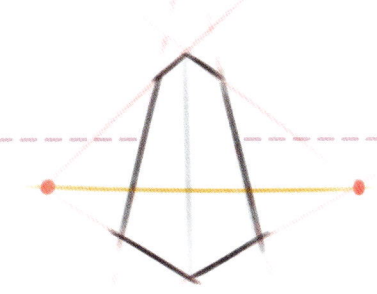

Three-Point Perspective (Three Vanishing Points)

For subjects that you see from a very low or very high angle, this creates vertical depth.

12 | PERSPECTIVE USING ONE VANISHING POINT

This perspective enables you to draw scenes and objects from the front. It's a perfect way to begin!

Frontal View

Let's take the example of a cube. The front is closest to the viewer. It's not distorted by perspective: It is a simple square. We'll work with three types of lines: vertical lines, horizontal lines, and vanishing lines. Only the lines that represent depth will converge at the vanishing point (see below).

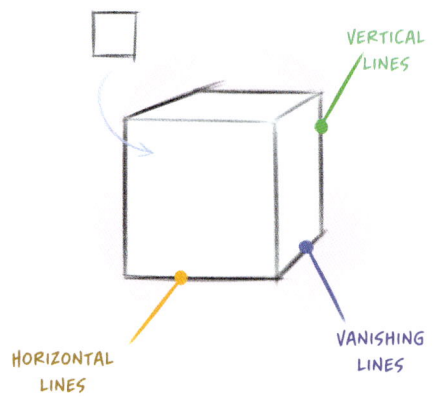

VERTICAL LINES

VANISHING LINES

HORIZONTAL LINES

🔥 HOW TO CREATE PERSPECTIVE WITH A VANISHING POINT

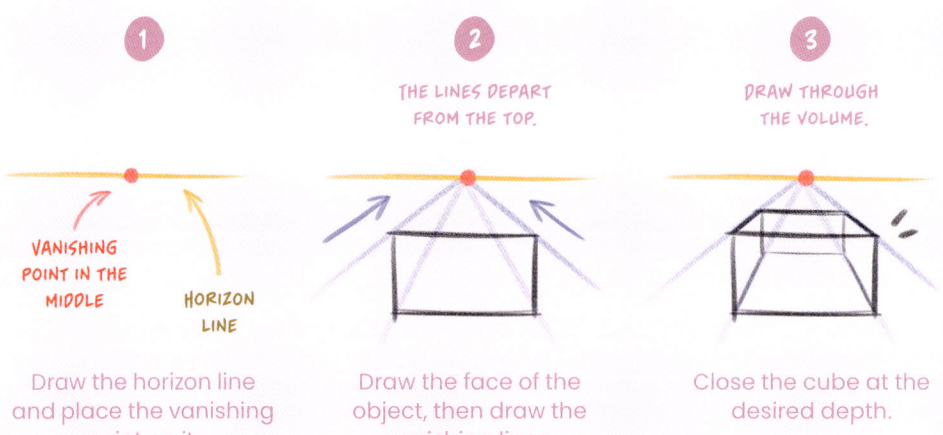

1

VANISHING POINT IN THE MIDDLE

HORIZON LINE

Draw the horizon line and place the vanishing point on it.

2

THE LINES DEPART FROM THE TOP.

Draw the face of the object, then draw the vanishing lines.

3

DRAW THROUGH THE VOLUME.

Close the cube at the desired depth.

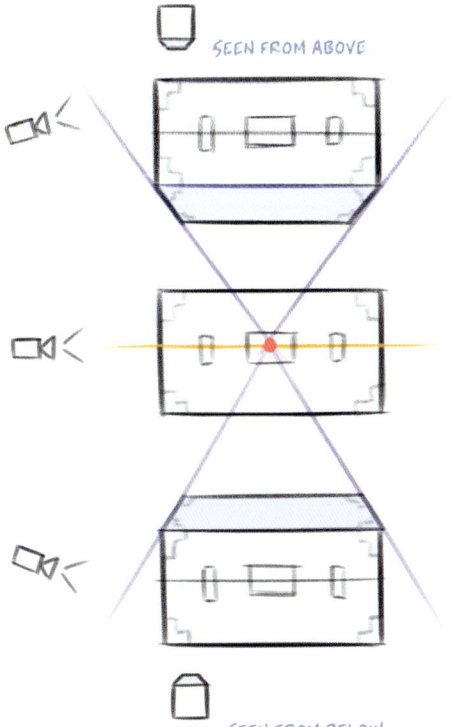

SEEN FROM ABOVE

SEEN FROM BELOW

Height of the Subject

Thanks to the vanishing point, you can control the position of the elements in your drawing. Let's take the example of a trunk. The horizon line, as we have seen, marks the height of the observer's point of view. If we draw the trunk above the horizon line (see the trunk on top), the trunk seems to float. If we draw it below the horizon line (see the trunk on the bottom), we have the impression that the trunk is resting on the ground.

Before drawing, reflect on the point of view you want to use to represent your model.

Distance from the Subject

Beyond the principle of convergence, perspective depends on two things: the distance between objects and the way that distance impacts the perception of the respective sizes of the objects. The closer an object is, the larger it seems. Conversely, the farther away an object is, the smaller it seems. This is how we perceive the world. And thanks to the vanishing point, you'll be able to give realistic depth to the flat paper.

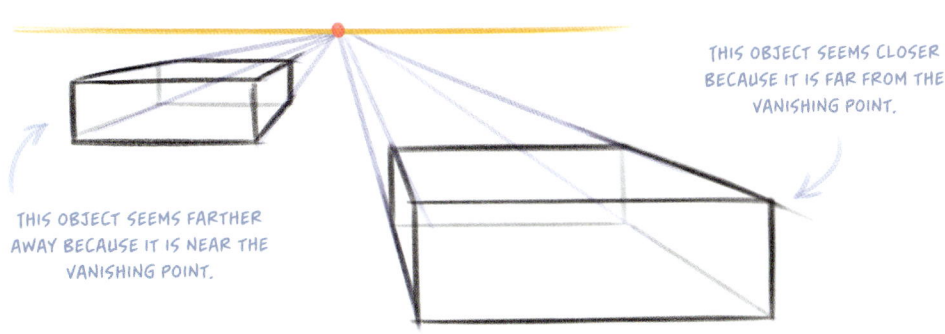

THIS OBJECT SEEMS CLOSER BECAUSE IT IS FAR FROM THE VANISHING POINT.

THIS OBJECT SEEMS FARTHER AWAY BECAUSE IT IS NEAR THE VANISHING POINT.

EXAMPLE

1

Create the foundation for perspective.

Our goal here is to create an urban scene. We begin by positioning the horizon line low on the paper to suggest that the viewer is looking up at the apartment buildings. Then, we draw the vanishing lines, creating the top and bottom of the buildings.

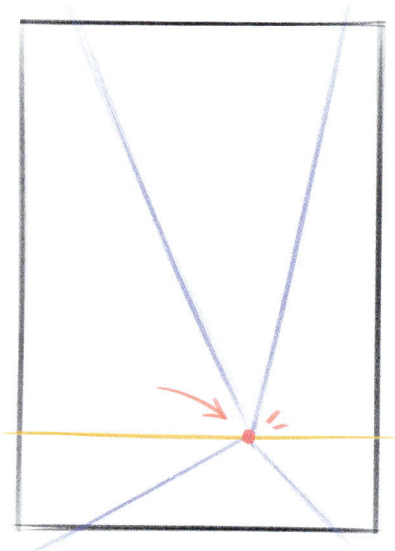

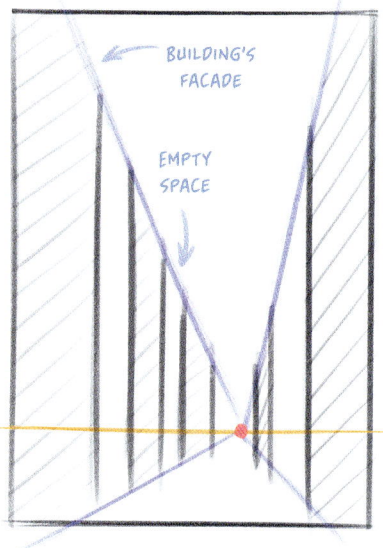

BUILDING'S FACADE

EMPTY SPACE

2

Place vertical lines.

Draw vertical lines to define each apartment building. As you do this, don't worry about making the divisions regular. On the contrary, asymmetry allows for a much more dynamic composition. Drawing buildings of different sizes creates a sense of variety and adds interest to the scene.

Draw horizontal lines.

Once the structure of the buildings is established, all that's left to do is add the volume by drawing horizontal lines at the top of the buildings and at the ground level. Next, go back over the vanishing lines to solidify the lines of the roof and ground.

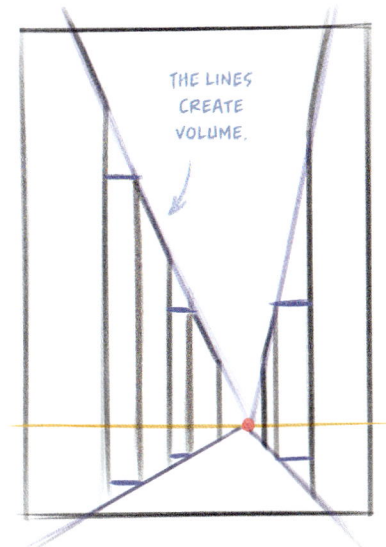

THE LINES
CREATE
VOLUME.

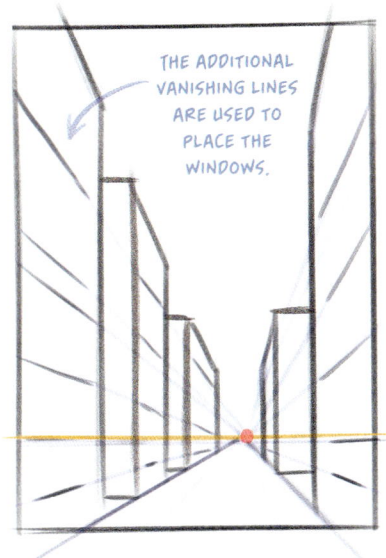

THE ADDITIONAL
VANISHING LINES
ARE USED TO
PLACE THE
WINDOWS.

Add windows.

Draw new vanishing lines where you wish to place windows and doors. Make sure to align these lines correctly so that the perspective will be accurate.

Add the final details.

Now that the perspective markers are drawn in, we can add secondary forms. Here, windows are rectangles that converge at the vanishing point. Stick to basic forms to simplify the task.

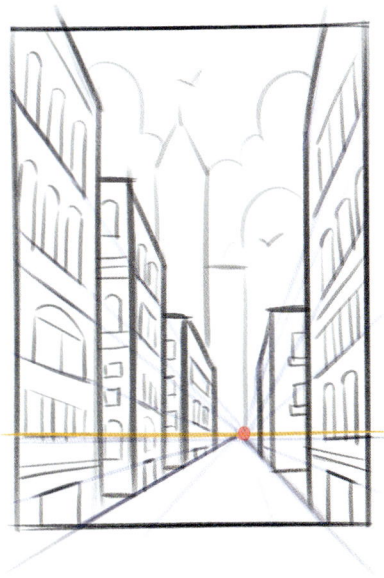

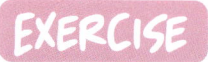

Draw an Object in Perspective with a Vanishing Point

It's time to dive into your perspective drawing! To do so, begin with simple cubic volumes. Suitcases are excellent subjects to practice with. In this exercise, you'll use a raised hand to draw two suitcases piled on top of each other.

You will need :

✳ Your sketchbook or a sheet of paper
✳ 3 colored pencils
✳ 1 drawing pencil
✳ 1 eraser

Analyze the Model

To create a perspective that is authentic to what you see before you, it's important to analyze the angle of the vanishing lines. As you can see, the vanishing lines only somewhat converge, indicating that the vanishing point is farther away. Given that the lines continue upward toward the top, we can infer that the horizon line is above the suitcases.

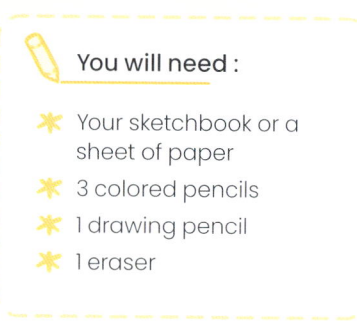

YOU CAN SIMPLIFY THE SUITCASES INTO TWO CUBIC VOLUMES.

THE VANISHING POINT IS FAR AWAY.

Only the sides of the suitcase converge at the vanishing point.

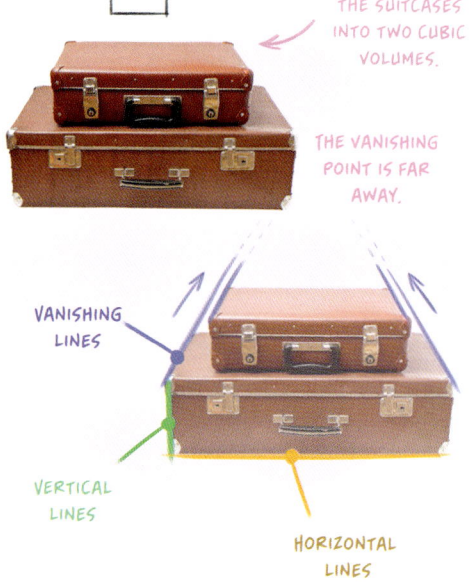

VANISHING LINES

VERTICAL LINES

HORIZONTAL LINES

The Drawing Step by Step

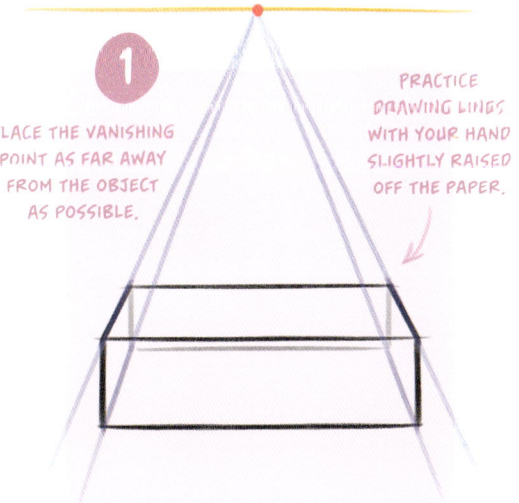

PLACE THE VANISHING POINT AS FAR AWAY FROM THE OBJECT AS POSSIBLE.

PRACTICE DRAWING LINES WITH YOUR HAND SLIGHTLY RAISED OFF THE PAPER.

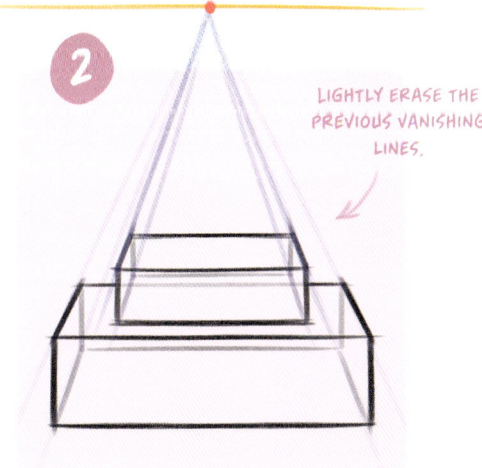

LIGHTLY ERASE THE PREVIOUS VANISHING LINES.

Draw the horizon line, placing the vanishing point, and draw the front of the suitcase (a simple rectangle). Then, draw the vanishing lines. Close the volume, adjusting the depth as you see fit.

Draw the second suitcase on top of the first. Be sure to maintain proper proportions by checking the width and adjusting for accurate spacing on either side.

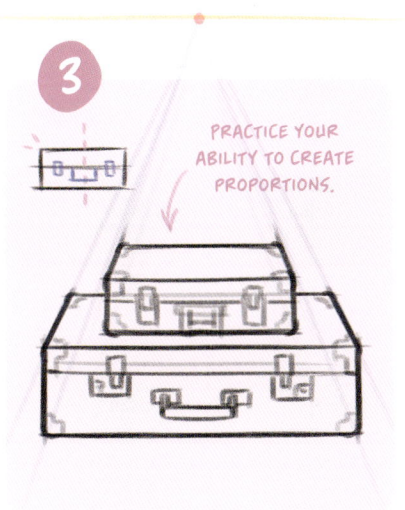

PRACTICE YOUR ABILITY TO CREATE PROPORTIONS.

Erase the vanishing lines and add details to the suitcases using basic forms. Use only rectangles to keep the drawing simple and practice drawing beautiful lines.

13 | PERSPECTIVE WITH TWO VANISHING POINTS

Perspective with two vanishing points gives a three-quarter view of the subject. Natural and dynamic, perspective with two vanishing points is close to human vision.

A Very Realistic Three-Quarter View

For this type of perspective, the vanishing lines we'll use to create depth converge at, or toward, two points: one on the left and one on the right. The vertical lines will be perfectly perpendicular to the horizon line.

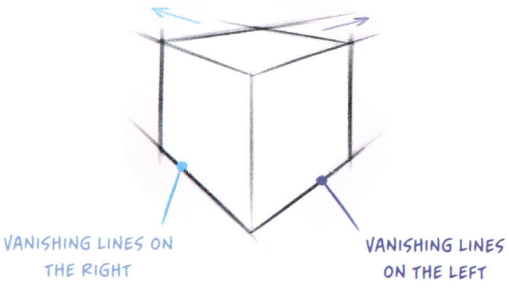

VANISHING LINES ON THE RIGHT

VANISHING LINES ON THE LEFT

🔥 HOW TO CREATE PERSPECTIVE USING TWO VANISHING POINTS

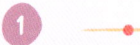

Draw the horizon line, then two vanishing points on either side.

Draw the vanishing lines to create a rectangle.

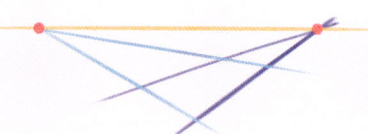

Next, draw vertical lines to define the height of the volume.

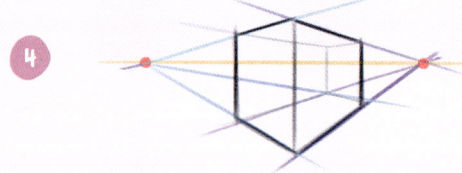

Starting at the top of the nearest vertical line, draw two vanishing lines and close the volume.

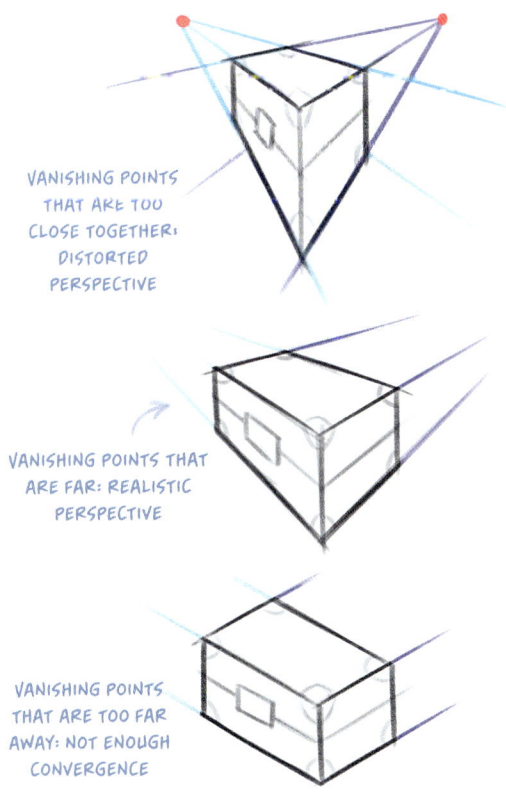

VANISHING POINTS THAT ARE TOO CLOSE TOGETHER: DISTORTED PERSPECTIVE

VANISHING POINTS THAT ARE FAR: REALISTIC PERSPECTIVE

VANISHING POINTS THAT ARE TOO FAR AWAY: NOT ENOUGH CONVERGENCE

Avoiding Distortions

How do you know where to position the two vanishing points on the horizon line? There are several ways to do so, all of which will have different results.

If the vanishing points are too close together, the volume will look distorted and not very realistic. Conversely, if the points are too far away from one another, the depth will not be effective. The goal is to strike a balance and achieve a light convergence without too much deformation.

When drawing an image based on a photograph, it's interesting to analyze the incline of the vanishing lines to discover, with more certainty, where the vanishing points are.

Varying Points of View

Instead of always centering the subject between two vanishing points, you can place the subject nearer to one vanishing point to create an even more natural perspective—rather than a rigid rendering. To vary the points of view, try modifying the position of the subject in different ways.

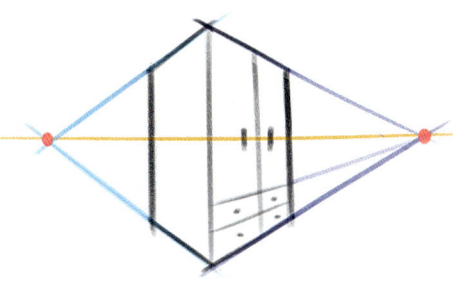

SYMMETRICAL VIEW: THE CORNER OF THE CABINET IS RIGHT IN FRONT OF US.

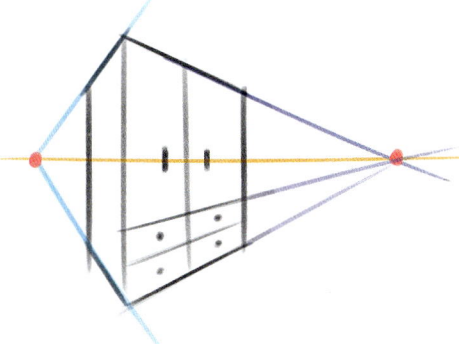

MORE DYNAMIC VIEW: WE CAN BETTER SEE THE FRONT OF THE CABINET.

1

Create the foundation of perspective.

Before drawing, always consider the angle of view that you wish to adopt. Here, we want to draw a bird's-eye view of a desk so that the top of it will be visible. The horizon line is thus placed above. Draw the vanishing points asymmetrically: the point on the left will be farther away from the object than the point on the right, which we imagine to be far off.

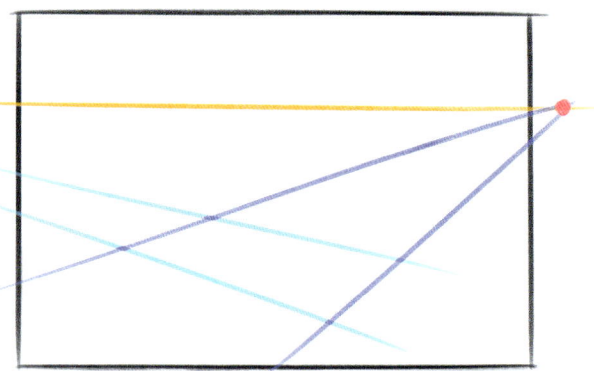

THE VANISHING LINES CROSS
TO FORM A RECTANGLE
ON THE GROUND.

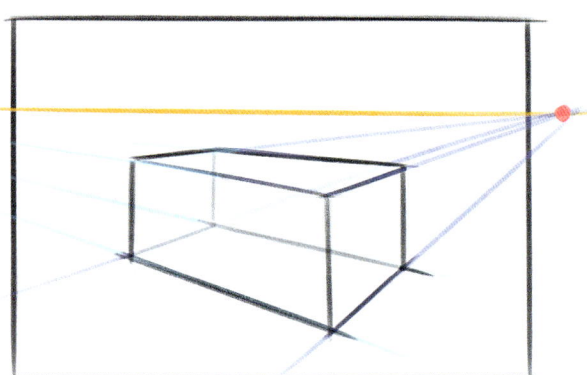

2

Draw the main volume.

Draw vertical lines to define the height of the volume. Next, close the shape by drawing lines that converge toward the point on the left—then, draw other lines that converge toward the point on the right.

First, draw a vertical line at the corner closest to you. Then, from the top of this line, draw vanishing lines to close the block off.

Break down the main volume.

Break the main volume down into several secondary volumes. In this example, we will divide it into three sections: two box sections on either side and one in the middle. Here, it's not about mathematical precision, but about developing your instinct.

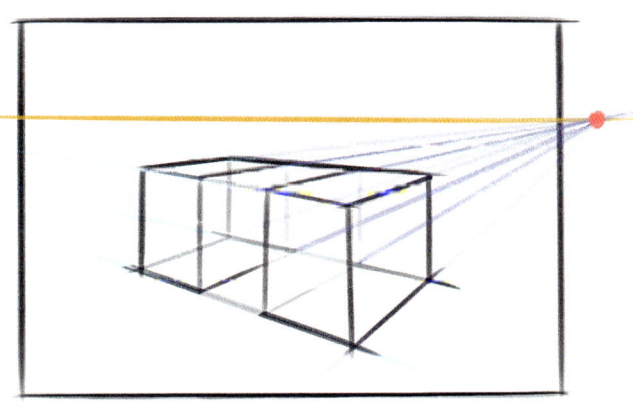

THE LINES SEPARATING THE SECONDARY VOLUMES ALSO CONVERGE TOWARD THE VANISHING POINTS.

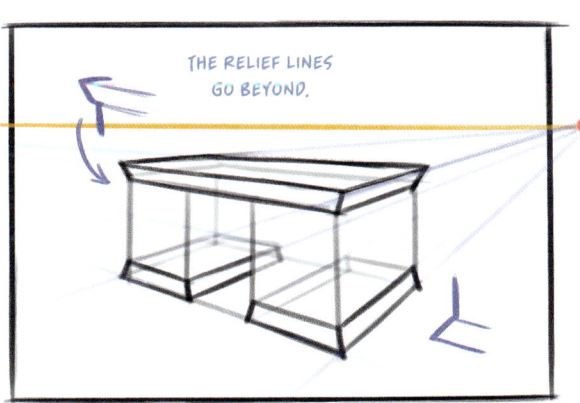

THE RELIEF LINES GO BEYOND.

Add relief.

Adding secondary volumes creates a more precise drawing of the desk. To add relief, we use oblique lines around the main volume.

Add the final details.

Adding details becomes easier now that the main elements are correctly positioned (in terms of perspective). To complete your drawing, add rectangles for the cabinet doors and the drawer, as well as circles for knobs. Let's keep it simple.

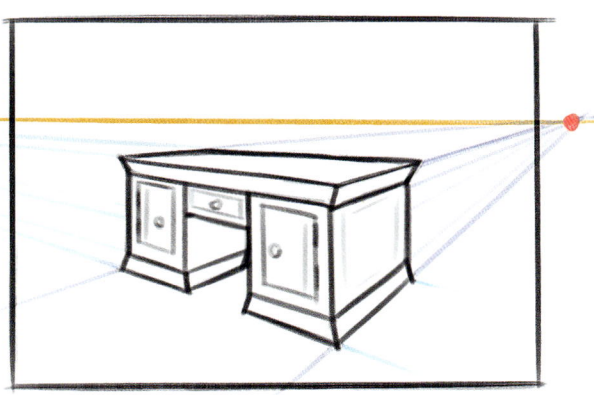

Draw an Object in Perspective Using Two Vanishing Points

To practice perspective using two vanishing points, it's important to practice drawing cubic forms, such as this chest. The goal here is to reproduce an angle of view that is as faithful as possible to the photograph.

You will need :

* Your sketchbook or a sheet of paper
* 1 drawing pencil
* 1 eraser

Analyze the Model

It's super easy to place the vanishing point when not drawing an image from a photo. However, when we *are* drawing from a photo, we should begin in the opposite way: by first analyzing the tilt of the vanishing lines. Then, extending the lines, we can discover the position of the vanishing points. Once we have found the vanishing points, we know they will be on the horizon line, allowing us to identify the position of the horizon line as well.

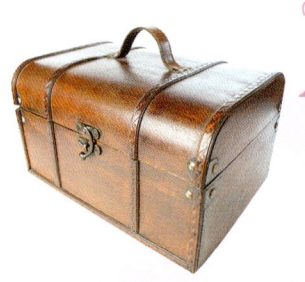

CHOOSE A MODEL WITH FEW DETAILS.

THE VANISHING LINE ON THE RIGHT SEEMS TO BE CLOSER.

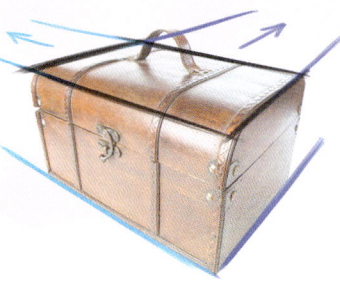

THE VANISHING LINE ON THE LEFT SEEMS TO BE FARTHER.

THE HORIZON LINE IS ABOVE THE OBJECT BECAUSE THE LINES CONVERGE TOWARD THE TOP.

Analyzing the three elements of perspective of an image allows us to know how to position the three elements—horizon line, vanishing points, vanishing lines—for the drawing.

The Drawing Step by Step

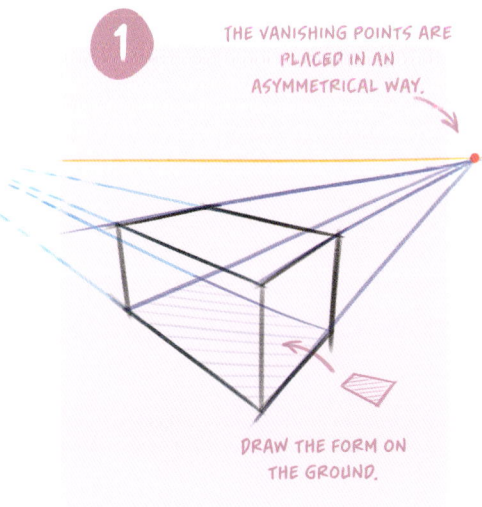

1 THE VANISHING POINTS ARE PLACED IN AN ASYMMETRICAL WAY.

DRAW THE FORM ON THE GROUND.

Trusting your observation and analysis, begin by positioning the horizon line, as well as the vanishing point that is closest to the object. Next, draw the main volume.

2 THE STRAPS RESEMBLE GRID LINES.

Add secondary volumes in the simplified form of rectangles. The lines must also go toward the vanishing point on the right. Check the spacing.

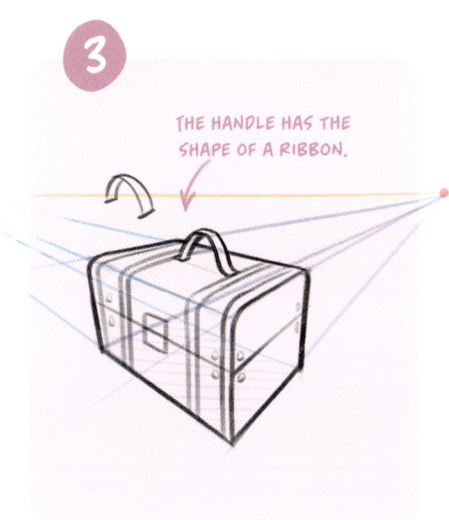

3 THE HANDLE HAS THE SHAPE OF A RIBBON.

Erase the vanishing lines and add details using basic forms. Erase the corners and draw them in with rounded lines to give a more natural and realistic finish to the object.

14

PERSPECTIVE WITH THREE VANISHING POINTS

Perspective with three vanishing points allows you to create a bird's-eye view and views from below, which are very impressive. We use the same principle as that of perspective with two points (one on the left, one on the right), and we add a third vanishing point outside the horizon line.

A View that Magnifies Height

As we have seen, objects in the distance seem smaller. For example, the taller a building is, the more the top of it seems to shrink and narrow as we look up at it from the ground. Adding a third vanishing point allows us to give greater effect to the perspective thanks to this extra point of convergence.

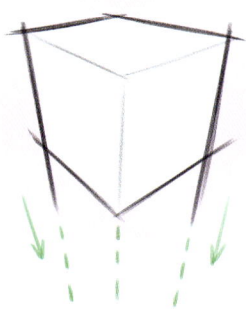

VERTICAL LINES ARE NOT PARALLEL; INSTEAD, THEY CONVERGE TOWARD THE THIRD VANISHING POINT.

✍ HOW TO CREATE PERSPECTIVE USING THREE VANISHING POINTS

1

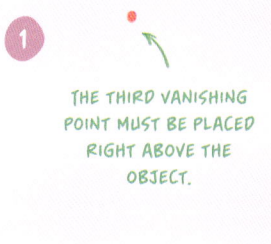

THE THIRD VANISHING POINT MUST BE PLACED RIGHT ABOVE THE OBJECT.

Draw the horizon line, the two vanishing points, and finally, the third vanishing point above.

2

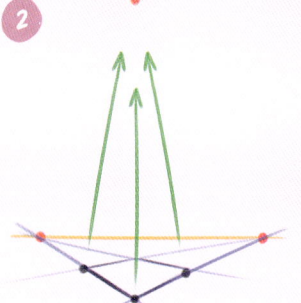

Draw the front on the ground, then draw vertical lines that converge toward the third vanishing point.

3

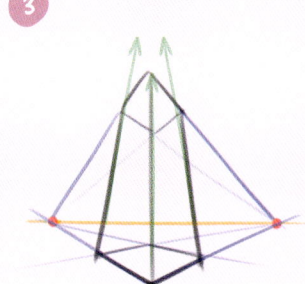

Using the vanishing lines on the left and right, close the block off.

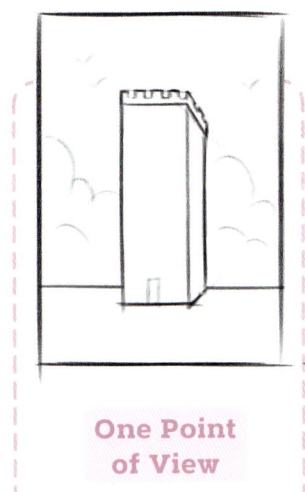

**One Point
of View**

Static vision

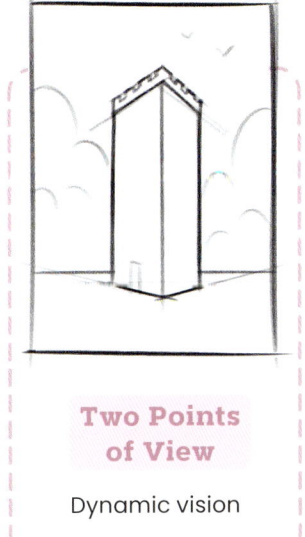

**Two Points
of View**

Dynamic vision

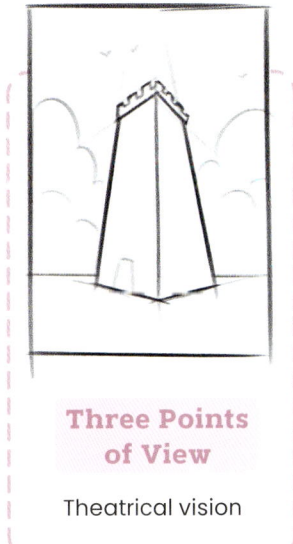

**Three Points
of View**

Theatrical vision

High-Angle View and Low-Angle View

To successfully create the illusion of depth, the third vanishing point must be placed either above (high-angle view) or below (low-angle view) the horizon line.

The closer the third vanishing point is to the horizon, the more distorted the object seems! To avoid this distortion, keep it as far away as possible from the horizon line.

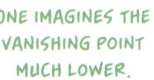

THE THIRD VANISHING POINT BELOW THE HORIZON LINE: AERIAL VIEW OR HIGH-ANGLE VIEW

THE THIRD VANISHING POINT ABOVE THE HORIZON LINE: GROUND VIEW OR LOW-ANGLE VIEW

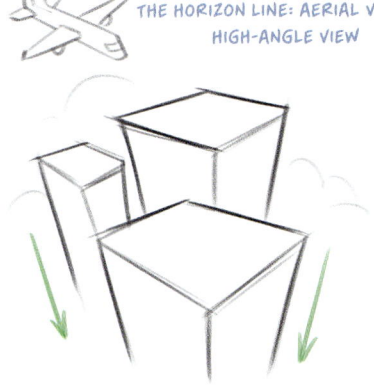

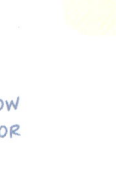

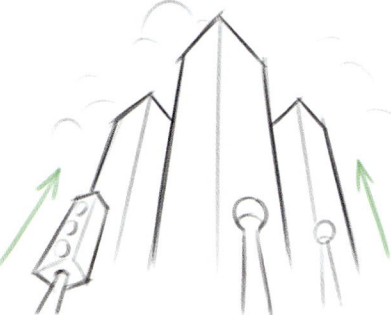

ONE IMAGINES THE VANISHING POINT MUCH LOWER.

EXAMPLE

Build the foundation for perspective.

We always begin by placing the horizon line and tracing the front side on the ground. This step helps to define the point of view of the scene and to establish the composition. It's important to devote some time to this phase—and restart as often as needed until you have the desired positioning.

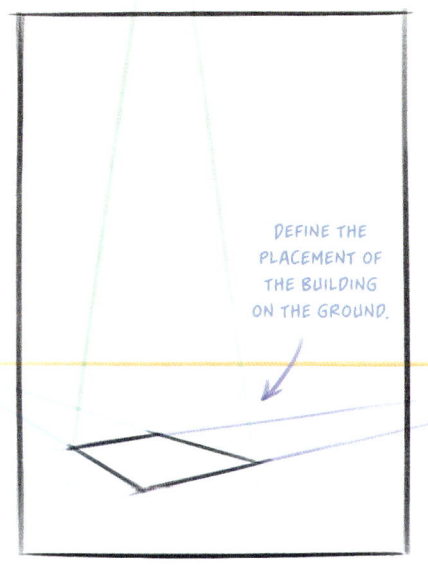

DEFINE THE PLACEMENT OF THE BUILDING ON THE GROUND.

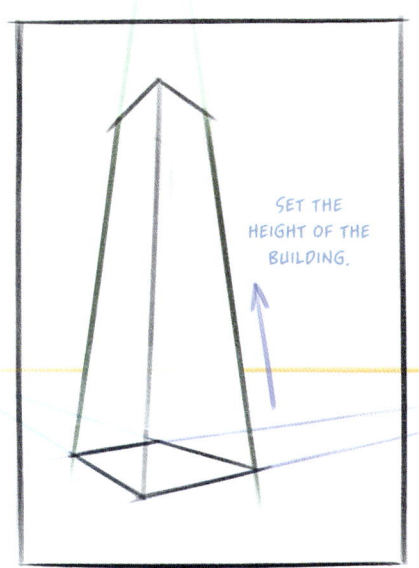

SET THE HEIGHT OF THE BUILDING.

Draw the main volume.

Once the front is placed on the ground, draw vertical lines, taking care to make them converge only slightly. They should not be parallel: instead, they should converge toward the same vanishing point. Close the volume at the desired height and don't forget to draw through the volume—this way, you can better see the object in the space and check if the perspective is correct.

3

Add reliefs.

Add reliefs that extend beyond the main frame of vanishing lines. Let the new lines converge on the left and right. The idea is to create volume and progressively detail the drawing, all while maintaining perspective.

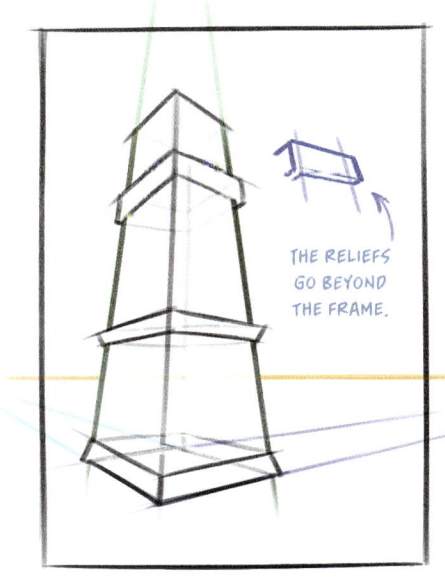

THE RELIEFS GO BEYOND THE FRAME.

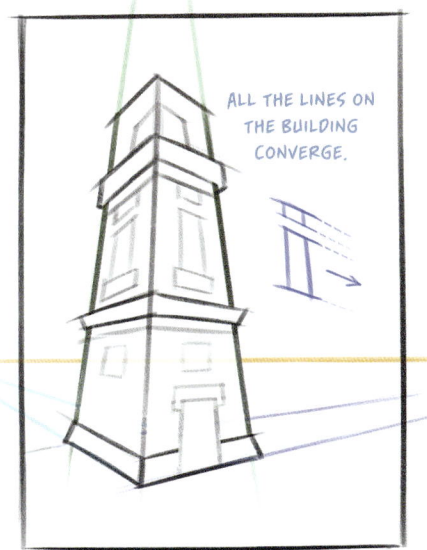

ALL THE LINES ON THE BUILDING CONVERGE.

4

Work at the building details.

Add details (windows, door) all around the building using basic shapes. Take care to ensure the convergence of lines and thus the perspective.

5

Add surrounding details.

The last stage, optional, involves detailing the environment surrounding the building. You can have fun creating details using simple forms (such as semicircles for clouds), varying the sizes, or adding rocks in the foreground.

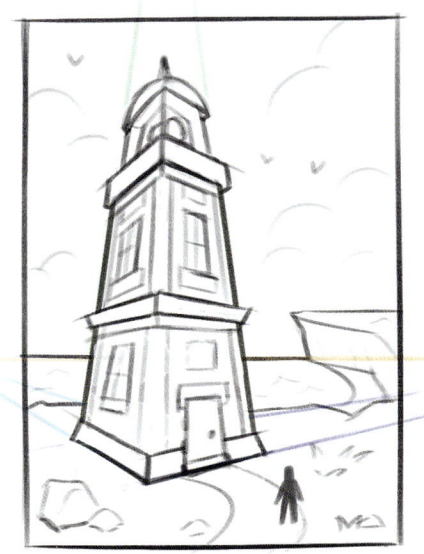

Draw a Monument with Perspective Using Three Vanishing Points

It's time to apply your newly acquired knowledge and draw a tower! The goal is to construct, step by step, a perspective that is believable and realistic, using a photo as a reference.

You will need :

✳ Your sketchbook or a sheet of paper
✳ 1 drawing pencil
✳ 1 eraser

Analyze the Model

For a solid start, analyze the direction of the vanishing lines. These lines will help you determine the position of the horizon line. The vanishing points are often too far off to be drawn on the sheet of paper. You will have to extrapolate the vanishing lines, imagining them far away.

Simplify the building by illustrating it as a box and eliminating details such as the reliefs and the molding.

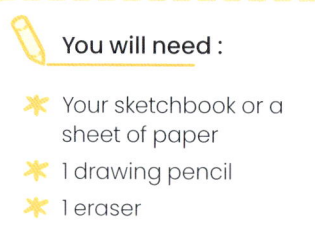

BIG BUILDINGS ARE OFTEN IN A PERSPECTIVE OF THREE VANISHING POINTS.

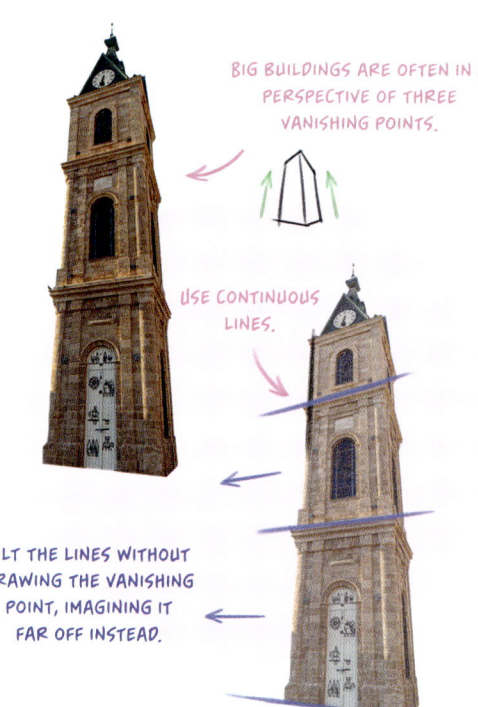

USE CONTINUOUS LINES.

TILT THE LINES WITHOUT DRAWING THE VANISHING POINT, IMAGINING IT FAR OFF INSTEAD.

The Drawing Step by Step

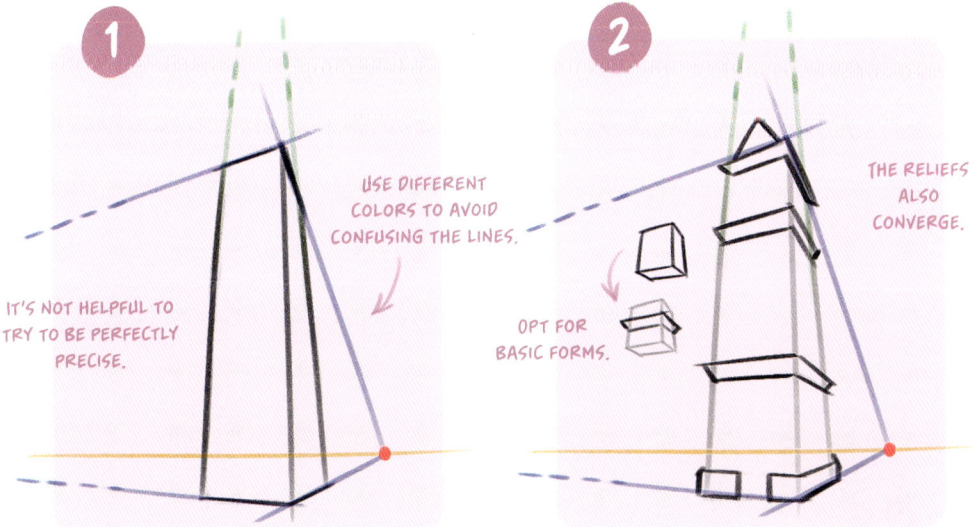

USE DIFFERENT COLORS TO AVOID CONFUSING THE LINES.

IT'S NOT HELPFUL TO TRY TO BE PERFECTLY PRECISE.

THE RELIEFS ALSO CONVERGE.

OPT FOR BASIC FORMS.

Draw the horizon line and the vanishing point that is visible. Next, draw the front on the ground, then draw vertical lines, from the bottom up, letting them lightly touch.

Add reliefs around the main volume. Be sure that the lines converge by taking your time to draw them one by one.

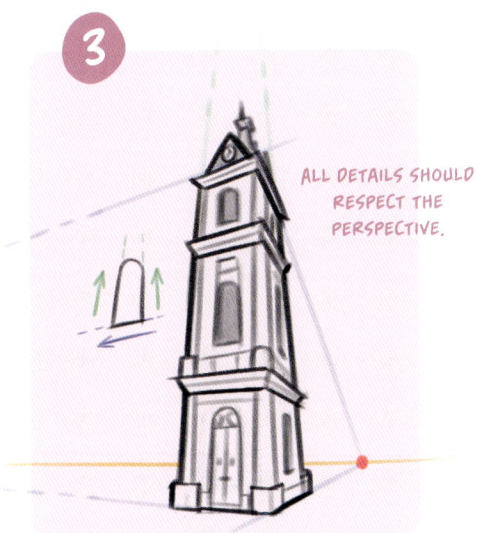

ALL DETAILS SHOULD RESPECT THE PERSPECTIVE.

Now that the structure is placed, you can add the details. Take care to ensure that all the lines converge!

15 | INTERIORS

You don't have to be an expert to draw interiors! Perspective with two vanishing points is all you need to help you conceive a whole room with elaborate furnishings.

The Main Room

To draw the furnishing and objects in a room, the *decor*, always begin by defining the point of view that you want to adopt by drawing a simple frame in perspective. You can choose between a perspective with one, two, or three vanishing points. All the elements of the decor will be placed inside the block!

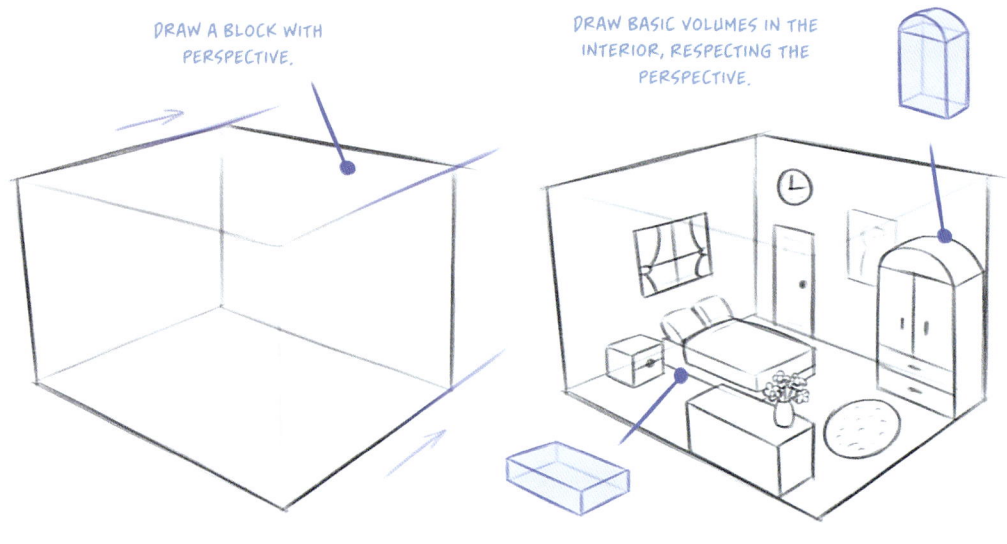

DRAW A BLOCK WITH PERSPECTIVE.

DRAW BASIC VOLUMES IN THE INTERIOR, RESPECTING THE PERSPECTIVE.

USE A PERSPECTIVE WITH TWO VANISHING POINTS FOR A NATURAL POINT OF VIEW.

DRAW THE VANISHING LINES WITH A RAISED HAND, IMAGINING THE VANISHING POINTS FAR OFF. THEY SHOULD ONLY SOMEWHAT CONVERGE.

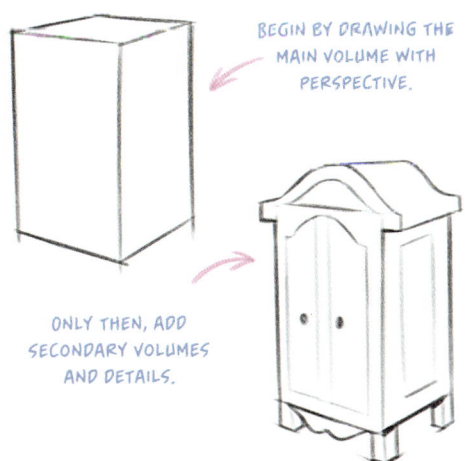

BEGIN BY DRAWING THE MAIN VOLUME WITH PERSPECTIVE.

ONLY THEN, ADD SECONDARY VOLUMES AND DETAILS.

From the Biggest to the Smallest

Defining the perspective of a main volume before adding details is absolutely essential, whether for a room or an object. Beginning with the basic volume, as in the example here, ensures the sense of the perspective. Drawing a detailed version directly—without this preliminary step—compromises the quality of the drawing. Add the larger elements of the decor before the smaller ones.

Choose Your Theme

To draw interesting decors, choose a theme along with objects to add. You can determine the position of the various elements in the composition by drawing rectangles in perspective: the rectangles should match the sides on the ground. And finally, draw the basic volumes to finish the sketch.

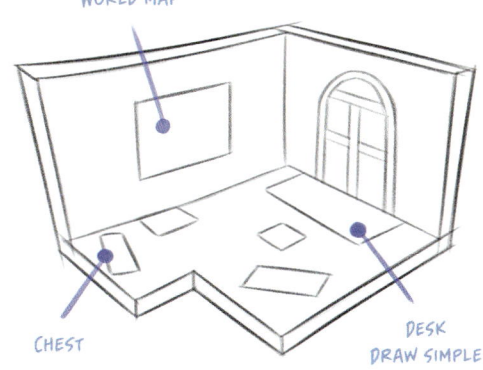

WORLD MAP

CHEST

DESK
DRAW SIMPLE

🐾 THEMES TO EXPLORE

* Desk with telescope
* Large, rounded window
* Desk chair
* World map
* Chest and scrolls

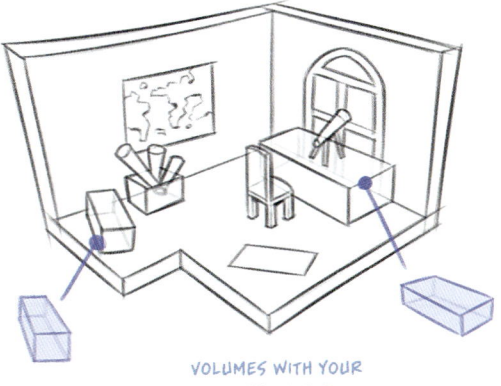

VOLUMES WITH YOUR HAND RAISED.

EXAMPLE

1

Create the perspective.

Begin by defining the perspective of the frame, or block, that will outline the room. As always, begin working on the volumes from the largest to the smallest.

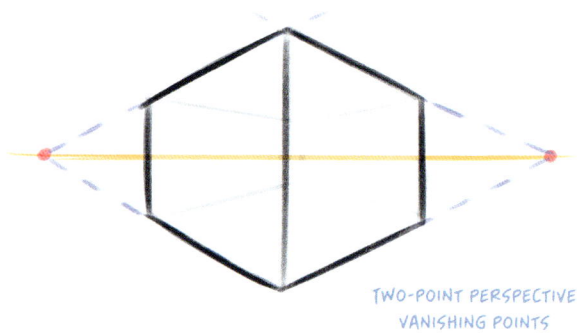

TWO-POINT PERSPECTIVE
VANISHING POINTS

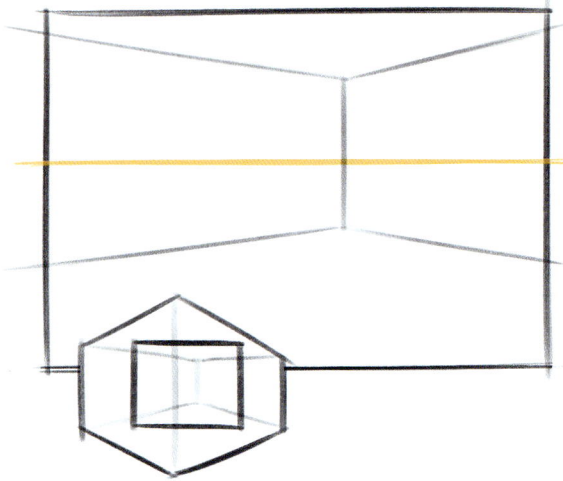

2

Frame the scene.

Define the frame of the block's interior. Imagine a camera focused on capturing an angle of the room—that is, a corner, including part of the ground and the ceiling.

IN THIS EXAMPLE, WE'VE
CHOSEN TO FOCUS ON THE
FARTHEST CORNER OF
THE ROOM.

The horizon line of the decor is the same as that of the block. The vanishing points are beyond the sheet of paper. Imagine the vanishing points far off to create only some convergence with the vanishing lines.

3

Position the front sides on the ground.

To position the furniture, draw the front sides that touch the ground. In this way, you will focus on the simplest shapes, which makes correct perspective much easier to achieve.

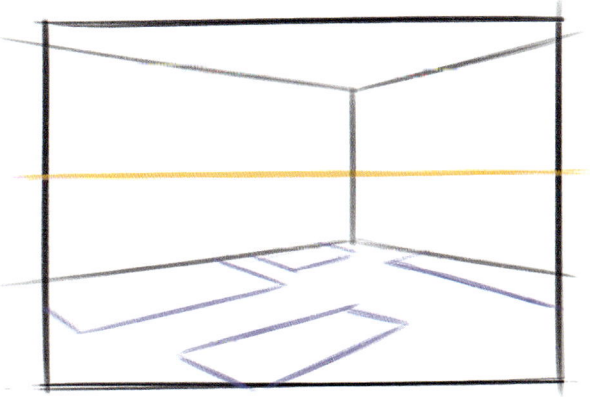

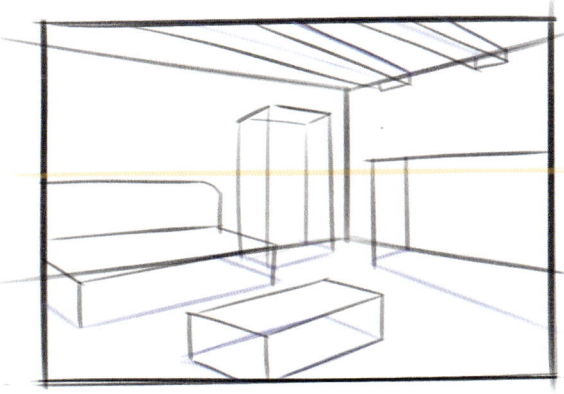

4

Draw the main volumes.

Next, draw vertical lines, going from the ground up, to create the volumes of the furniture. Paying attention to the convergence of lines, draw simple blocks. Imagine a far-off point and lightly slant the lines in that direction. The tilt does not have to be perfect!

5

Add secondary volumes and details.

The most technical stages are complete! The only thing left to do is to focus on the secondary volumes. Then, you can give "life" to the scene by adding curves and details.

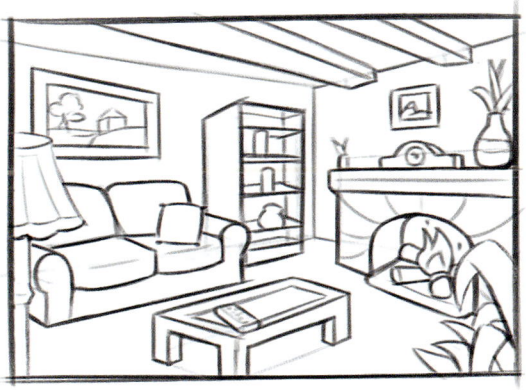

7

CONSTRUCTION

16 CONSTRUCTION

Construction, a principle of drawing, consists of assembling basic volumes, such as building blocks (for example, LEGOs), in a progressive way. Thanks to your competency in perspective, you can strengthen this principle even more.

A Hierarchy of Volumes

To build different volumes or blocks in a methodical way, we apply the same principle as that of the basic forms in 2D: we begin with the largest volume to progressively move toward the smallest. We will prioritize volumes according to three categories: main volume, secondary volume, and tertiary volume.

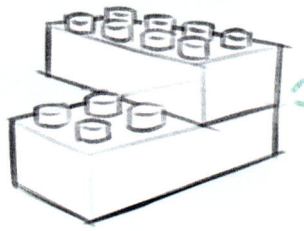

Main Volume	Secondary Volumes	Tertiary Volumes
This is the focus of the sketch. It's the most imposing volume of the subject.	These are the average-size volumes surrounding the main volume. They distinguish the subject in a more precise way.	The smaller volumes are not essential, but they allow you to enhance the subject and design of the drawing.

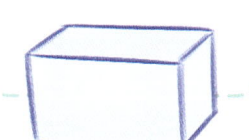

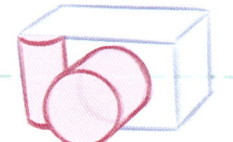

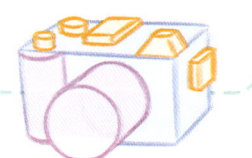

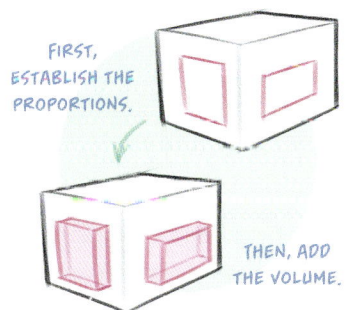

FIRST, ESTABLISH THE PROPORTIONS.

THEN, ADD THE VOLUME.

Relying on 2D Forms

To position the secondary and tertiary volumes on the main volume, the first step is always to lay them down in 2D using simple shapes, such as squares and rectangles. In this way, you can specify the position and proportions of the elements before transforming them into volumes.

Conserving the Perspective

Placing the 2D forms in the main block also allows you to control the perspective. In this way, you can better align all the volumes, including those you add to the main volume, with this perspective. This approach simplifies the construction of your drawing because it helps you to let all the lines converge in the same direction.

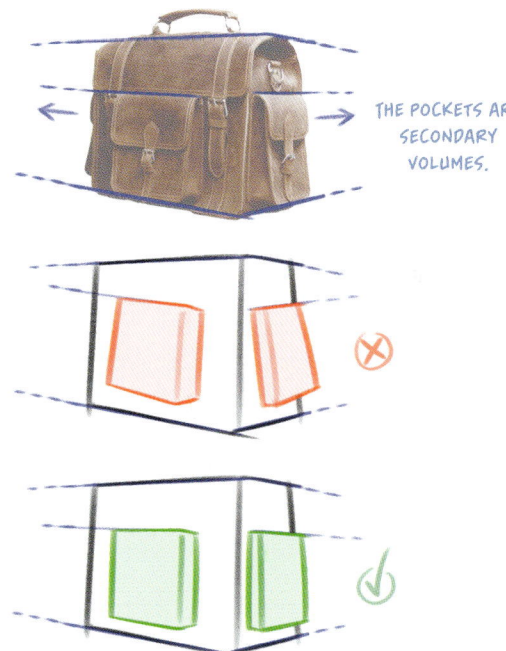

THE POCKETS ARE SECONDARY VOLUMES.

In this example, the pockets of the satchel will follow the same perspective as that of the main volume.

🖐 IN THE KNOW

Here's a tip for controlling both proportions and perspective in your construction: Draw a cross at the midpoint of the main volume.

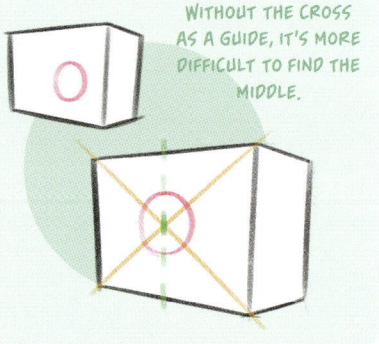

WITHOUT THE CROSS AS A GUIDE, IT'S MORE DIFFICULT TO FIND THE MIDDLE.

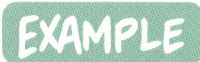

Draw the main block.

We always begin by drawing the largest volume of the object, the main block. In this example of a satchel, we'll take the time to establish the desired perspective so that we have a solid base for what follows. Then, using the cross technique, we will mark the middles of the sides to then center the secondary volumes.

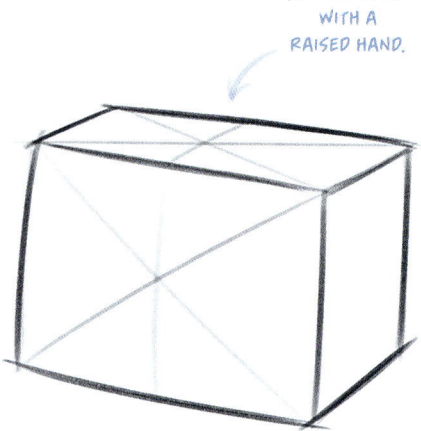

ALWAYS DRAW WITH A RAISED HAND.

Place the rectangles.

Lightly erase the marks of the cross and draw rectangles to better position the pockets. Marking the middle of the sides makes it much easier to place them in a symmetrical way. The goal is to respect the placements by following the principles of proportion.

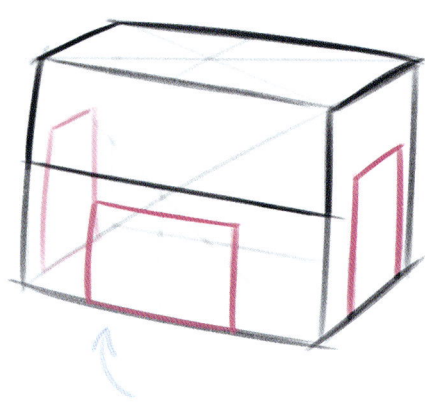

MARK THE POSITION OF THE POCKETS WITH RECTANGLES.

Draw lines that are not visible, imagining the volume as if it were transparent, to position the secondary volumes.

③ Add secondary blocks.

Once the placements are marked, you can add volume to the secondary elements, keeping in mind the perspective. Without drawing the vanishing point, you can simply converge the lines in the same direction, on the left and on the right. This is a good exercise for developing your instinct while practicing spontaneous and natural lines.

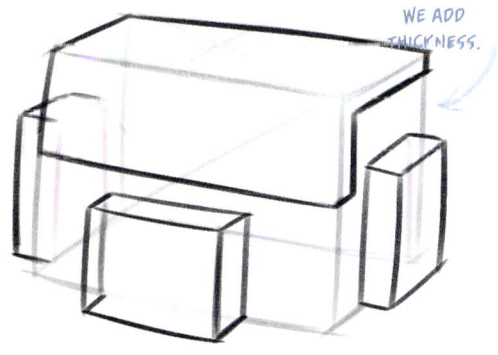

WE ADD THICKNESS.

CREATE RELIEF ON THE TOP OF THE SATCHEL.

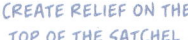

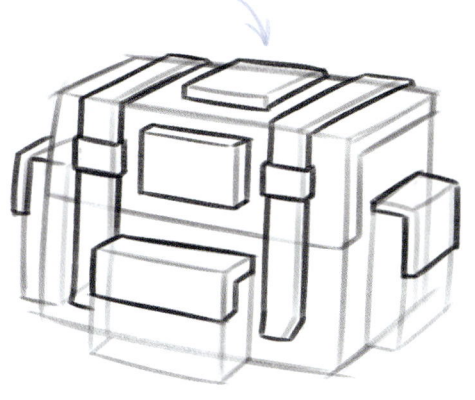

④ Add tertiary blocks.

Now that the structure of the satchel is in place, it's time to add the final volumes. Always draw cubic blocks to make this task simple. Our only concern here is to give the illusion of volume to the sketch while keeping the proportions in check.

DRAW OVER THE STRUCTURAL SKETCH.

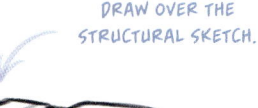

⑤ Finalize the sketch.

Finally, lightly erase the structural sketch to create a final drawing over top of it. The focus here is on the quality of your lines. Give preference to the straight and lightly curved lines. Keep a light touch to control the movement, going over the lines several times to add the desired thickness.

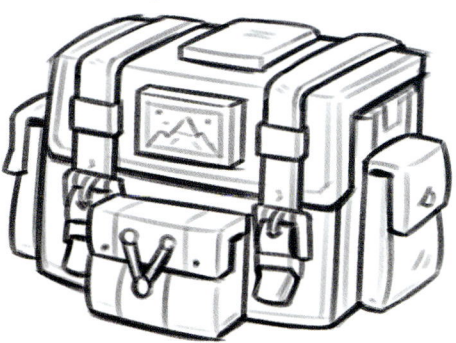

Draw an Object Using Basic Volumes

Let's practice now! The goal of this exercise is to use the principle of construction to assemble different basic volumes while respecting the hierarchy of different elements.

You will need :

* Your sketchbook or a sheet of paper
* 1 drawing pencil
* 1 eraser

Analyze the Model

Whatever you choose for a model, the first step is to analyze the perspective of the main volume. Here, we'll create a perspective with two vanishing points. Observe the incline of the vanishing lines to reproduce them. Then, deconstruct the bag into three types of volumes: main, secondary, and tertiary.

Print a photo of the model to draw over it. This makes the analysis of perspective and of the direction of vanishing lines easier.

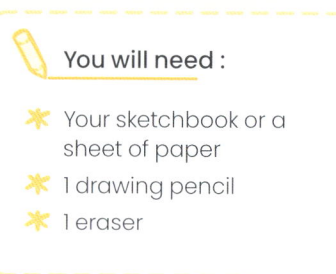

IDENTIFY THE VANISHING LINES.

PRIORITIZE THE BASIC VOLUMES.

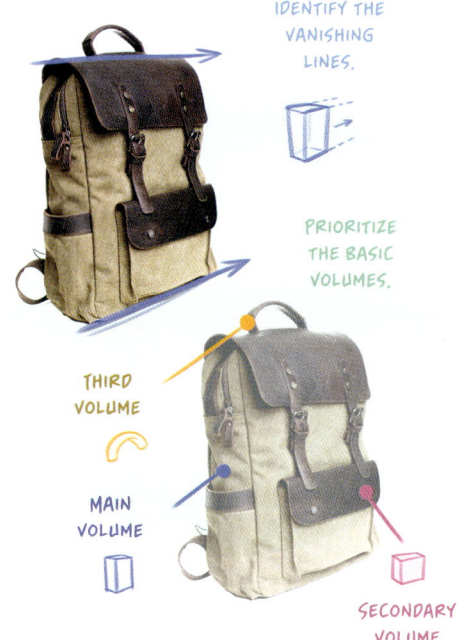

THIRD VOLUME

MAIN VOLUME

SECONDARY VOLUME

The Drawing Step by Step

1 LIGHTLY CURVE THE LINE OF THE FRONT OF THE BAG BEFORE ADDING ROUNDNESS TO THE VOLUME.

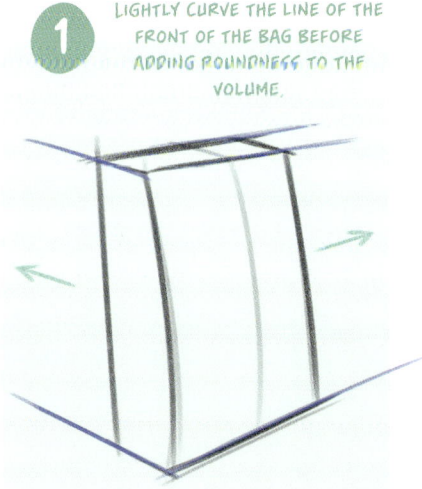

Begin by drawing the main volume in perspective. Take the time to identify the height and width of the block to achieve proportions that match those of the model.

2 CONSIDER ADDING THICKNESS TO YOUR BLOCKS

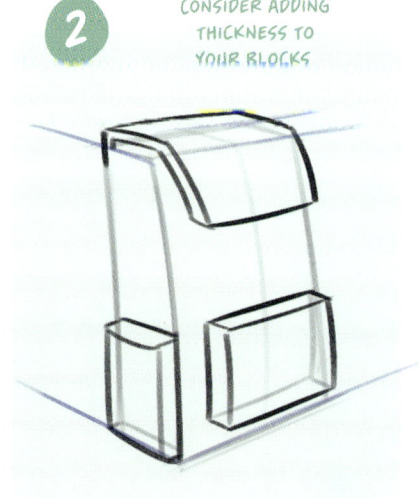

Add the secondary volumes while simplifying the basic ones. The pockets can be simplified into flattened blocks.

3 THE DETAILS THEMSELVES ARE ALSO VOLUMINOUS.

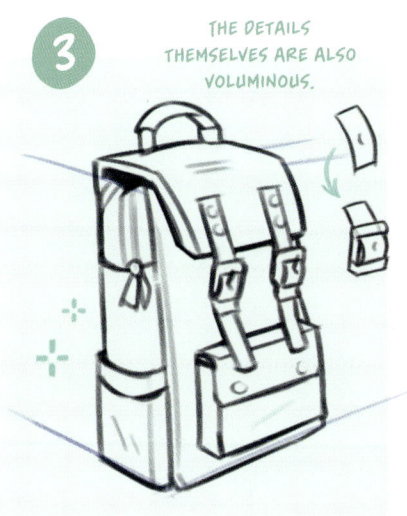

Finish with the smallest volumes, such as the straps. Keep the proportions in mind to position the various volumes accordingly. Always go with the simplest way.

17

THE BOX SYSTEM

To help you lay the first lines of a structural sketch, begin by first drawing a box. Framing provides an accurate perspective that will empower you to draw more complex subjects.

Creating from a Box

Boxes are cubic volumes of varied shapes and sizes. They can contain anything at all because any object can be held in a cubic volume, whether an animal, decor, or object. Boxes are useful tools when starting from a blank page and drawing any complex subject in perspective. Once the box is drawn, you can create the structural sketch by gathering the volumes inside it.

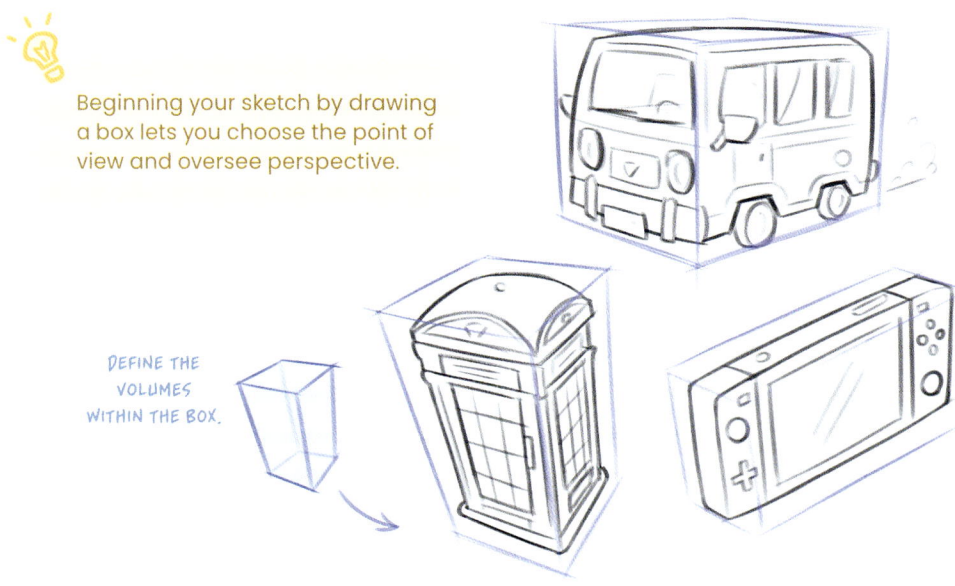

Beginning your sketch by drawing a box lets you choose the point of view and oversee perspective.

DEFINE THE VOLUMES WITHIN THE BOX.

Sculpting the Curves

Drawing rounded volumes in perspective can be difficult. Since cubic volumes are easier to create in perspective than rounded volumes, it's best to begin by drawing a box. Once the perspective of the box is set, you can then focus on the roundness.

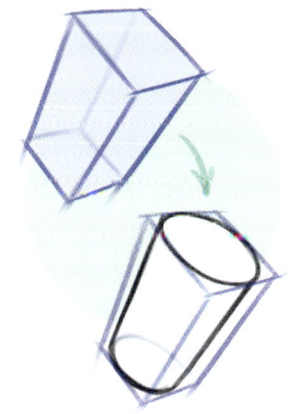

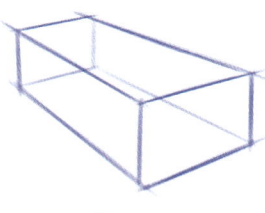

BEGIN BY
DRAWING A BOX.

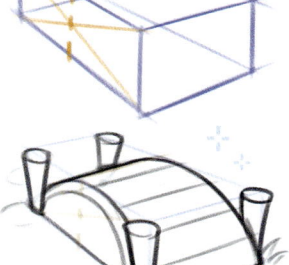

YOU CAN FIND THE
MIDDLE OF THE VOLUME
USING A CROSS.

If we had immediately drawn the bridge without first having drawn a box, it would have been much more difficult to achieve the desired angle afterward.

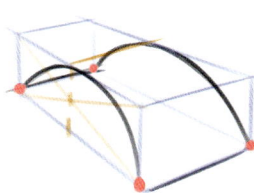

MARK THE FARTHEST
POINTS AND CONNECT THEM
WITH CURVES.

LIGHTLY ERASE, THEN DRAW THE
FINAL SKETCH OVER TOP.

🐾 IN THE KNOW

Practice tracing ellipses inside squares and rectangles in perspective to feel more at ease with curved lines.

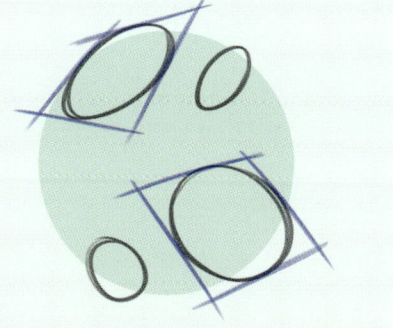

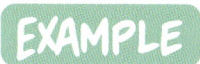

Draw the box in perspective.

Let's take the example of a car, which is a complex model. To simplify, begin by drawing a box in perspective with the desired dimensions. Cars are longer than they are wide, so adjust the format of the box accordingly.

DRAW THROUGH THE BOX AS IF IT WAS TRANSPARENT.

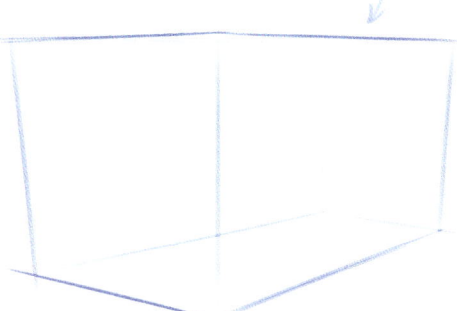

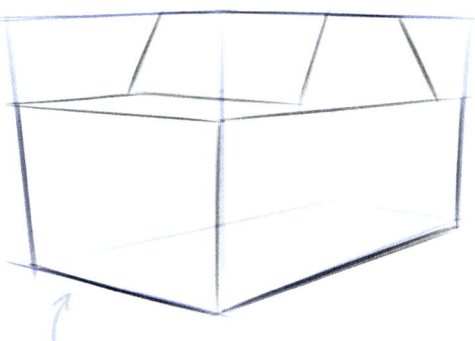

LIGHTLY ERASE THE TRACES OF THE BOX: THESE WILL SERVE AS MARKERS.

Draw the main volumes.

Create your drawing inside the box with the principle of construction in mind. The box defines the size of the object, allowing you to maintain the correct perspective. Draw the main volume of the car, as well as the upper part, which is lightly inclined.

3

Work on the secondary volumes.

In a construction drawing, it's often necessary to add blocks to the structure, but this is not always the case. Sometimes, it's better to sculpt the main blocks to define the secondary ones. Here, for example, drawing rectangles helps to determine the position of the wheels, windshield, and windows.

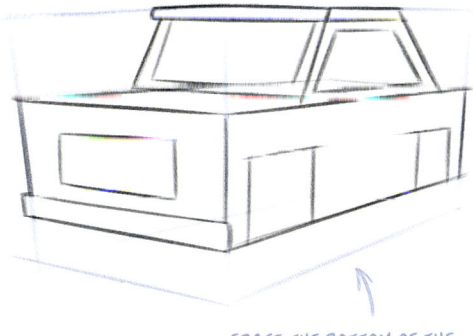

ERASE THE BOTTOM OF THE BOX TO BETTER POSITION THE WHEELS.

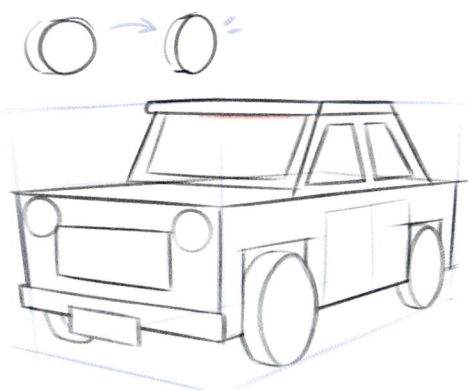

4

Add the tertiary volumes.

Since the general structure is complete, we can now incorporate the last elements such as the headlights, wheels, and so on. The bottom of the box is the ground, which helps to position the wheels on this same line.

SINCE THE BASE OF THE SUBJECT IS POSITIONED, THE SKETCH IS EASIER TO REALIZE.

Finalize the sketch.

Finally, you can lightly erase the structural sketch to create the final drawing with a pencil or pen. Add the curves on the roof and detail the wheels and frontal elements of the car, as much as you like.

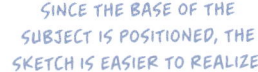
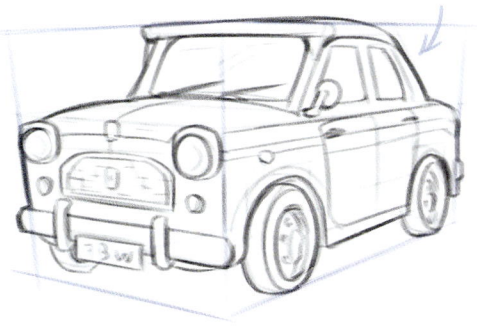

Draw a Ladybug Using a Box

It's time to practice by using a model that embodies round forms. Studying insects is an excellent exercise for this. Because they often have rounded bodies, they are ideal models for working on perspective.

You will need :

✳ Your sketchbook or a sheet of paper

✳ 1 drawing pencil

✳ 1 eraser

Analyze the Model

Let's take the example of a ladybug. You can simplify it into a sphere that is cut in two, with a domed lid sitting on top. Next, identify the secondary and tertiary volumes. Then, analyze the perspective to determine the angle from which the ladybug is viewed.

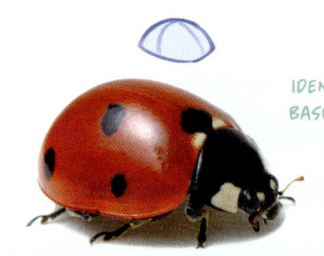

IDENTIFY THE BASIC FORMS.

ENVISION A BOX SURROUNDING THE LADYBUG.

Devote some time to creating various sketches of boxes, drawn from different angles, to reproduce the most faithful perspective of the model.

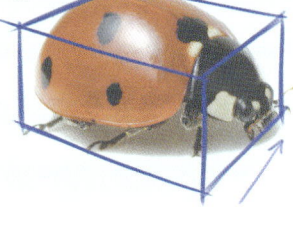

The Drawing Step by Step

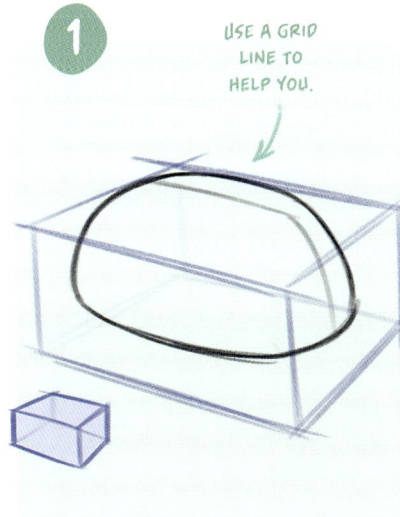

USE A GRID
LINE TO
HELP YOU.

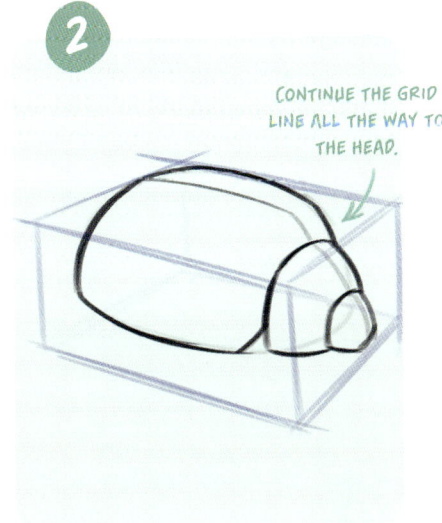

CONTINUE THE GRID
LINE ALL THE WAY TO
THE HEAD.

Begin by drawing a box in perspective. Next, draw an egg-shaped volume for the body and then join the contours to the box.

Erase the front of the volume and sculpt it into three parts to create the anatomy of the insect. Use basic and rounded volumes.

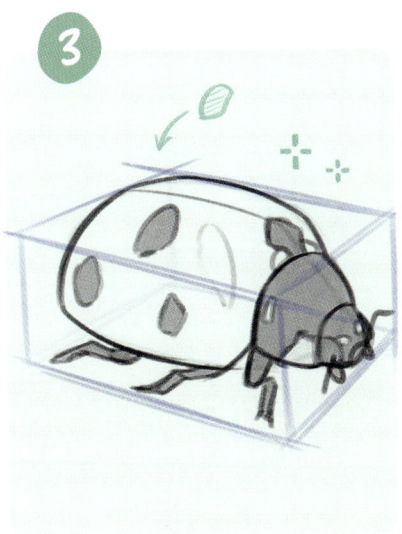

Add final details such as the ladybug's feet, which are simple cylinders, and the black dots.

PRINCIPLE

PRINCIPLE 18 | ANGLES OF VIEW

Thanks to all that you have learned about volumes, you're now able to draw the same model from various angles. It's as easy as simplifying the model into a cubic form.

Two Parameters to Take into Account

Drawing an object from different angles can seem intimidating. It is your first step toward drawing from the imagination. To make this task easier, consider varying two parameters to establish a point of view.

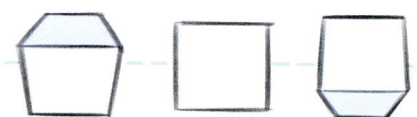

Vertical Incline

You can adapt the point of view by varying the incline of a cube, following its vertical axis whether on the top, the front, or the bottom. Keep in mind the principle of perspective and modify the position of the horizon line accordingly.

Horizontal Incline

Imagine a camera encircling a cube on a horizontal axis. Depending on where the camera is positioned, you might see the cube from the right, front, or left side.

When you master each type of incline, you can then combine the two! By varying the vertical incline as well as the horizontal one, you'll be able to create more nuanced angles.

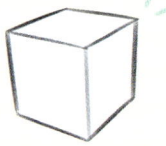

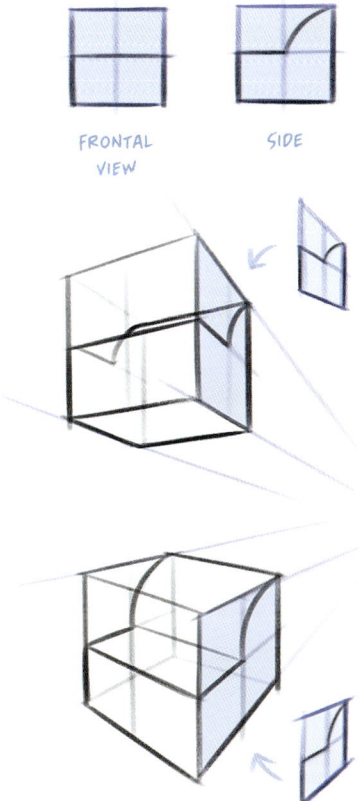

FRONTAL
VIEW

SIDE

Creating 2D Plans

To draw more complex objects, it's best to begin with a sketch in 2D. Create the front and side view of the object within a simple square.

Let's take the example of the armchair (see left). We start by drawing the frontal view, placing the chair in the middle of the square. Next, for the side, divide the square into two—this allows you to place the backrest of the chair at an appropriate depth. By positioning the marks on the cube to create perspective and marking the center of each side of the cube, you'll be able to draw this armchair from any angle whatsoever.

Drawing based on boxes is the key to drawing from your imagination. You can simplify any object in a simple box!

Practice with a Raised Hand

To develop your instinct and progress further in your understanding of volumes and perspective, the most important thing to do is practice with a raised hand. Explore and have fun with drawing objects from different angles—without looking for perfection.

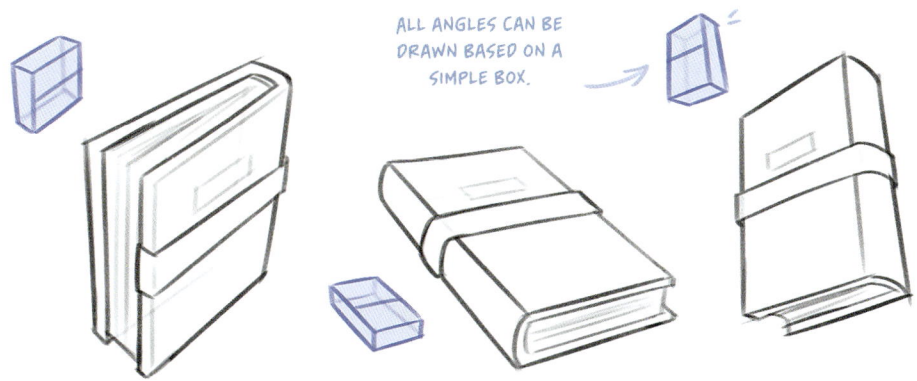

ALL ANGLES CAN BE
DRAWN BASED ON A
SIMPLE BOX.

EXERCISE

Draw an Object from Different Angles

The goal of this exercise is to draw an object of your choice from several angles, combining principles 17 and 18. Train yourself with one simple object, such as a teacup.

 You will need :

* Your sketchbook or a sheet of paper
* 1 drawing pencil
* 1 eraser

Analyze the Model

Begin by simplifying the object into basic volumes. The less there are, the easier the exercise will be. Next, analyze the perspective to determine the point of view. You can create several small sketches from different angles before choosing the one you like.

 Pay attention to the width, height, and depth of the box.

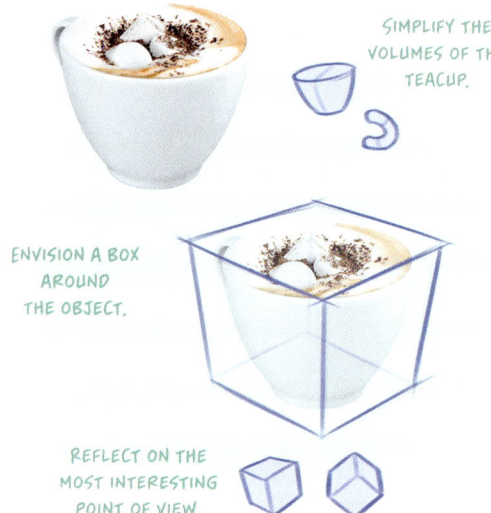

SIMPLIFY THE VOLUMES OF THE TEACUP.

ENVISION A BOX AROUND THE OBJECT.

REFLECT ON THE MOST INTERESTING POINT OF VIEW.

The Drawing Step by Step

1

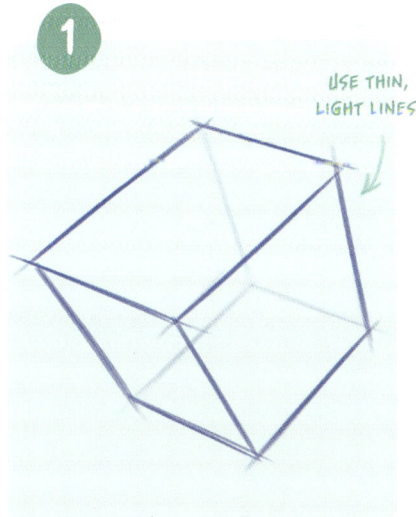

USE THIN,
LIGHT LINES.

2

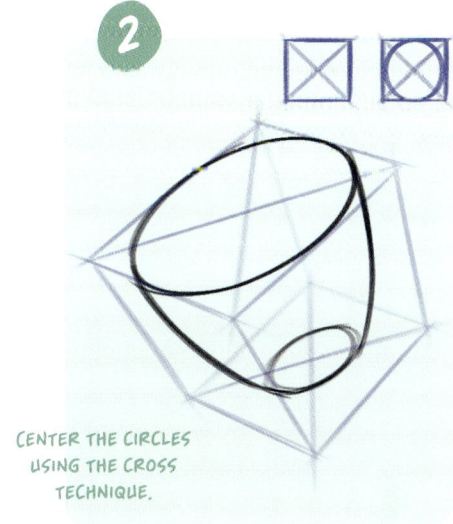

CENTER THE CIRCLES
USING THE CROSS
TECHNIQUE.

Start by drawing a cube from a different angle than the model. Make the lines converge to vanishing points in the distance.

Lightly erase your sketch and draw a slightly rounded cylindrical shape inside. Center the ends of the cylinder on the faces of the cube.

3

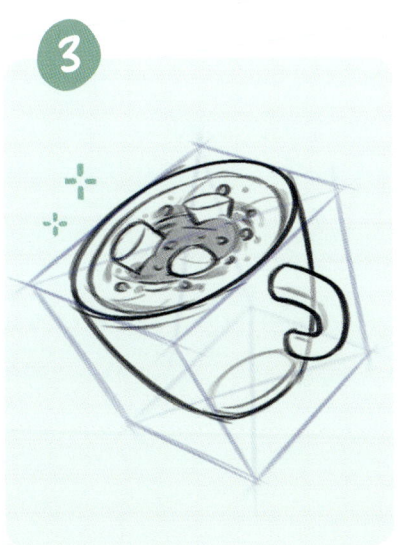

Draw the secondary volume in the location of your choice. Then, draw the details, such as the marshmallows, envisioning them as cylinders.

8

DETAILS

19 THE ILLUSION OF DETAILS

The addition of details is the last step (or the last layer) of a sketch. It's not about reaching a precise photo-like image, but rather about creating designs and infusing them with realism. Creating detail in your drawings follows a very different strategy than that of identical reproduction.

Two Categories of Details

There are two major categories of details: textural and environmental. When used together, they help you create a complete and refined drawing, one that gives the impression of a wealth of information.

Details of Texture

Decoration, embellishment, and design imitate texture (wood, fur, metal, etc.). They help to distinguish the model, giving it more precision. You can draw these details on the surface of the model.

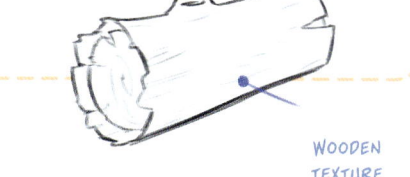

WOODEN
TEXTURE

Details of the Environment

These elements are added around the main subject, allowing you to contextualize the drawing, tell a story, or enhance the scene.

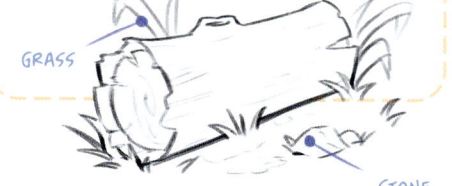

GRASS

STONE

It's always interesting to think about what (story) you want to tell in your drawing. This helps you to select the details in a more reflective way.

Giving a View of the Whole

When we begin drawing, we often prioritize the details, which can be detrimental to the drawing's design and slow our progress. To spend less time on the details and still get effective results, maintaining a global view of the ensemble is essential. In reality, the human eye does not perceive every detail. For example, if we look at a fish, we don't see each individual scale at the same time. We perceive the texture of the scales in their entirety, and it is precisely this view of the whole that our brain interprets as being most realistic.

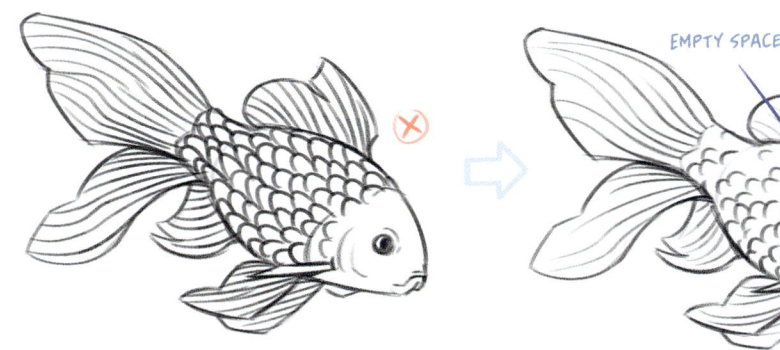

DRAWING ALL THE DETAILS IS TEDIOUS, AND THE RESULT IS NOT NECESSARILY AESTHETICALLY PLEASING.

BY ADDING DETAILS IN CERTAIN PLACES AND IN VARYING THE THICKNESS OF THE LINES, YOU CAN OFFER JUST ENOUGH INFORMATION TO THE EYE TO REPRESENT THE TEXTURE.

Working in Details Using Groups of Shapes

To give a realistic impression to your drawing without overloading it, you can group subjects together in groups of two or three. For the best balance, leave two-thirds as empty space. The eye will seize upon the global whole, creating the illusion of reality on its own. This approach is both effective and quick!

Light plays an important role. Well-lit areas offer less detail—thus the need to leave some empty spaces.

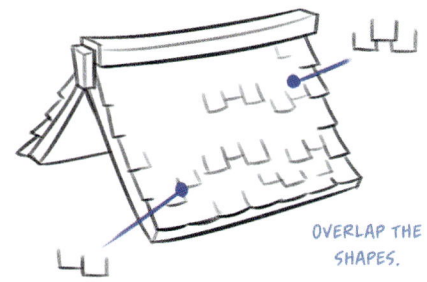

OVERLAP THE SHAPES.

PRINCIPLE

20 CONTRAST

As with the previous principle, it is crucial to not overload your drawing with details. The other important aspect is striking a balance between your design and the amount of detail. To get there, you'll have to establish a hierarchy of lines.

Prioritize the Information

Prioritizing the elements of a design is indispensable to emphasizing details and encouraging a sense of logic. The most important elements stand out, and the details stay in the background.

Fundamental Elements: Thick Line	Secondary Elements: Average Line	Detail Elements: Fine Line
Emphasize the main elements of a drawing using thicker lines.	For secondary or less important elements, maintain lines of average thickness.	Even though it isn't crucial to the clarity of the design, detail elements help embellish it. We use fine lines to keep the details subtle.
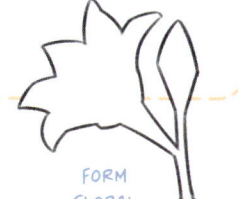 FORM GLOBAL	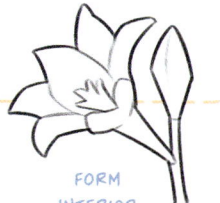 FORM INTERIOR	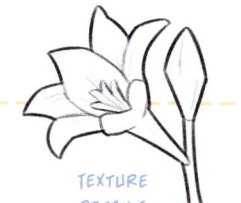 TEXTURE DETAILS

Adding Depth with Solid Black

We add solid black, small geometric shapes worked with a 2B pencil, as a final touch to the drawing, to create contrast and depth. We just need to place a few of them strategically, especially where the shadows are most pronounced. In the example opposite, we position them at the level of the hollows between the blueberries, for an overlay effect.

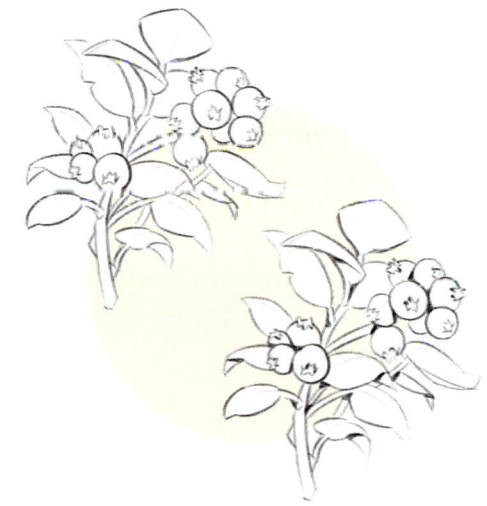

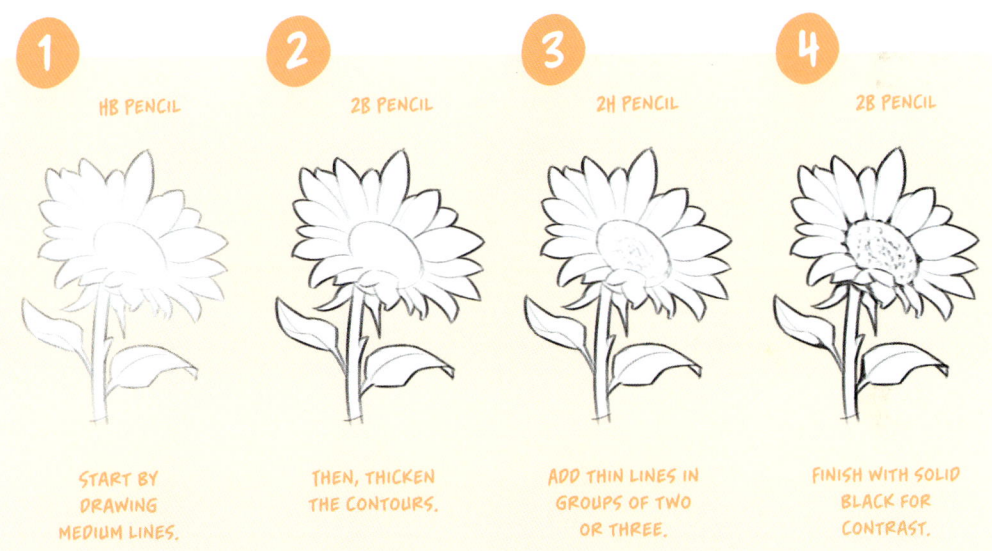

1 HB PENCIL

START BY DRAWING MEDIUM LINES.

2 2B PENCIL

THEN, THICKEN THE CONTOURS.

3 2H PENCIL

ADD THIN LINES IN GROUPS OF TWO OR THREE.

4 2B PENCIL

FINISH WITH SOLID BLACK FOR CONTRAST.

 Place the black shading carefully, keeping in mind the principle of layering. Since they symbolize the most pronounced shadows, we always place them on the elements located in the background.

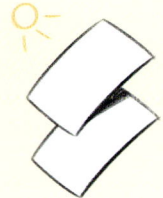

Draw the Details of a Flower

The goal of this exercise is to add details to the sketch by maintaining harmony and balance. You'll want to keep empty spaces to allow the drawing to breathe, while adjusting the thickness of lines to prioritize the elements.

You will need :

* Your sketchbook or a sheet of paper
* 3 drawing pencils (HB, 2B, and 2H)
* 1 eraser

Analyze the Model

To effectively place details in the sketch, you'll want to examine the elements of the flower to determine the thickness of the lines used for each component. Also keep in mind the principle of grid lines (see p. 54). The texture of the petals follows their curvature, like grid lines.

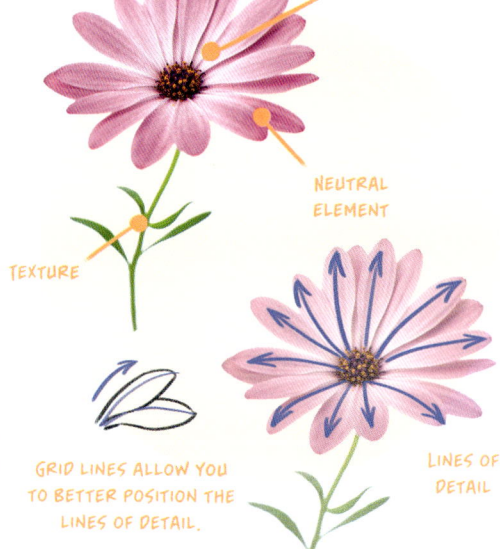

IMPORTANT ELEMENTS

NEUTRAL ELEMENT

TEXTURE

GRID LINES ALLOW YOU TO BETTER POSITION THE LINES OF DETAIL.

LINES OF DETAIL

This is not the only approach! You are free to express the lines differently. So long as your choices are consistent, the design will be credible.

The Drawing Step by Step

1

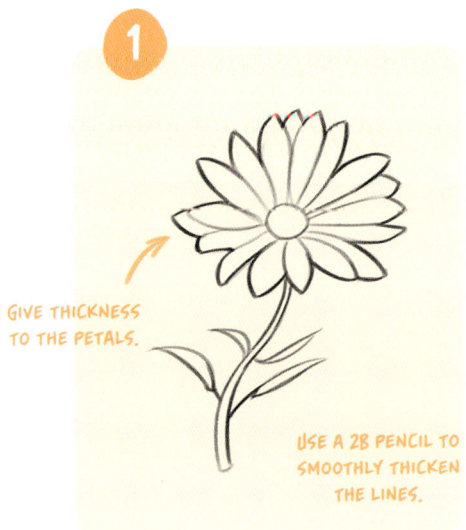

GIVE THICKNESS
TO THE PETALS.

USE A 2B PENCIL TO
SMOOTHLY THICKEN
THE LINES.

Make an initial sketch focusing on the proportions. Next, lightly thicken the contours to showcase the entire form.

2

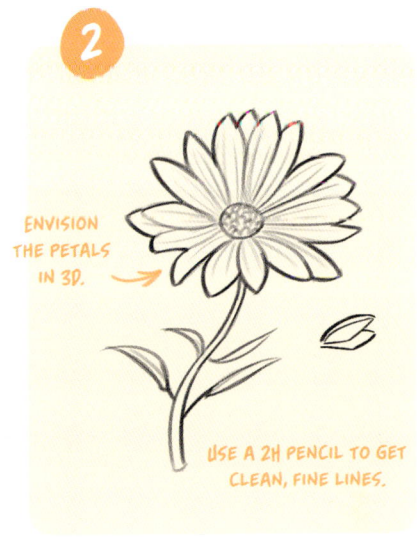

ENVISION
THE PETALS
IN 3D.

USE A 2H PENCIL TO GET
CLEAN, FINE LINES.

Add fine lines on the petals, following their curves. Leave some white spaces between the lines.

3

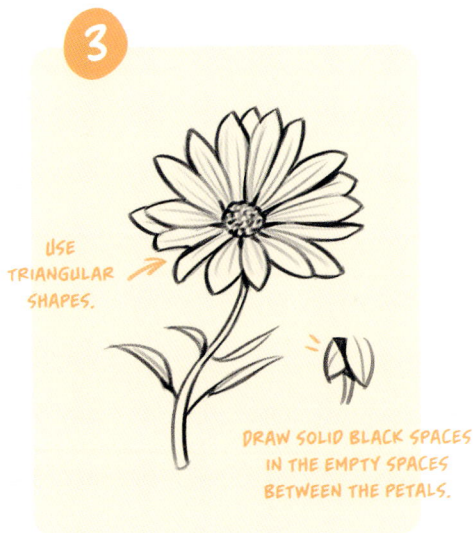

USE
TRIANGULAR
SHAPES.

DRAW SOLID BLACK SPACES
IN THE EMPTY SPACES
BETWEEN THE PETALS.

Finish by adding solid black spaces using a 2B pencil. Draw these in an area that seems to be darker, like the center of the flower. Test out different positions!

21 | TEXTURES

Soft, coarse, granular . . . thanks to the repetition of designs, you can reproduce the surface of objects. Textures add a sensory dimension to your drawing, making it more realistic.

Draw Two Types of Textures

Repeated Patterns

Uniform textures that are regular (such as fur, water, and grass) can be drawn using the same pattern all over the surface of the subject.

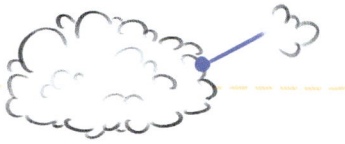

Multiple Patterns

For irregular and more unpredictable textures (like wood, metal, or rock), the drawing will need to include variations in order to create an accurate drawing.

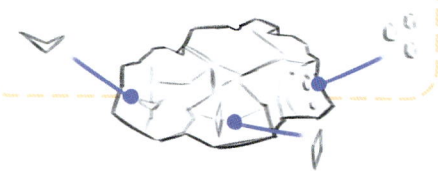

🔥 IN THE KNOW

When you draw a texture, whether with a repeated patten or multiple patterns, you must break the continuity of contours. Erase the straight lines and draw them back in over top. Here (right), we're using short, straight lines to represent fur.

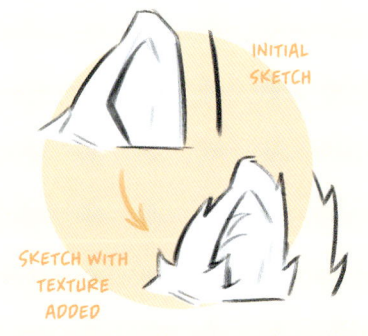

INITIAL SKETCH

SKETCH WITH TEXTURE ADDED

Creating a Simplified Pattern

To add texture to your sketches, it's essential to learn to identify and simplify patterns. This approach involves studying the texture you wish to represent by identifying the repeating patterns, then seeking to simplify them into their most elementary form.

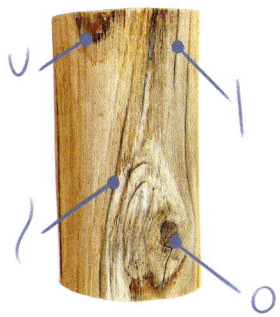

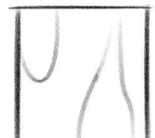 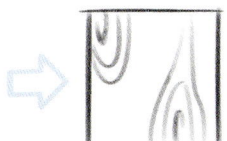 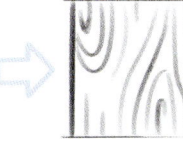

FIRST, DRAW THE LARGER FORMS.

REPEAT THE CURVES SEVERAL TIMES.

ADD SHORT, STRAIGHT LINES.

OBSERVE THE PRESENCE OF VARIOUS PATTERNS.

Working on patterns in 2D in a square allows you to evaluate the drawing. If it's convincing, add volume.

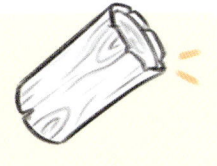

Integrating Four Parameters

To draw a realistic texture, it's important to take into account four parameters: size, incline, thickness of lines, and spacing of patterns. Let's take the example of grass, a repeated pattern with a single texture. To make grass more realistic in your drawing, you will need to introduce some disorder, varying the parameters. Avoid any symmetry to produce more natural sketches.

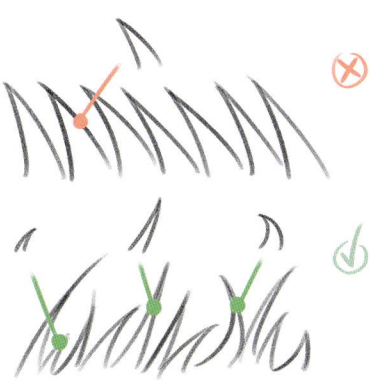

THE LINES HERE GREATLY VARY IN SIZE, INCLINE, THICKNESS, AND SPACING.

EXAMPLE

1

Analyze the texture.

When observing this image, in addition to identifying the silhouette and the main shapes, now analyze the texture. Is it uniform or irregular? And is it repeated? Here, the texture of the fur is in a unique pattern that is repeated all over the animal's body

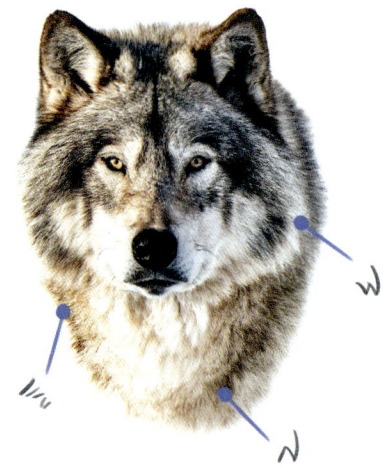

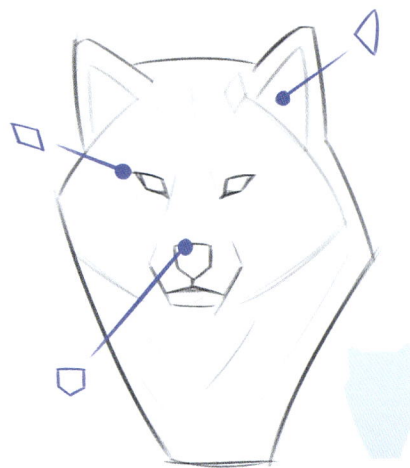

2

Make your first sketch.

First, draw the silhouette. Then, add the details in the interior with simple shapes, such as a trapezoid for the eyes and triangle for the ears. Respect the proportions by checking the width and height of each element.

Add texture to the contours.

Break up the contours using different line sizes, tilt, and spacing. Don't add too many textured lines to the silhouette. In areas where there is less long fur, such as on the ears and the muzzle, keep the lines straight.

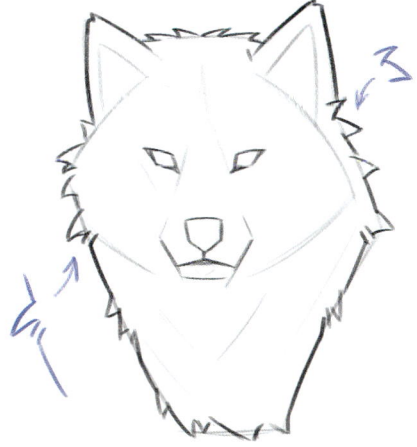

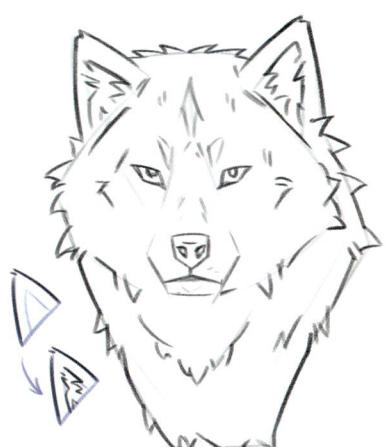

Work on the interior of the sketch.

Now draw the interior of the silhouette to create the effect of texture. Unlike the contours, use thinner and finer lines for the inside.

Reinforce the contrast.

Finish the sketch by adjusting the thickness of the lines and adding the final details. Apply solid black to the darkest areas, such as the ears. Remember that the textures are determined by the thickness and length of the lines.

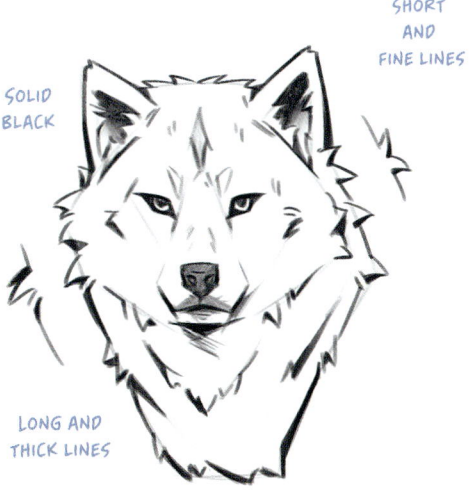

SHORT AND FINE LINES

SOLID BLACK

LONG AND THICK LINES

EXAMPLE

1

Analyze the texture.

Grass represents a dense mass formed of individual strands. Each strand follows the same pattern: a long, thin triangle shape. The aim is to recreate the impression of density without drawing each individual strand of grass.

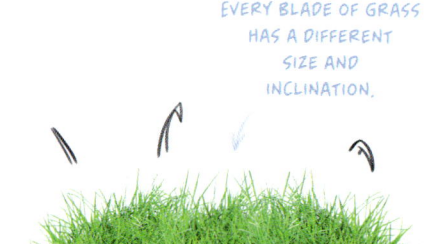

EVERY BLADE OF GRASS HAS A DIFFERENT SIZE AND INCLINATION.

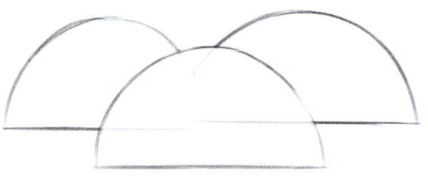

HERE, THREE TUFTS OF GRASS ARE USED TO GIVE RELIEF.

2

Make your first sketch.

For the first sketch, use basic shapes, such as semicircles, for the tufts of grass. It is beneficial to divide the texture into groups of shapes to generate relief. Overlapping the shapes will give the illusion of depth and volume.

Add texture to the contours.

Slightly erase the semicircles to apply texture along the contours. Use triangle shapes in different sizes and shapes and leave some empty space in between. Plants are organic forms with chaotic and asymmetrical texture; therefore, make the lines irregular in shape.

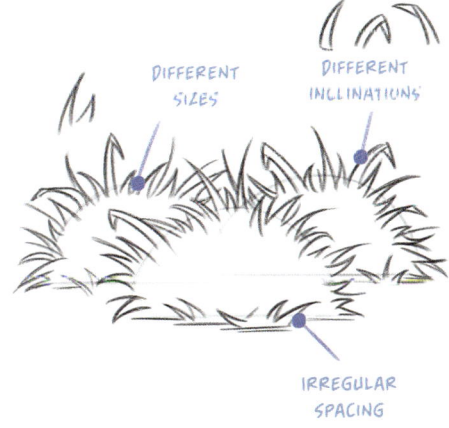

DIFFERENT SIZES

DIFFERENT INCLINATIONS

IRREGULAR SPACING

Work the interior of the sketch.

Now draw the details of the interior of the sketch of the silhouette to create the effect of texture. Use both single lines and triangles for the blades of grass. As you near the ground, the definition decreases because the mass is denser at the bottom. Make sure to leave some empty spaces.

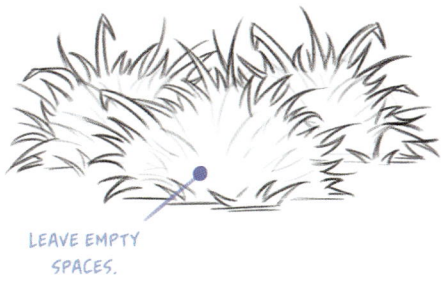

LEAVE EMPTY SPACES.

Reinforce the contrast.

Finish the sketch by adjusting the thickness of the lines. Do not thicken the entire contour but only a few strands that appear larger or detached from the mass for contrast. Add solid black to the areas where the strands overlap and the sketch is complete!

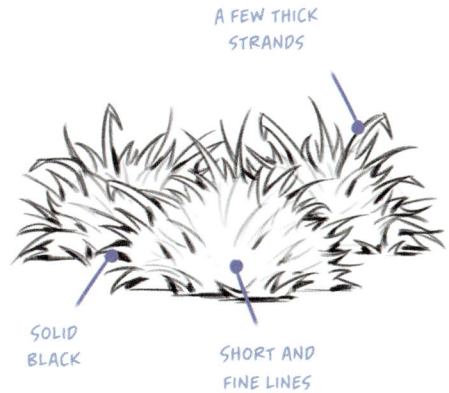

A FEW THICK STRANDS

SOLID BLACK

SHORT AND FINE LINES

EXAMPLE

Analyze the texture.

Trees present two distinct textures: the foliage and the bark. The foliage has a repeated pattern. The leaves can be simplified into semicircles of different shapes, sizes, and incline. On the other hand, the pattern on the bark is varied. To make the task easier, use S lines to represent the bark.

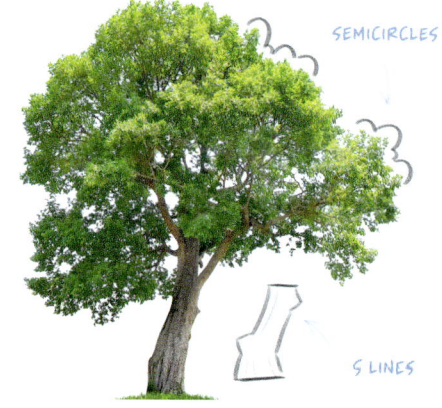

SEMICIRCLES

S LINES

Make your first sketch.

Base your first sketch on the tree's silhouette. Separate the foliage into three blocks and simplify the negative spaces to make the silhouette pop. Smooth the tree's structure as much as possible, without any texture. This sketch forms the skeleton of the design, so it's important to spend sufficient time on this first step.

SMOOTH OUT THE CONTOURS.

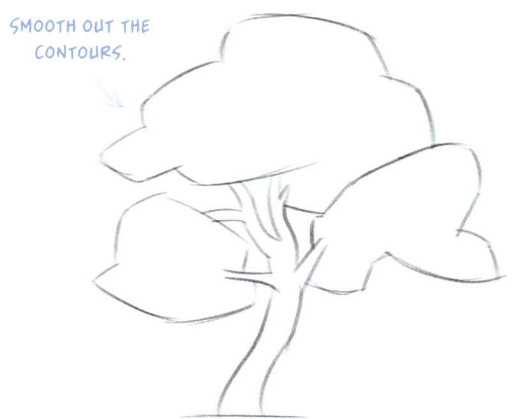

We'll only draw some of the branches in order to simplify the sketch.

Add texture to the contours.

Add small semicircles to the contours of the foliage, taking care to vary the size and intensity of the curvature. As we are aiming to create a natural look, avoid symmetry. Draw continuous lines for the branches and trunk and create two reliefs to represent the knots in the wood.

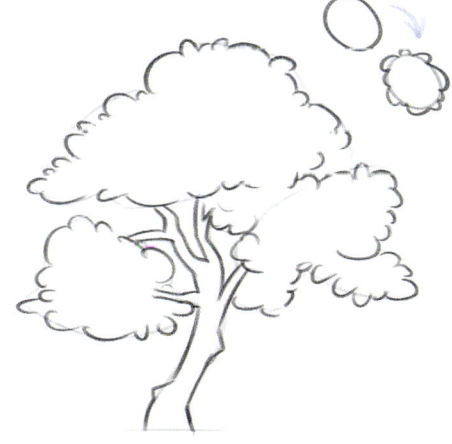

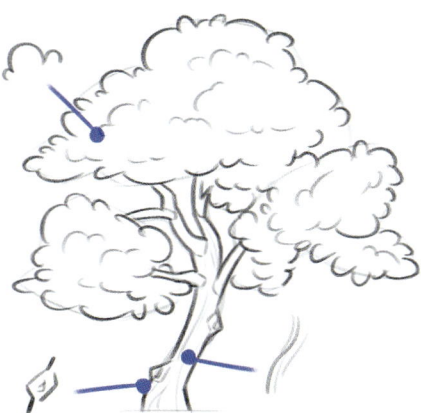

Work the interior of the sketch.

Now draw the interior of the silhouette to create the effect of texture. For the interior of the foliage, create groups of three semicircles. For the wooden texture, draw fine S lines by following the curves of the trunk. Finally, add volume to the knots.

Reinforce the contrast.

Finish the sketch by adjusting the thickness of the lines. Go over certain contours to create more contrast. The parts under the foliage are darkened with solid black to give relief. Take equal care to leave some negative spaces to give lightness to the drawing.

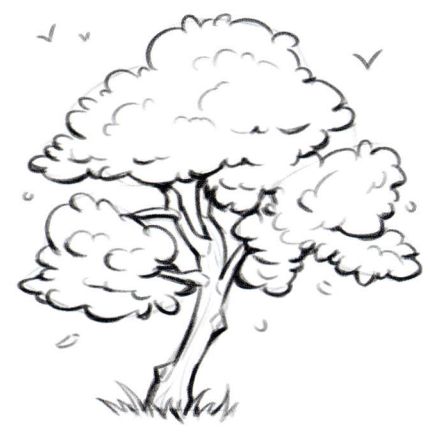

Draw a Detailed and Realistic Texture

It's time to put your ability to observe and create patterns of texture to the test! In this exercise, you'll apply a leafy texture on a cube to perfect the technique of adding details to a volume.

You will need :

✳ Your sketchbook or a sheet of paper
✳ 1 colored pencil
✳ 1 drawing pencil
✳ 1 eraser

Analyze the Model

Choose a texture to work on—for example, foliage. Observe the type of texture to determine if the pattern is repeated or not. In this example, we see one pattern. However, we see that the contours present twigs that are longer than others and that stick out from the mass.

Feel free to choose whatever texture you want. The important thing is to identify the pattern and simplify it, regardless of what you choose..

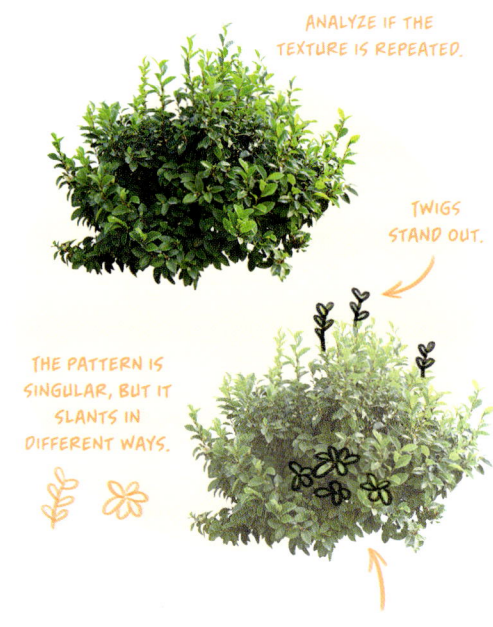

ANALYZE IF THE TEXTURE IS REPEATED.

TWIGS STAND OUT.

THE PATTERN IS SINGULAR, BUT IT SLANTS IN DIFFERENT WAYS.

WE CAN SEE DIFFERENT INCLINES WITHIN THE PATTERN.

The Drawing Step by Step

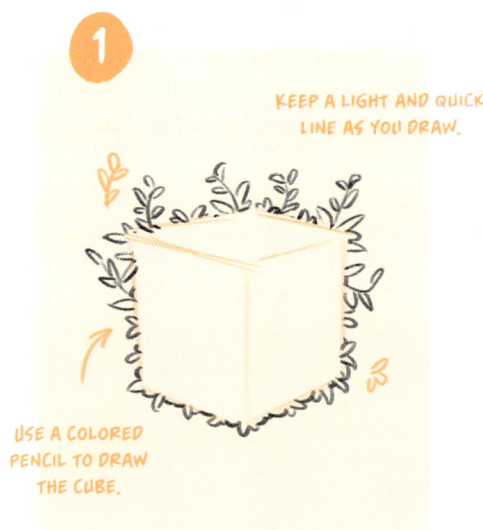

1

KEEP A LIGHT AND QUICK
LINE AS YOU DRAW.

USE A COLORED
PENCIL TO DRAW
THE CUBE.

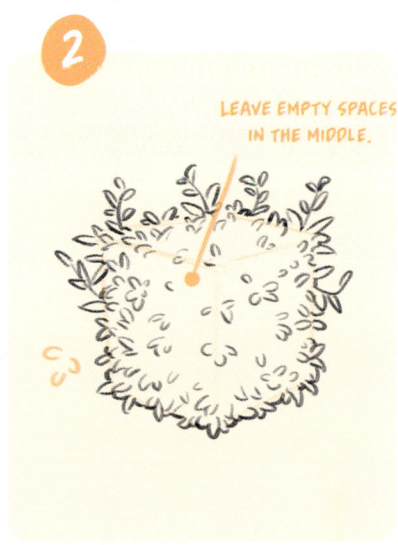

2

LEAVE EMPTY SPACES
IN THE MIDDLE.

Draw a cube and apply the texture along the contours. Draw twigs that stick out on top by varying their incline and the pattern size.

Add the pattern to the interior of the form by varying the density this time. Apply more patterns along the cube's border to create relief and depth.

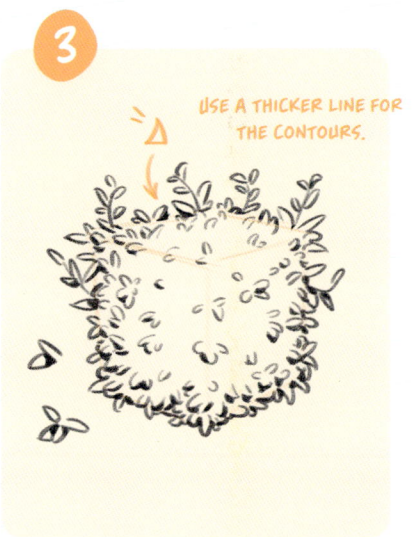

3

USE A THICKER LINE FOR
THE CONTOURS.

Play with the thickness of lines to create the best readability. Add black spaces under the leaves to create some volume.

9

ANATOMY

22 | MOVEMENT

Drawing a human body requires that we first understand the essence of a pose to give it life. Creating a sketch of movement is crucial for a dynamic foundation before working on proportions and anatomy.

Line of Action

The first line to draw when drawing a dynamic pose is the principal axis, which we call the *line of action*. This line represents the main action of the pose. It always follows the movement of the torso and generally proceeds along one of the legs. This line is the first essential step in drawing a dynamic pose.

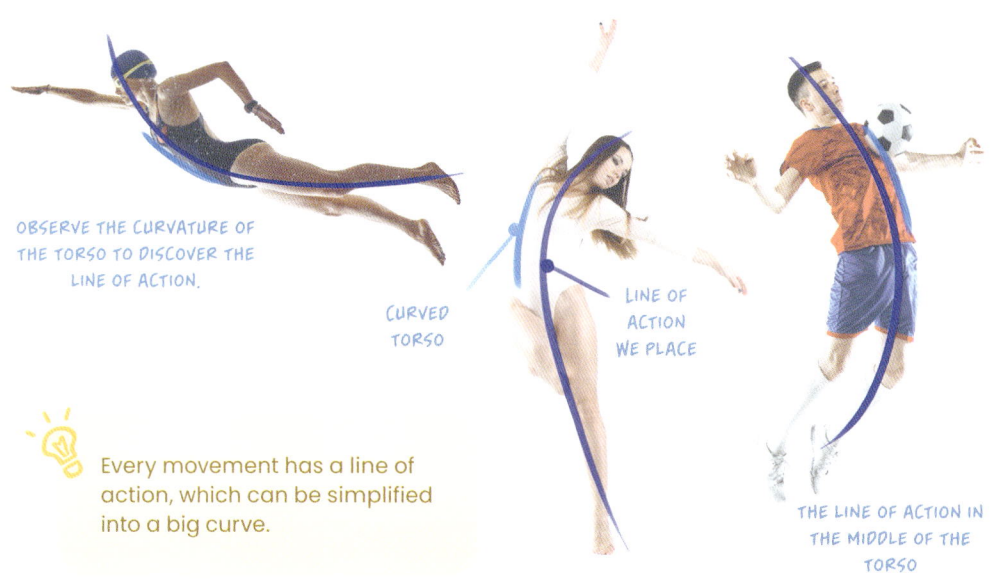

OBSERVE THE CURVATURE OF THE TORSO TO DISCOVER THE LINE OF ACTION.

CURVED TORSO

LINE OF ACTION WE PLACE

Every movement has a line of action, which can be simplified into a big curve.

THE LINE OF ACTION IN THE MIDDLE OF THE TORSO

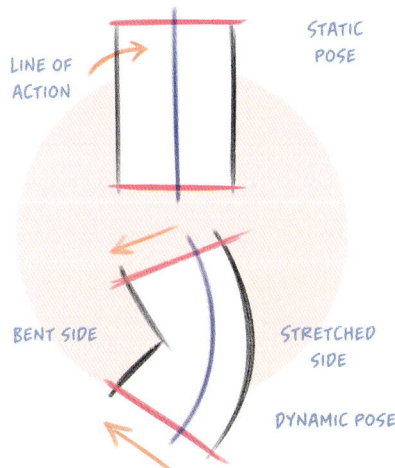

LINE OF ACTION

STATIC POSE

BENT SIDE

STRETCHED SIDE

DYNAMIC POSE

The Movement of the Torso

Once the line of action is placed, you'll want to analyze the torso because the dynamics of the pose depend upon it. We can simplify this into a rectangle. The top line indicates the position of the shoulders, while the bottom line indicates that of the pelvis. For a static pose viewed from the front, the lines are parallel. However, in movement, they tilt, creating an asymmetry of the torso with the stretched side (following the line of action) and a bent side.

Adding Body Parts

To sketch an entire human body, we usually use curves and S lines to represent the fluidity of movement. We want dynamism without worrying about proportions as we did previously. Begin with a line of action, then the torso, head, and pelvis using simple forms. Next, add the arms and legs with fluid, curved lines.

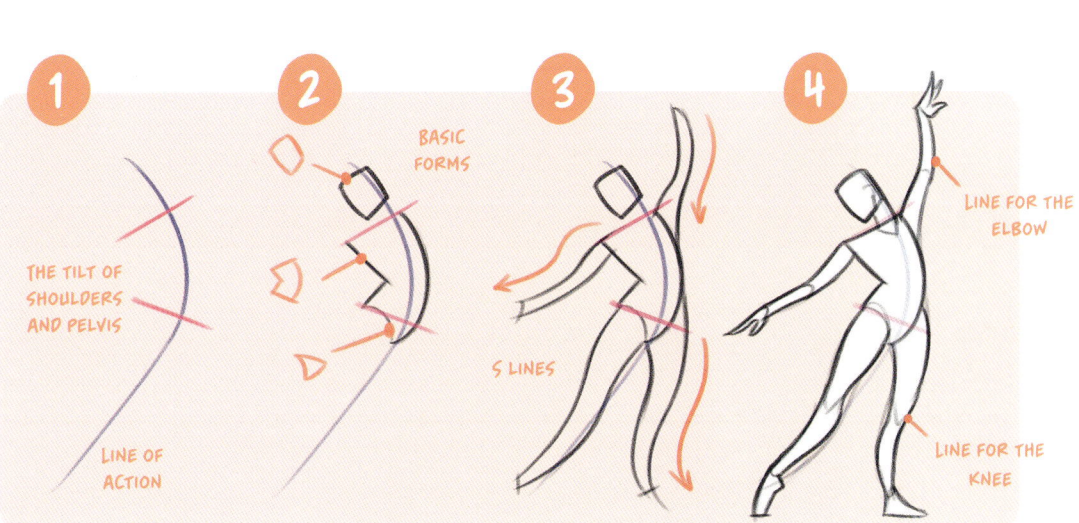

1

THE TILT OF SHOULDERS AND PELVIS

LINE OF ACTION

2

BASIC FORMS

3

S LINES

4

LINE FOR THE ELBOW

LINE FOR THE KNEE

23 | PROPORTIONS

Proportions are key to a drawing a realistic human body. Rather than fussing over exact lengths of each body part, you can use the principle of ratios to simplify your vision of the human body.

Breaking It Down to Simple Ratios

We can create fairly simple proportional relations between different parts of the body. The key point is the pubic bone, placed at the center of the body, which ensures a good balance between the top and bottom of the body. The top part is divided into three equal sections: the head, thoracic cavity, and pelvis. The knees are at the middle of the legs.

These proportions apply to all people, whatever their gender, size, or body shape!

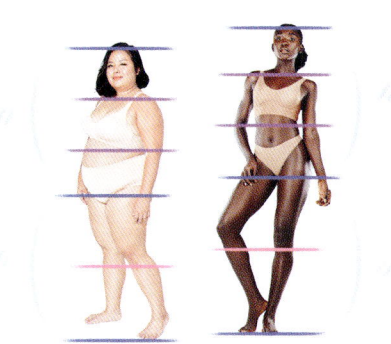

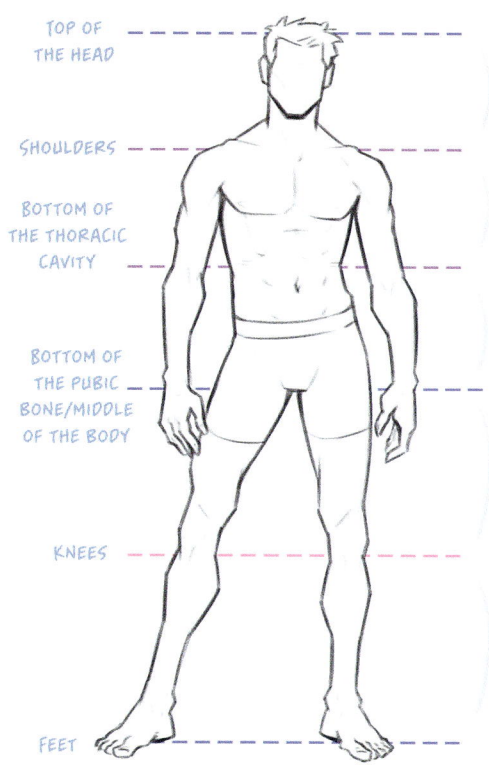

TOP OF THE HEAD

SHOULDERS

BOTTOM OF THE THORACIC CAVITY

BOTTOM OF THE PUBIC BONE/MIDDLE OF THE BODY

KNEES

FEET

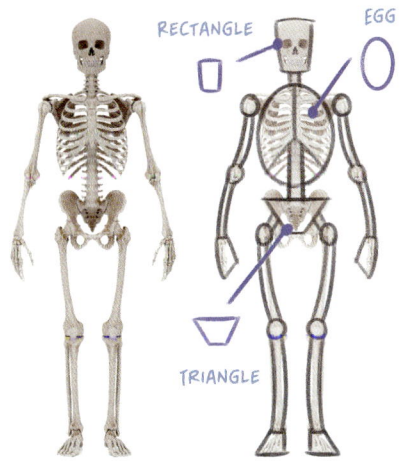

RECTANGLE

EGG

TRIANGLE

Simplify the Forms

Drawing a skeleton is ideal for studying proportions while learning anatomy. We can find many basic forms in the human body: the head is a rectangle, the thoracic cavity resembles an egg, and the pelvis becomes a triangle. To add dynamism, draw the bones with S shapes for the arms and legs.

The Three Major Elements

The head, thoracic cavity, and pelvis make up the three main parts of the human body. They are tied together with the spinal column. Collectively, they form the top of the body and have the same height. Using these markers, it becomes easier to articulate the arms and legs with the correct proportions.

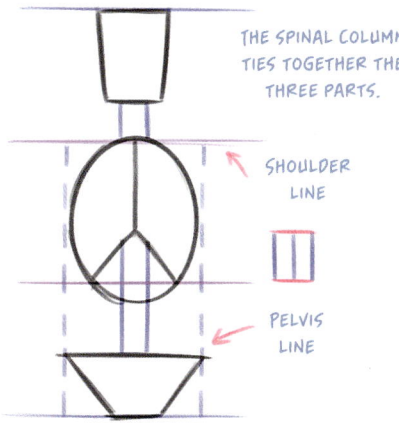

THE SPINAL COLUMN TIES TOGETHER THE THREE PARTS.

SHOULDER LINE

PELVIS LINE

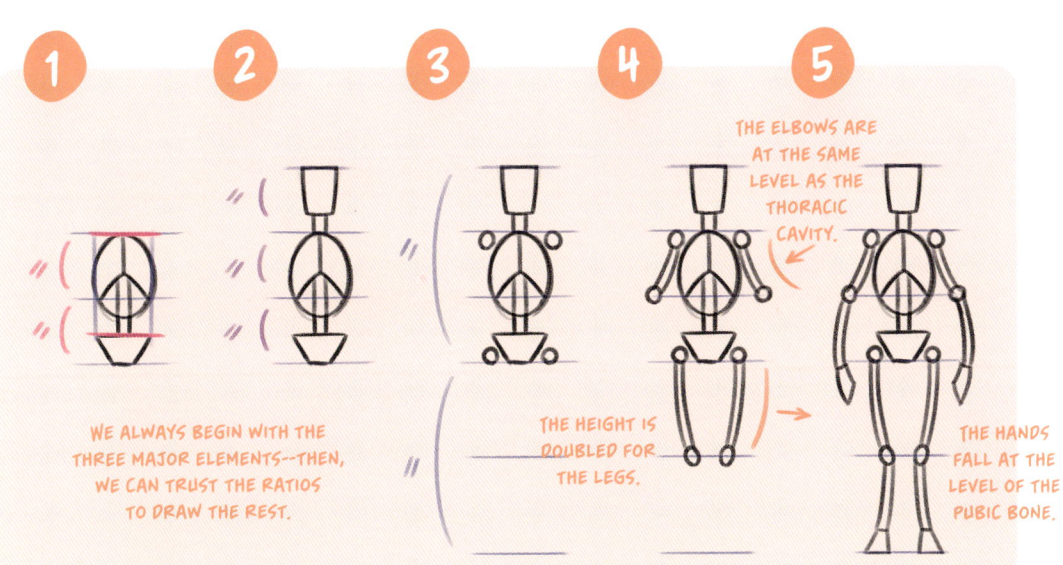

1

2

3

4

5

WE ALWAYS BEGIN WITH THE THREE MAJOR ELEMENTS--THEN, WE CAN TRUST THE RATIOS TO DRAW THE REST.

THE HEIGHT IS DOUBLED FOR THE LEGS.

THE ELBOWS ARE AT THE SAME LEVEL AS THE THORACIC CAVITY.

THE HANDS FALL AT THE LEVEL OF THE PUBIC BONE.

24 MUSCLES

To create a realistic drawing, three key concepts must be mastered: gesture, proportions, and anatomy. It's not required that you know all the muscles to create a good drawing. What is more important is your understanding of their form and positioning.

Tying Muscle to Form

To begin mastering anatomy, simplify the muscles into basic forms, such as triangles, rectangles, or trapezoids. These simple forms are suitable for all genders and body shapes. We can play with forms to create distinctions: using the form of an hourglass will give a more well-proportioned shape to the waist, while a rectangle will make the body seem more robust.

Varying the sizes of the forms, you can create a multitude of shapes while maintaining a believable anatomy.

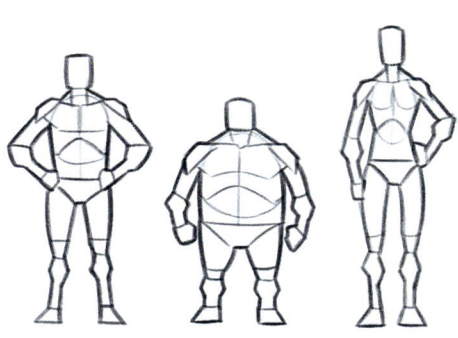

WHATEVER THE SHAPE, THE ANATOMY REMAINS THE SAME FOR ALL!

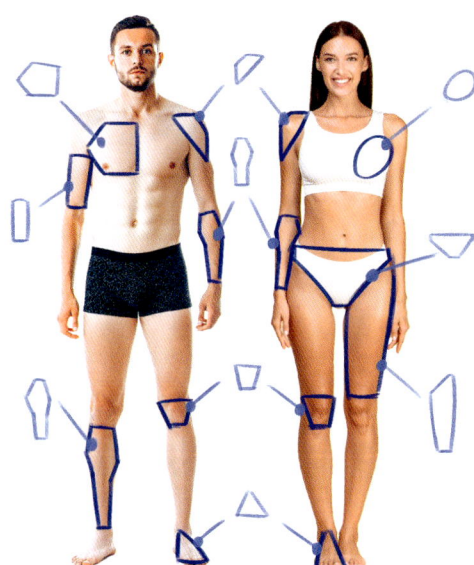

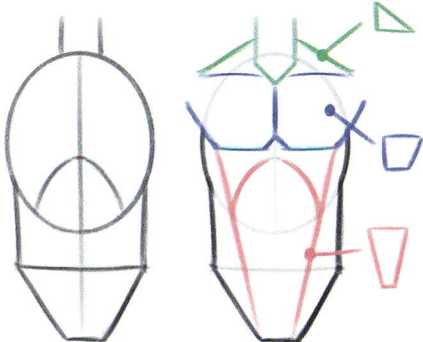

Defining the Chest

You can find the three main muscles within the chest. The trapezoids form a triangle, connecting the neck to the shoulders. The pectorals cover the top of the thoracic cavity, and the abdominals descend to the pubic bone.

The Four Parts of the Arms and Legs

The arms and legs can be simplified in a similar way. To represent them, identify four main parts: trapezoid, rectangle, a keel shape (in the form of a boat keel), and triangle.

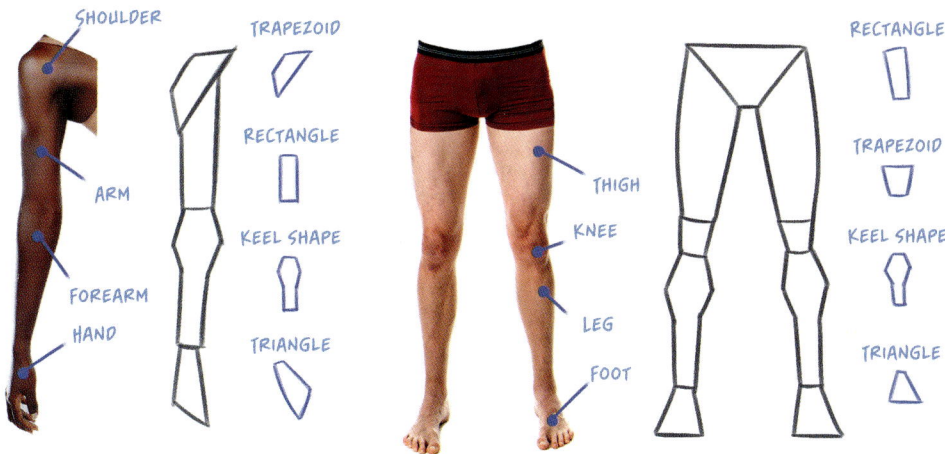

🦋 IN THE KNOW

To improve your drawings, study each muscle individually to add more detail and give them volume. Consult medical or artistic illustrations to deepen your knowledge!

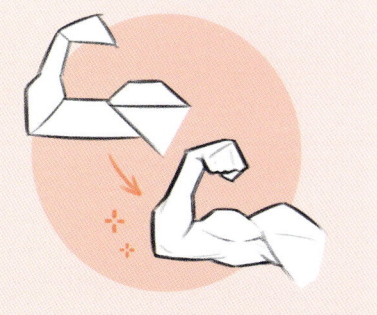

137

EXAMPLE

1

Draw the line of action.

The torso slightly tilts to the left, while the pelvis leans toward the right. To represent this movement, draw an S line as well as two points to mark the height of the body.

Marking the middle of the body allows you to better estimate the size of the drawing and to proportion it accordingly.

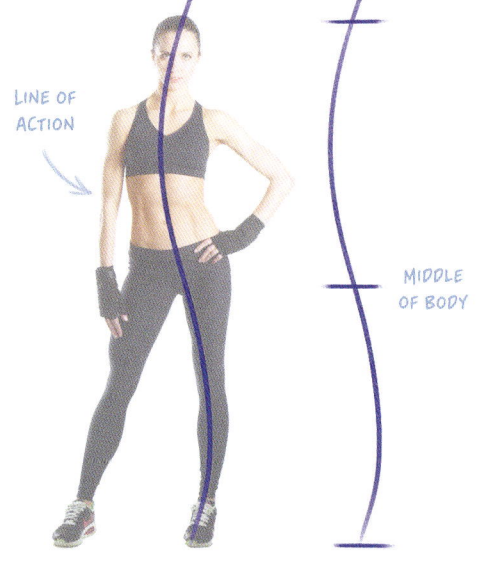

LINE OF ACTION

MIDDLE OF BODY

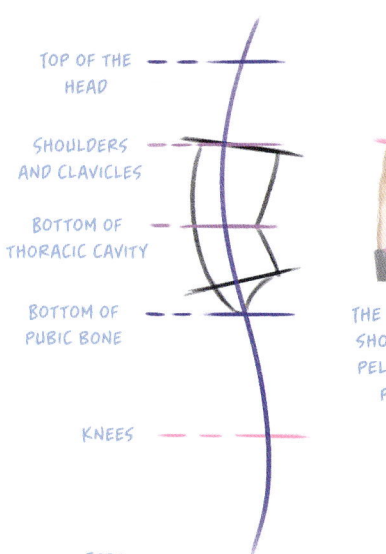

TOP OF THE HEAD

SHOULDERS AND CLAVICLES

BOTTOM OF THORACIC CAVITY

BOTTOM OF PUBIC BONE

KNEES

FEET

THE LINES OF THE SHOULDERS AND PELVIS ARE NOT PARALLEL.

2

Mark the points of proportions.

We can use the proportion markers to divide the top of the body into three parts and the bottom into two. Next, we draw the lines of the shoulders and the pelvis by tilting them for a more dynamic quality. To simplify the torso's movement, we can sketch a lengthened side and a bent side.

Sketching movement.

Now that we have established the proportions, sketching movement is easier. Lightly erase the points to draw over top of them. Next, draw S lines to give fluidity to the arms and legs, then mark the placement of knees and elbows with a curve.

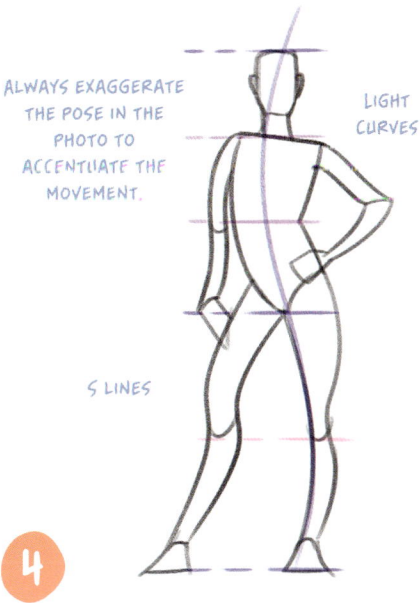

ALWAYS EXAGGERATE THE POSE IN THE PHOTO TO ACCENTUATE THE MOVEMENT.

LIGHT CURVES

S LINES

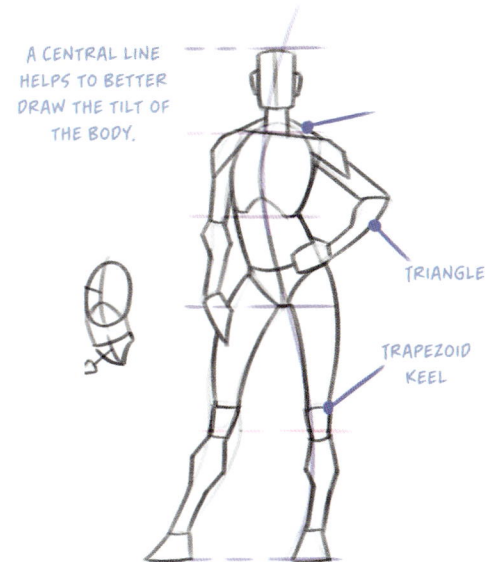

A CENTRAL LINE HELPS TO BETTER DRAW THE TILT OF THE BODY.

TRIANGLE

TRAPEZOID KEEL

Using simplified forms.

Once again erase the sketch, leaving it slightly visible to use as a guide. Next, define the anatomy with basic forms. It's also crucial to think of volume to capture the angles of the head, torso, and pelvis.

Thicken the lines and add details.

Finally, go over the preceding sketch, taking care to lightly erase. Use thick lines to emphasize the important volumes, like the torso. Inside the silhouette, maintain fine lines to lightly give volume to the muscles.

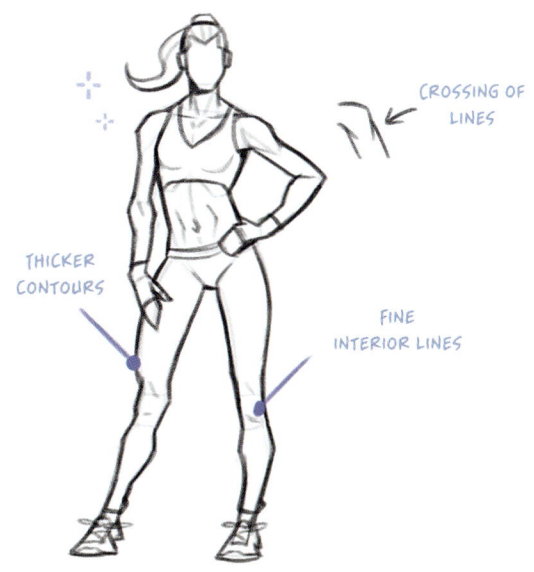

CROSSING OF LINES

THICKER CONTOURS

FINE INTERIOR LINES

25 | PORTRAITS

To make portraits more accessible, it's important to master certain techniques. It all depends on the position and simplification of various elements of the face.

Head Shapes

It is essential to understand that there's no anatomy type for the face. The forms and proportions vary according to the shape of each individual. As an artist, you'll need to first envision the simple form that most closely matches the model's head.

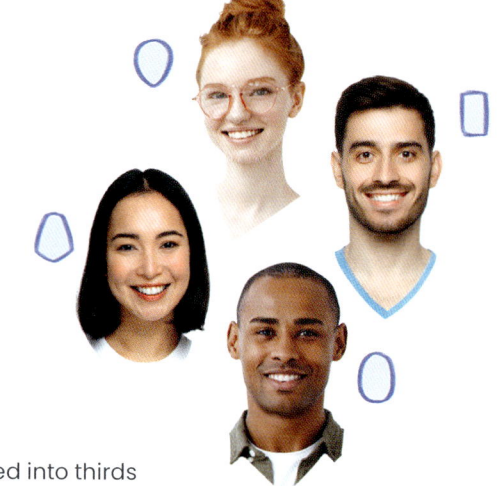

The Basic Proportions

The proportions of the face can be simplified into thirds to identify the position of the main elements of the face. These three parts do not have to be perfectly equal. By varying their size, you can create different shapes.

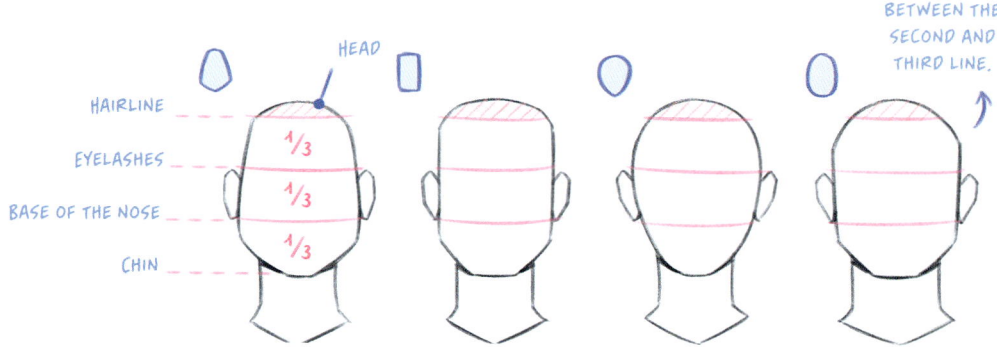

THE EARS FALL BETWEEN THE SECOND AND THIRD LINE.

HAIRLINE

EYELASHES

BASE OF THE NOSE

CHIN

HEAD

$^1/_3$

$^1/_3$

$^1/_3$

🔥 IN THE KNOW

We can explore the inclines by simplifying the head into two volumes: a sphere for the head and the shape of a piece of paper for the face. Next, add the points of proportion on the paper sheet form to achieve a well-proportioned face.

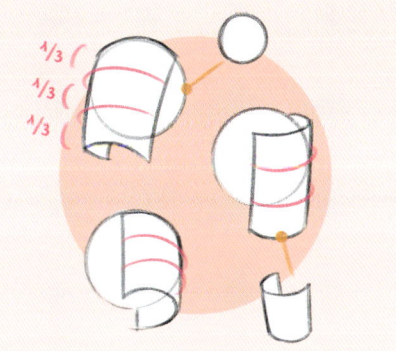

TRAPEZOID

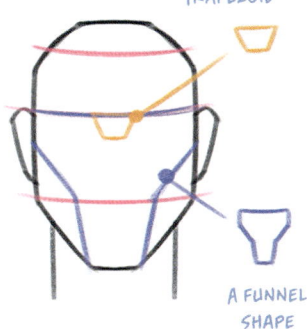

A FUNNEL SHAPE

The Elements of the Face

To position the elements of the face, you can use two basic forms: a funnel shape and a trapezoid. The funnel shape represents the zone where we will add the eyelashes, eyes, nose, and mouth. The trapezoid allows us to define the space between the eyebrows and to proportion them correctly on the face. This simplified structure is key for creating correct proportions for the different parts of the face.

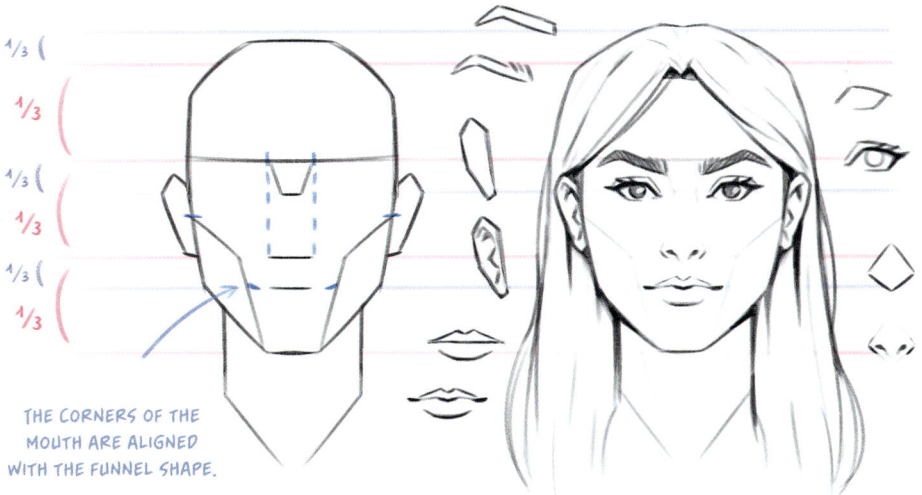

THE CORNERS OF THE MOUTH ARE ALIGNED WITH THE FUNNEL SHAPE.

THE SHAPES VARY ACCORDING TO GENDER AND SHAPE.

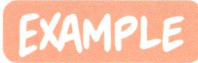

Analyze the model.

Generally, we want to use a neutral model, avoiding big smiles or dramatic facial expressions. We can observe the three parts of the face, taking care to respect their proportions. For example, here, the zone for the forehead is smaller than the zone for the eyes and nose.

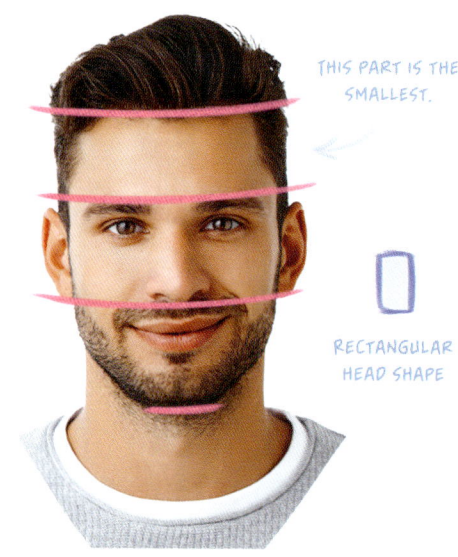

THIS PART IS THE SMALLEST.

RECTANGULAR HEAD SHAPE

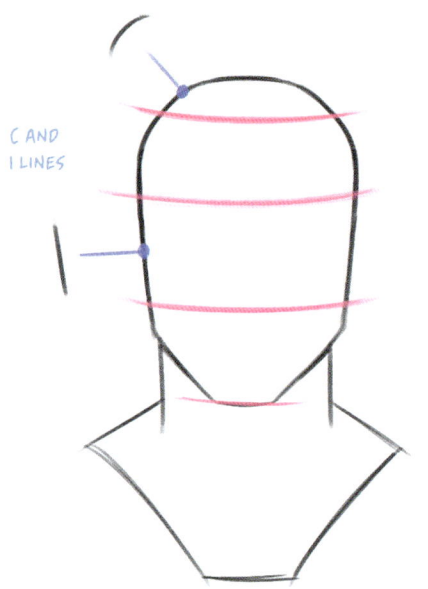

C AND I LINES

Define the form of the head and the proportions.

We begin the sketch with the basic shape of the head. In this case, the model has a rectangular head. We draw the jaw with two straight lines, then we add a horizontal line for the chin. To bring more dynamism to the portrait, we use two V-shaped lines to close the chest.

We mark the points of proportions, respecting the same spacings as the model.

3

Frame the face.

Draw the ears between the points marking the eyebrows and the base of the nose. To frame the zone of the face, draw a funnel shape, starting from the middle of the ears, continuing to the angles of the chin. Add a trapezoid in the middle to define the space between the eyebrows.

MIDDLE OF
THE EARS

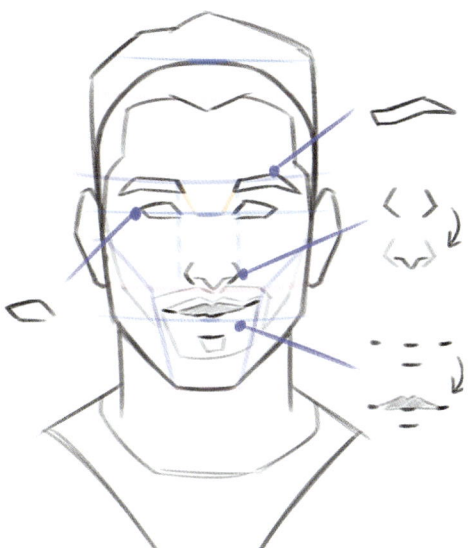

4

Add simplified forms.

To detail the face, place the facial elements with simplified forms. Use the points to correctly position the eyebrows, eyes, nose, and mouth. Trapezoids, rectangles, and triangles can help to represent them.

5

Add the final details.

The only thing left to do is to detail each element, taking care to maintain simple lines. Break the continuous line near the hairline, beard, and eyebrows using fine lines. To create contrast, darken certain places, like the eyes and upper lip.

WE BREAK
THE LINES.

BLACK
SPACE

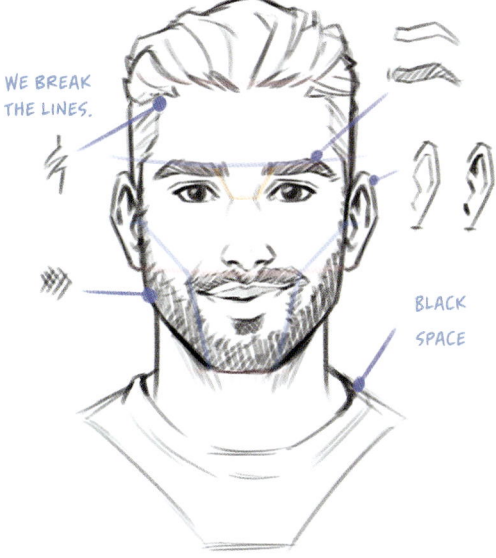

Draw a Portrait with Good Proportions

Use your new knowledge of proportions and simplified forms to sketch a portrait. Rather than drawing the elements of the face directly, begin by establishing the structure of the head by respecting the proportions of the model.

You will need :

✳ Your sketchbook or a sheet of paper
✳ 1 drawing pencil
✳ 1 eraser

Analyze the Model

Observe the form of the head, which, here, looks like an upside-down raindrop. Pay particular attention to the proportions of the face and the size of the three main sections. These elements will help you to correctly establish your sketch.

For your first drawings, print images of the models you want to use and draw over top of them to get familiar with the proportions.

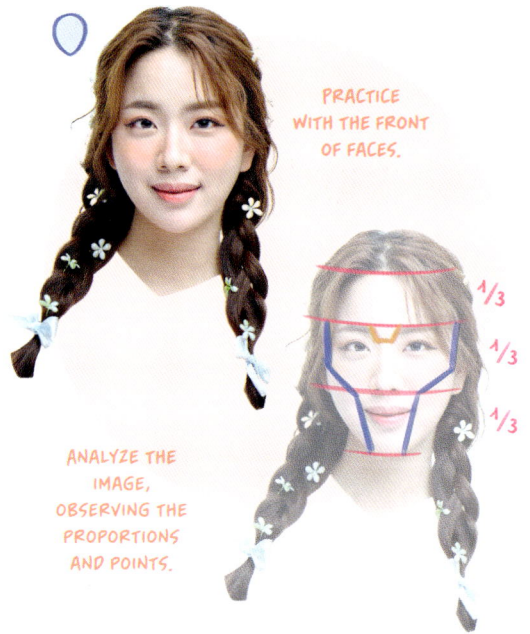

PRACTICE WITH THE FRONT OF FACES.

ANALYZE THE IMAGE, OBSERVING THE PROPORTIONS AND POINTS.

$^1/_3$
$^1/_3$
$^1/_3$

The Drawing Step by Step

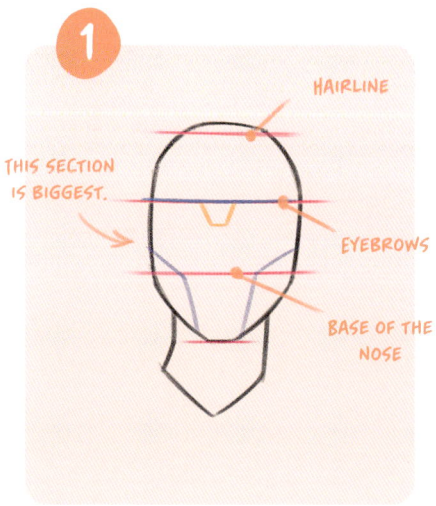

1

HAIRLINE

THIS SECTION IS BIGGEST.

EYEBROWS

BASE OF THE NOSE

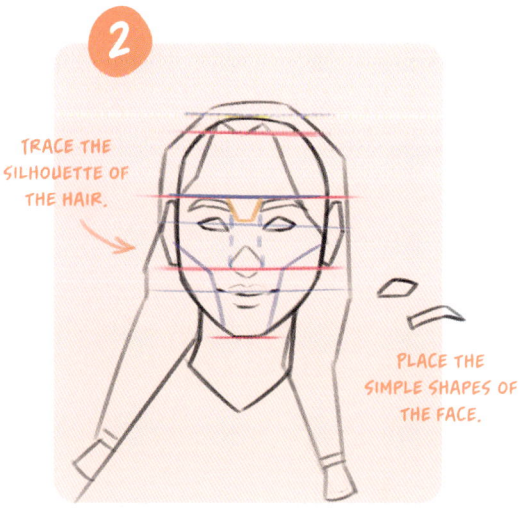

2

TRACE THE SILHOUETTE OF THE HAIR.

PLACE THE SIMPLE SHAPES OF THE FACE.

Draw the form of the head and neck. Place the lines of proportions to define the three sections. Next, add the funnel form and trapezoid.

Draw the facial elements using simplified forms and focusing on their positioning. Draw the silhouette of the hair with two straight lines.

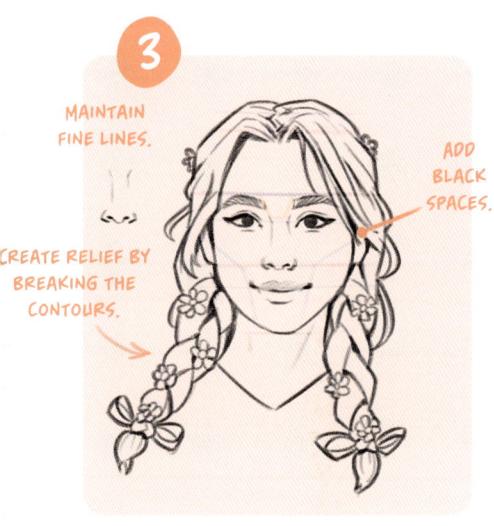

3

MAINTAIN FINE LINES.

ADD BLACK SPACES.

CREATE RELIEF BY BREAKING THE CONTOURS.

Lightly erase your drawing, then go over the contours with more precision. Define the volume of the braids and use fine lines for the details, like the lips, eyebrows, and nostrils. The precise position of the facial elements is key for achieving a realistic drawing.

10

SHADOW
AND LIGHT

26 THE ROLE OF LIGHT

To create realistic shadows, it's crucial to understand the role of the light source, which will guide you as you place shadows in a logical way. Without light, shadows do not exist.

The Light Source

Light always comes from a specific source, like the sun or a lightbulb. The rays of light leave from point A and reach point B in a straight line. Understanding the light's direction is essential to position the shadows in the sketch.

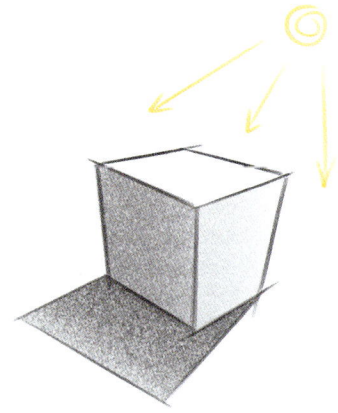

The Position of Light

The first step in shading is to locate the light source, which determines the position of the shadows. The shadows are always situated opposite the light source.

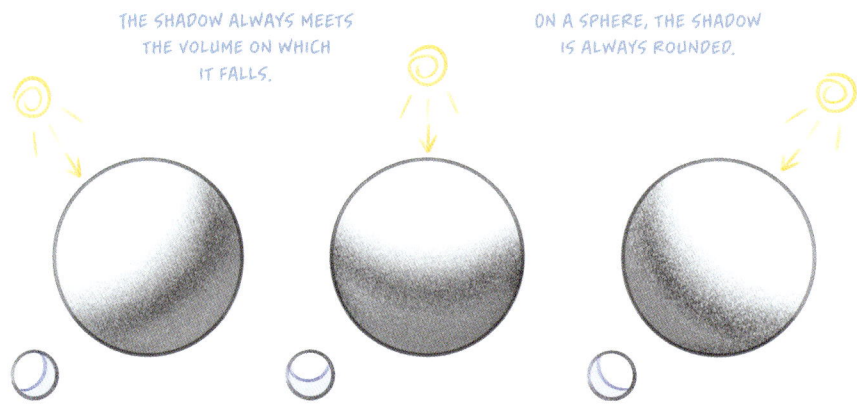

THE SHADOW ALWAYS MEETS THE VOLUME ON WHICH IT FALLS.

ON A SPHERE, THE SHADOW IS ALWAYS ROUNDED.

Two Distinct Zones

After locating the light source, we can identify two different zones: shadow and light. Draw a line to demarcate these zones and prepare the shading. This separation, drawn here darker, allows you to define the shaded and lit parts of the drawing. This sets the position of the main shading, which we will do next.

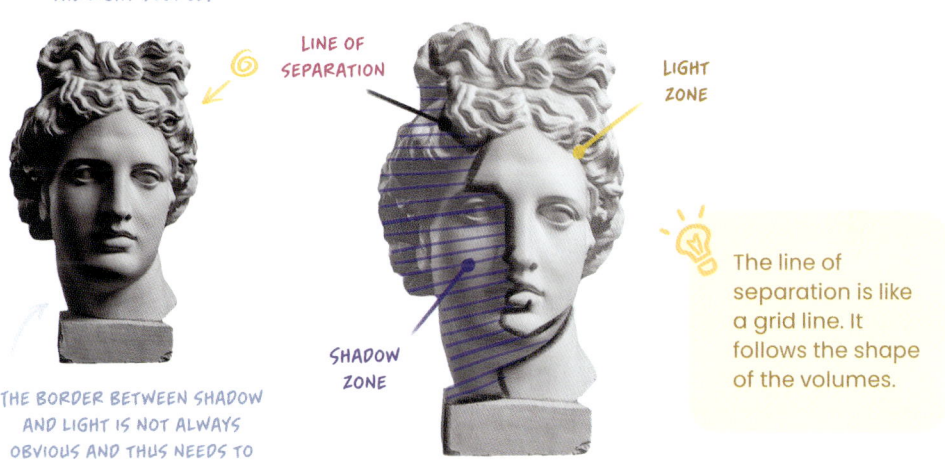

FIRST, ANALYZE THE POSITION OF THE LIGHT SOURCE.

LINE OF SEPARATION

LIGHT ZONE

SHADOW ZONE

THE BORDER BETWEEN SHADOW AND LIGHT IS NOT ALWAYS OBVIOUS AND THUS NEEDS TO BE DEFINED.

The line of separation is like a grid line. It follows the shape of the volumes.

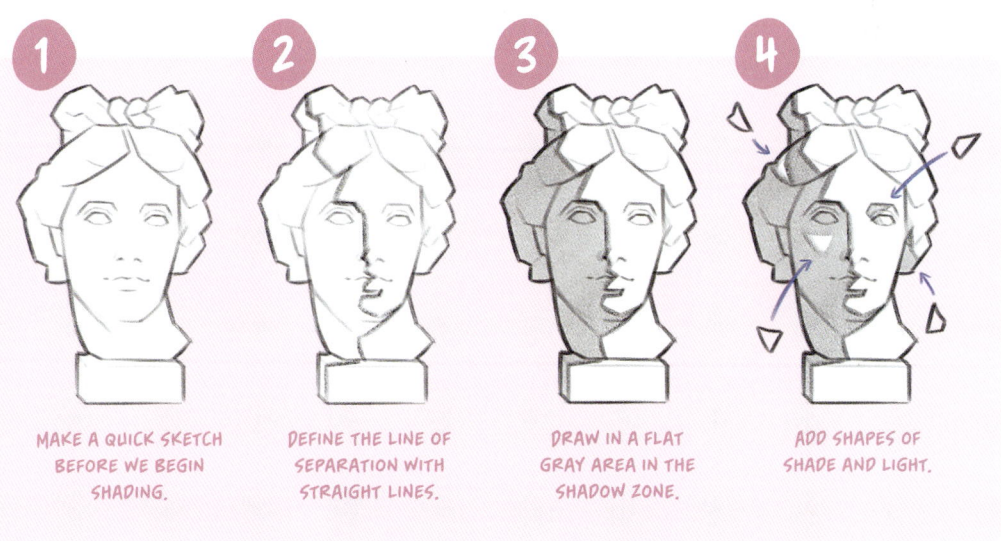

1 MAKE A QUICK SKETCH BEFORE WE BEGIN SHADING.

2 DEFINE THE LINE OF SEPARATION WITH STRAIGHT LINES.

3 DRAW IN A FLAT GRAY AREA IN THE SHADOW ZONE.

4 ADD SHAPES OF SHADE AND LIGHT.

EXERCISE

Lay the Foundation for Shading in Drawing

Practice observing and analyzing a model to identify the shade and light zones. The goal is to draw a line of separation by simplifying the model and interpreting what you see.

You will need :

* Your sketchbook or a sheet of paper
* 3 drawing pencils (HB, 2B, and 4B)
* 1 eraser

Analyze the Model

In this exercise, you'll have to examine a simple object to practice identifying the shaded zones. A line of separation follows the curves of rounded forms, much like a grid. Your job is to determine its position and ensure a clean separation between the two areas.

Print out a photo of a model and draw a line of separation right on it. This will help you to focus on your perception of shadows.

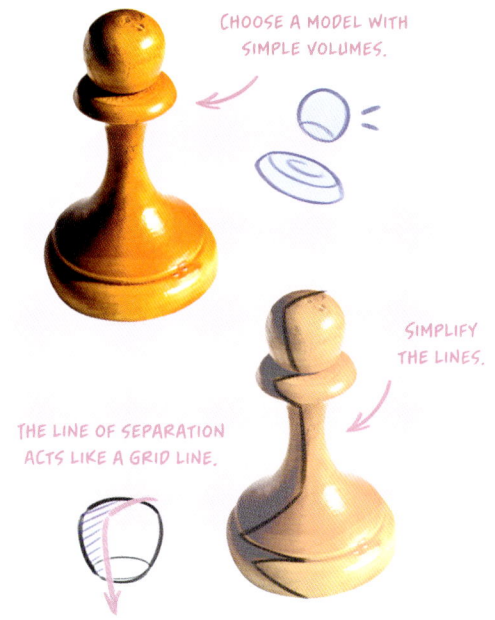

CHOOSE A MODEL WITH SIMPLE VOLUMES.

SIMPLIFY THE LINES.

THE LINE OF SEPARATION ACTS LIKE A GRID LINE.

The Drawing Step by Step

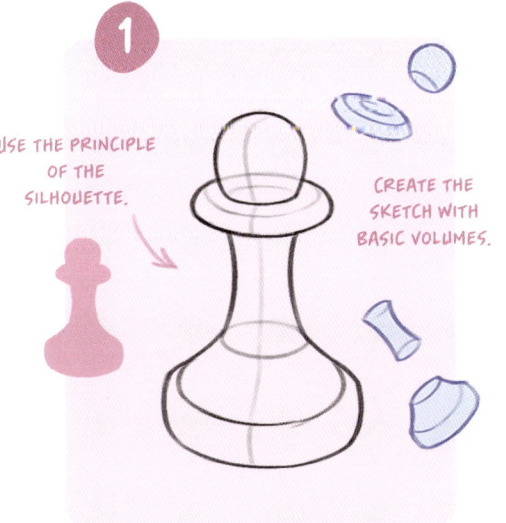

1

USE THE PRINCIPLE OF THE SILHOUETTE.

CREATE THE SKETCH WITH BASIC VOLUMES.

Begin by sketching a simple sketch with an HB pencil. Apply what you have learned about forms, proportions, and volumes.

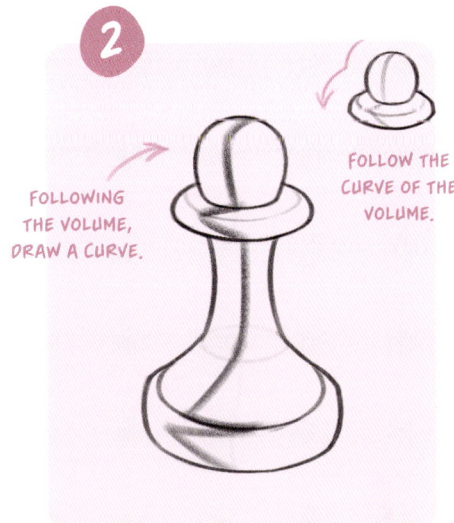

2

FOLLOWING THE VOLUME, DRAW A CURVE.

FOLLOW THE CURVE OF THE VOLUME.

Draw the line of separation with a 4B pencil, relying on your analysis. Use your knowledge of grid lines to portray the volume.

Shade the left part of the drawing with a 2B pencil to separate the two zones. Don't press too hard on the pencil to ensure a uniform flat shade throughout the area.

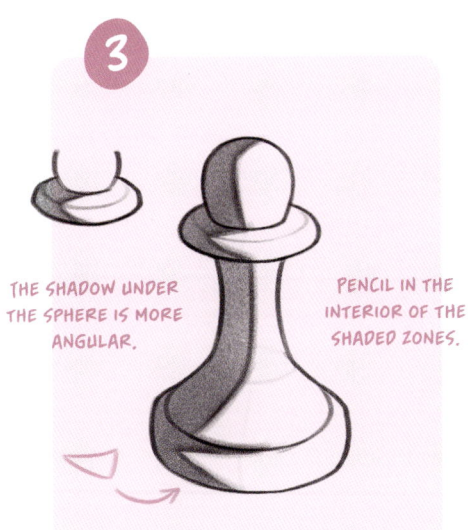

3

THE SHADOW UNDER THE SPHERE IS MORE ANGULAR.

PENCIL IN THE INTERIOR OF THE SHADED ZONES.

27 | TYPES OF SHADOWS AND LIGHT

It is essential to master the technique of shading. There are eight categories of light and shadow to explore: live, bright, and attenuated light and dark, medium, light, deep, and projected shadow.

The Eight Simplified Categories

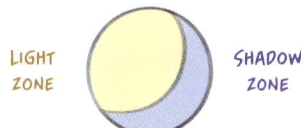

LIGHT ZONE

SHADOW ZONE

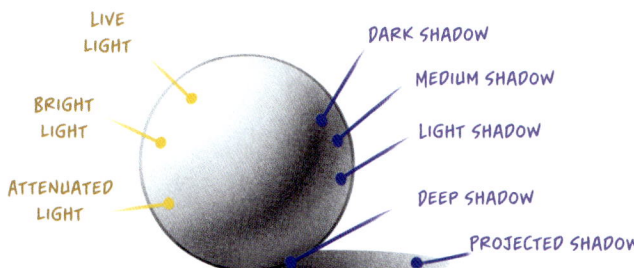

LIVE LIGHT

BRIGHT LIGHT

ATTENUATED LIGHT

DARK SHADOW

MEDIUM SHADOW

LIGHT SHADOW

DEEP SHADOW

PROJECTED SHADOW

Family of Lights

1. **Live light,** or *direct light*, is the area that receives direct light.

2. **Rays of light** that are intense reflections from a light source are called *bright light*.

3. **Attenuated light**, also called *middle tones*, is the area that is neither in direct light nor in the shadowed zone.

The Family of Shadows

1. **Dark shadow**, also called *form shadow*, is found at the border between the shaded and the light zones.

2. **Medium shadow** is the main shaded area. It's the area of transition between the dark and light shades.

3. **Light shadow**, or *reflected light*, is the lightest shadow. Here, light has bounced off other surfaces and lights this shadow area.

4. **Deep shadow**, or *occlusion shadow*, is the darkest shadow. It's found in crevices where light cannot penetrate.

5. *Projected shadow* is the shadow the object creates on the ground.

Bounce Lights

The variety of shades comes from the way light behaves. When light touches the ground, we say it "bounces." These bounces create a gradual shift in the shadows. The shadow is therefore darkest at the center of the object and softer at the ground.

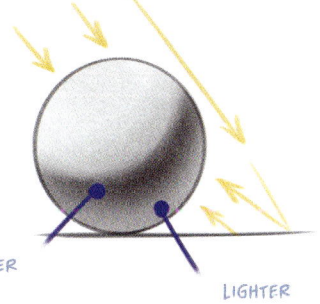

DARKER

LIGHTER

Balancing Contrasts

It's important to maintain two distinct zones: the gray nuances in the light zone must always be lighter than those in the shaded zone. This balance is crucial. You want to avoid contrasts that are too strong so the drawing has a natural feel. On the other hand, take care to not join the two zones together so much that the drawing becomes flat and lacking in volume.

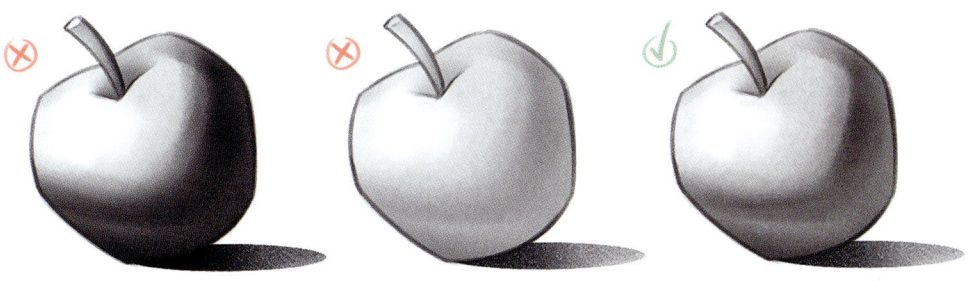

TOO MUCH CONTRAST: THE SHADOWS ARE TOO DARK, AND THE LIGHT IS TOO WHITE.

NO CONTRAST: THERE IS VERY LITTLE DIFFERENCE BETWEEN THE SHADOWS AND LIGHT.

BALANCED SHADING WORK: THE ZONES ARE DISTINCT BUT NATURAL.

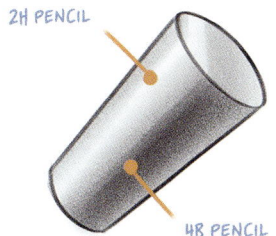

2H PENCIL

4B PENCIL

Using Different Pencils

For distinct contrasts, we use pencils of different grades: soft pencils (2B and above) are perfect for shading, while hard lead pencils (2H and above) are ideal for nuanced light. Rather than pressing harder on the pencil, we can use different grades of pencils for the desired effect.

Apply Different Types of Shadows to Your Drawing

To practice recreating the different types of light and shadow, choose a simple model. Basic volumes like those found on a piece of fruit are perfect for learning how to overlap shadows one by one. Use different grades of pencils to create contrast and create more interesting shading.

You will need :

* Your sketchbook or a piece of paper
* 5 pencils (2H, HB, 2B, 4B, and 6B)
* 1 eraser

Analyze the Model

Choose a well-lit subject and analyze it to identify the light source. In this example, the light comes from the left, as evident by the position of the shadows. Next, locate the separation between the zones of light and shade, then draw a line of separation on the photo.

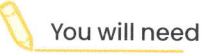
IDENTIFY THE POSITION OF THE LIGHT SOURCE.

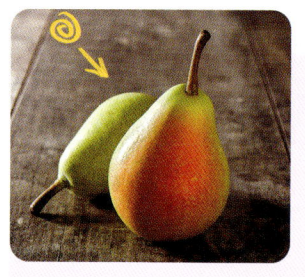

SHADOWS ON THE LEFT: LIGHT ON THE RIGHT

Take time to pinpoint the different types of light and shade. This careful observation is the most important step.

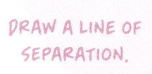
DRAW A LINE OF SEPARATION.

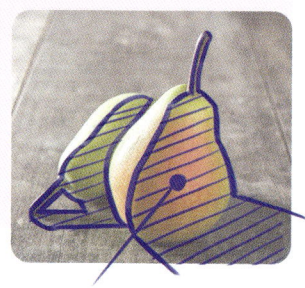

SHADED ZONE

The Drawing Step by Step

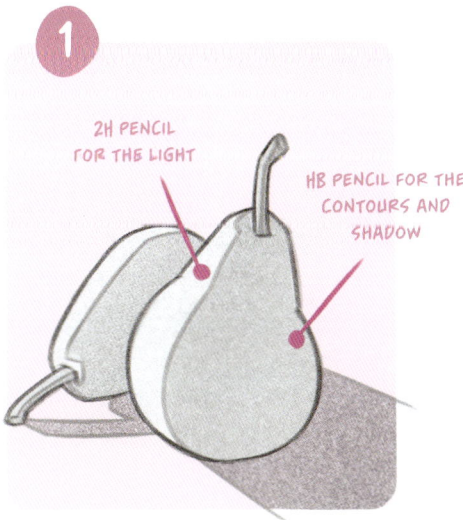

2H PENCIL
FOR THE LIGHT

HB PENCIL FOR THE
CONTOURS AND
SHADOW

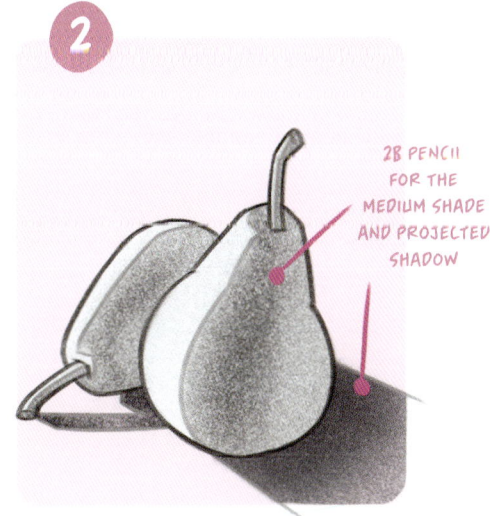

2B PENCIL
FOR THE
MEDIUM SHADE
AND PROJECTED
SHADOW

Draw the pears and the line of separation without pressing hard on your pencil. Add a light gray area for the light and a darker gray area for the light shadow and projected shadow.

From the line of separation, add medium shade. Then, create a light shadow zone to the right of the pears. Lastly, darken the projected shadow.

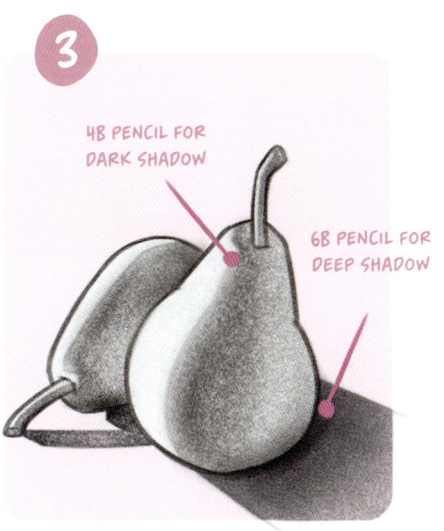

4B PENCIL FOR
DARK SHADOW

6B PENCIL FOR
DEEP SHADOW

Finally, darken the zones at the edge of the light to create a strong shadow. Add a deep shadow under the pears to create contrast.

28 CLEAN AND DIFFUSED SHADOWS

The shape of the shadow varies according to the volume. The shadow of a cube does not resemble that of a cylinder. Shadows can be drawn in two ways: clean or blurred.

Clean Shadows

In terms of an angular volume such as a cube, when the light hits the flat sides, it creates shadows that are delineated, or clean. The edges of the shadows are well-defined, creating a more distinct contrast.

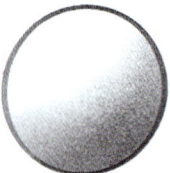

Diffused Shadows

Imagine a rounded volume such as a sphere. When the light hits the curved surface, it creates a diffused shadow. The contours of the shadow are thus not clean—they are blurred.

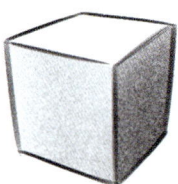

The Definition of a Shadow

When drawing a shadow, it's important to take into consideration the nature of the volume as well as its curvature. Because there is a vast array of volumes—from the sphere to the cube—we must adapt the definition of the shadow. The principle of grid lines will help you to better understand the intensity of the curvature.

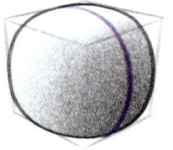 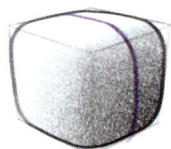 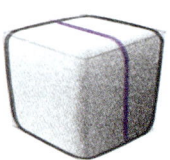 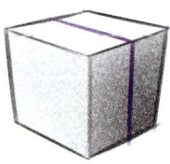

DIFFUSED SHADOW   CLEAN SHADOW

Analyze the Shades

Objects are often made up of several volumes. The shadows are thus sometimes diffused, sometimes clean. It is crucial to observe the subject to analyze the hardness of the shadows. On a piece of fabric, for example, the places where the folds are more pronounced have the most delineated shadows.

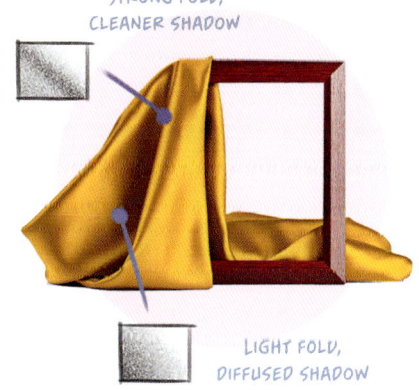

STRONG FOLD,
CLEANER SHADOW

LIGHT FOLD,
DIFFUSED SHADOW

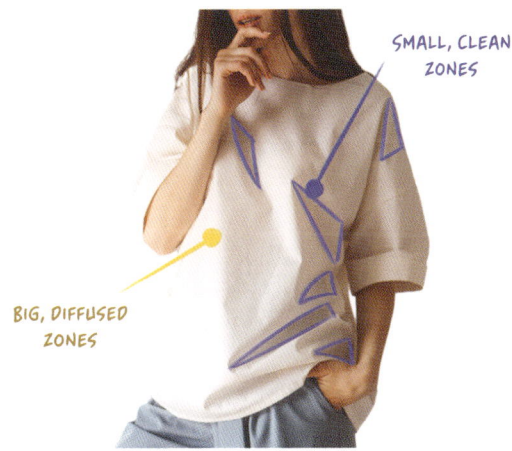

SMALL, CLEAN
ZONES

BIG, DIFFUSED
ZONES

Using the Two Types of Shadow

To make realistic shadow zones, you'll need to also take into account the type of volume on which they are found. This will help you to practice controlling the shading. For powerful drawings, you'll want to create the right mix of diffused and clean shadows. In general, diffused shadows will cover more area, while areas with clean shadows will be smaller.

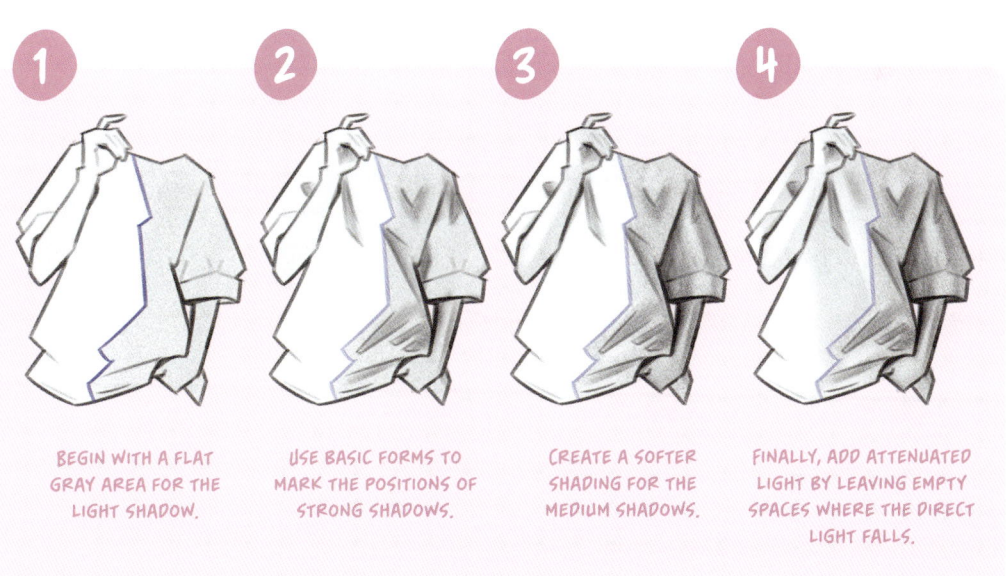

1 BEGIN WITH A FLAT GRAY AREA FOR THE LIGHT SHADOW.

2 USE BASIC FORMS TO MARK THE POSITIONS OF STRONG SHADOWS.

3 CREATE A SOFTER SHADING FOR THE MEDIUM SHADOWS.

4 FINALLY, ADD ATTENUATED LIGHT BY LEAVING EMPTY SPACES WHERE THE DIRECT LIGHT FALLS.

EXAMPLE

1

Distinguish the two zones.

The first step is to define the light source. Here, we have chosen to position it at the top right. Next, identify the direction of the light to identify the shadow areas. It's important to pay attention to the volume of the object. Because the apple is round, the shadow will also have a rounded form.

USE A 2H PENCIL FOR THE LINE OF SEPARATION.

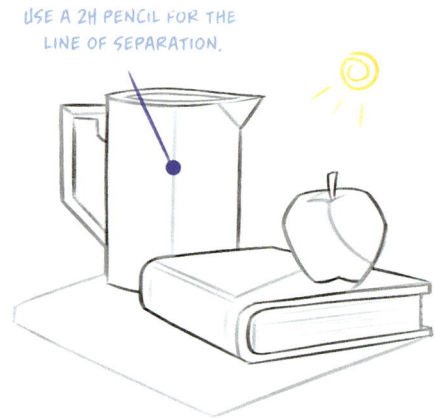

USE A 2H PENCIL FOR THE LINE OF SEPARATION.

HB PENCIL

2H PENCIL

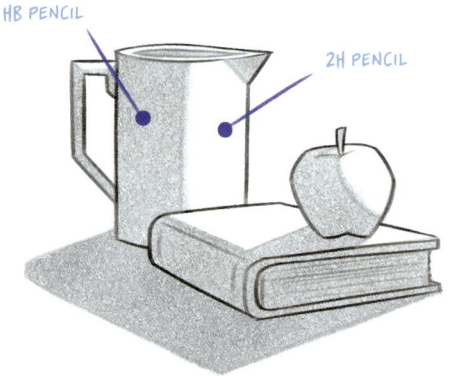

2

Draw the light shadow and the direct light.

Add the first layer of gray in the shaded zones. This gray tone will serve as both the light shadow and the projected shadow. It is the lightest hue amongst the shadows and should not be too dark. Also, add a very light gray to the zone where the light falls to create live light—you'll want to reserve any all-white areas for rays of light.

 Go over the line of separation so that it blends into the light shadow.

3

Mark the medium and dark shadows.

First, we create medium shadows using our shading technique. Next, we reinforce the dark shadow at the line of separation. Because the pitcher and apple are rounded shapes, the shadows are diffused. On the other hand, we will use clean shadows for the book and under the pitcher spout due to their angles.

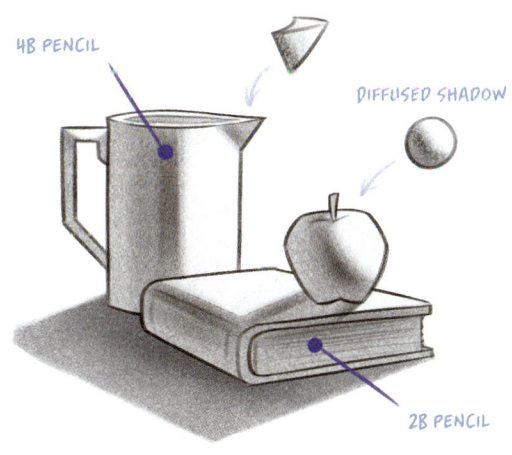

CLEAN SHADOW

4B PENCIL

DIFFUSED SHADOW

2B PENCIL

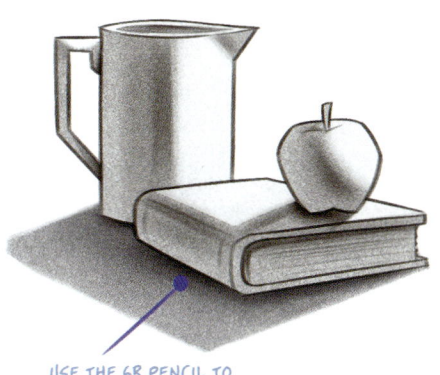

USE THE 6B PENCIL TO ACCENTUATE THE CONTRAST.

4

Add deep shadows.

The last shadows will be the deepest. These shadows fall under the objects and are the darkest. Thanks to their inclusion, the drawing has more contrast. These shadows are also helpful when darkening the projected shadow to achieve a uniform shading.

5

Bring the light in.

To finish, work on the light zones. Using a very light and diffused application of gray, create attenuated light. Lightly darken the zone near the dark shadows to create a softer transition. You can also create highlights by erasing a small rectangular area.

USE A 2H PENCIL TO NUANCE THE LIGHT.

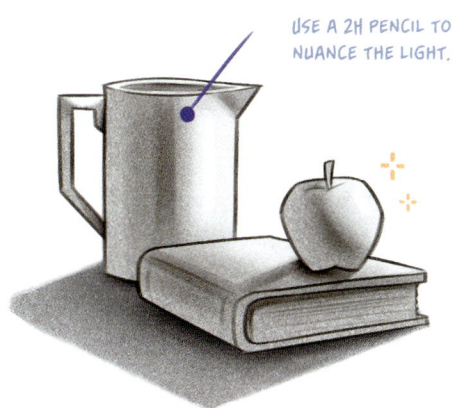

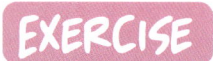

Shade Your Complete Drawing

To practice your work on shadows, it's best to work with a simple model that offers a well-contrasted light. Put what you have learned to work with basic volumes, focusing on the shadows rather than on the drawing.

> **You will need :**
>
> ✳ Your sketchbook or a piece of paper
> ✳ 1 colored pencil
> ✳ 5 pencils (2H, HB, 2B, 4B, and 6B)
> ✳ 1 eraser

Analyze the Model

Always choose a well-lit subject to focus more easily on the light source and the shaded areas. Take time to identify each type of shadow and determine whether the shadow is diffused or clean. Here, the projected shadows are clean, while the attenuated shadows are blurrier.

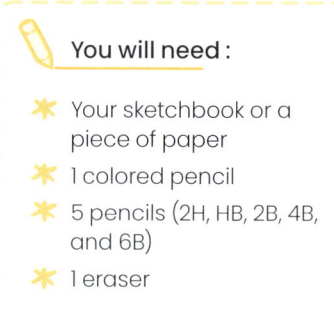

ATTENUATED LIGHT (DIFFUSED)

PROJECTED SHADOW (CLEAN)

DARK SHADOW (DIFFUSED)

The shadowed areas can be simplified into an abstract shape, which you can then transfer to your sketch.

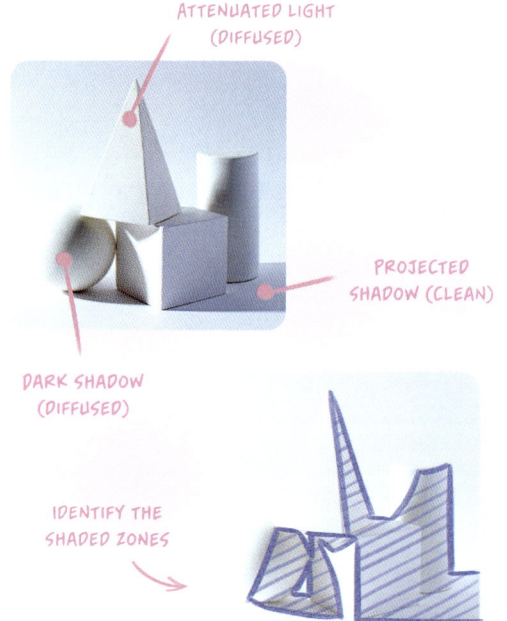

IDENTIFY THE SHADED ZONES

The Drawing Step by Step

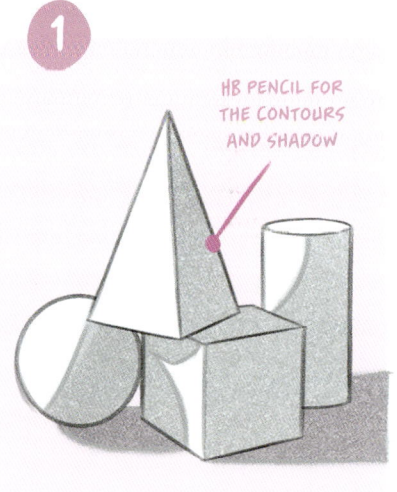

HB PENCIL FOR
THE CONTOURS
AND SHADOW

4N PENCIL FOR
DARK SHADOWS

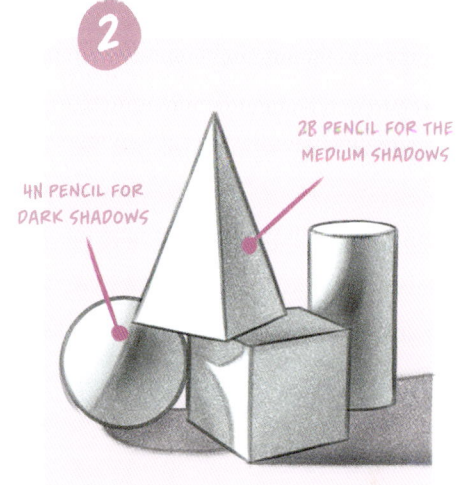

2B PENCIL FOR THE
MEDIUM SHADOWS

Create your sketch of volumes, then add the line of separation to mark the shaded area. Next, add a light gray area for the light shadow.

Add medium shadows by going over the light shadow with light shading. Then, strengthen the dark shadows, which will be more visible on the rounded forms.

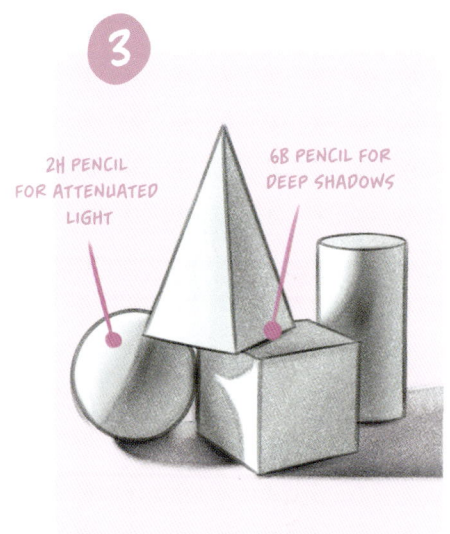

2H PENCIL
FOR ATTENUATED
LIGHT

6B PENCIL FOR
DEEP SHADOWS

Finally, add the shadows that fall under the objects. Darken the faces of the cube and pyramid. Then, add some nuance with a very light gray for the attenuated light.

11
COLOR

29 CHARACTERISTICS OF COLOR

In order to create a successful drawing, it is crucial to understand the role of colors. The color wheel is a visual key that clarifies the relationships between colors. This too is often used in drawing to help us understand how to combine colors in a harmonious way. It's very helpful to create coherent and balanced palettes.

THE WHEEL ILLUSTRATES 12 COLORS.

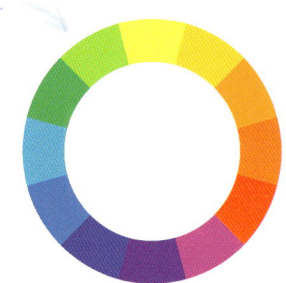

The Color Wheel

The color wheel is a visual tool that shows the relationships between colors. It is frequently used in drawing to understand how to harmoniously combine colors. It is very useful for creating cohesive and balanced palettes.

Primary, Secondary, and Tertiary Colors

The color wheel is divided into three categories of colors: primary, secondary, and tertiary. Secondary colors are a mix of primary colors, while tertiary colors are a mix of secondary colors. The twelve colors of the wheel allow for the creation of all other colors.

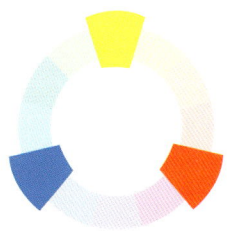

PRIMARY COLORS

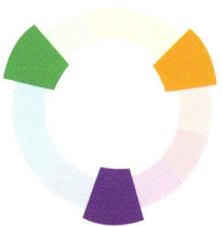

SECONDARY COLORS

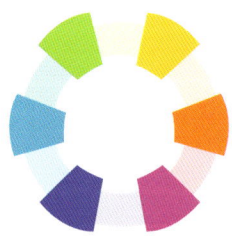

TERTIARY COLORS

Hue, Value, and Saturation

Let's take a closer look at the three fundamental characteristics of a color: hue, value, and saturation. Each color exhibits distinct levels of these dimensions, which makes it unique.

Hue

The hue corresponds to the nature of the color, allowing us to easily identify reds, blues, yellows, and so on.

THE 12 HUES

Value

The value (or luminosity) of a color indicates its degree of clarity or obscurity. The closer the color is to white, the lighter it will be; and the closer it is to black, the darker it will be.

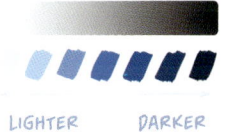

LIGHTER   DARKER

Saturation

The saturation (or intensity) corresponds with the strength of the color. This is determined by the level of gray in the color.

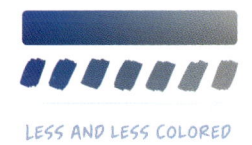

LESS AND LESS COLORED

The Temperature of a Color

Each color expresses a temperature: warm or cool. Using the color wheel, it's easy to divide the colors into two categories: warm tones and cool tones. Green, blue, and purple are considered cool tones, while orange and pink are considered warm tones. Knowing how to categorize the colors makes harmonizing your color palette easy.

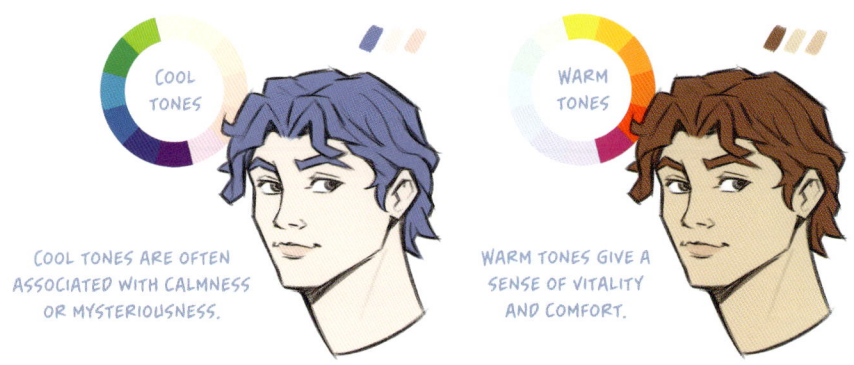

COOL TONES

WARM TONES

COOL TONES ARE OFTEN ASSOCIATED WITH CALMNESS OR MYSTERIOUSNESS.

WARM TONES GIVE A SENSE OF VITALITY AND COMFORT.

30 COLOR HARMONIES

How do we select and combine colors? There are some helpful rules for creating harmonious palettes. By employing these, your use of color will be balanced and aesthetically pleasing.

Creating and Testing Palettes

Before adding color to your drawings, some thought and research will go a long way. You can begin by choosing five or six colors to create a baseline reference. This prior preparation of your palette frees you to experiment with different combinations and make any necessary adjustments to ensure the harmony of the colors.

DRAWING SQUARES OF COLORS, SIDE BY SIDE, IS A GOOD WAY TO TEST A PALETTE.

Harmonizing the Value and Saturation

To create logical color palettes, let's go back to the three fundamental characteristics: hue, value, and saturation. The hues can vary, but their value and saturation must be similar to have good harmony. Radical differences in value and saturation between the colors creates imbalance.

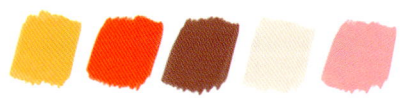

THE COLORS GO TOGETHER WELL, BUT THE DIFFERENCES IN VALUE AND SATURATION MAKE THE PALETTE LESS HARMONIOUS.

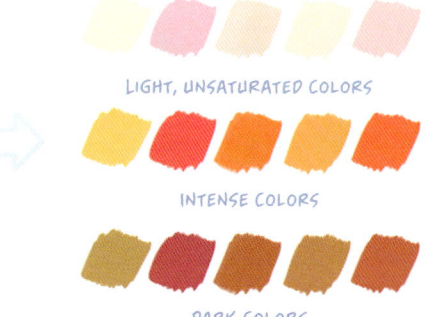

LIGHT, UNSATURATED COLORS

INTENSE COLORS

DARK COLORS

Four Formulas for Creating Harmony of Color

Rather than choosing hues at whim, simple formulas based on the color wheel can be used. After using these formulas to choose the colors of your palette, you'll be able to work with them by varying their values (lighter or darker) and saturations (more intense or less intense).

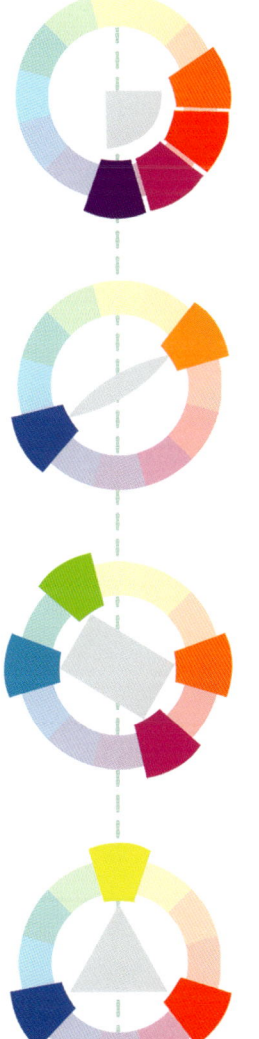

Analogous

These colors are adjacent to each other on the color wheel and create a soft and harmonious feel.

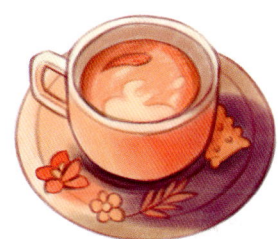

Complementary

These colors are opposite one another on the wheel. We use these to accentuate a specific part of the drawing. Here, the orange tea has touches of blue.

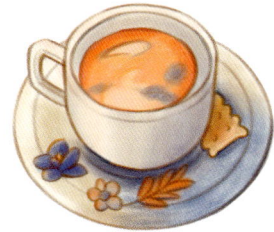

Double-complementary

These colors expand the range of colors. They also bring more depth and create a warm/cool effect that is interesting.

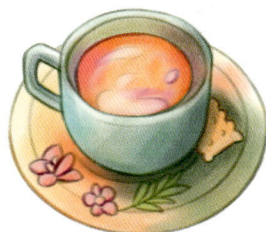

Triad

This is a group of three colors that are equally positioned on the color wheel. They create a dynamic effect, bringing a touch of fantasy to the drawing.

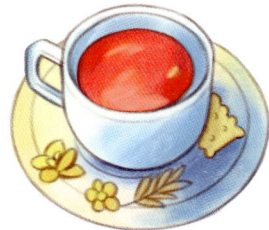

31 | SHADING IN COLOR

Whether we are using colored or drawing pencils, shading and the harmony of colors abide by the same principle. There are simple rules to follow to give depth to shadows in colored drawings, thus giving you a more intense and realistic drawing.

Prioritize Analogous Colors

When we begin to draw, we have a tendency to choose colors based on instinct. We lighten with white, and we shade with black. While this approach seems logical, it leads to dull drawings. To shade and lighten a drawing in color, it's best to use colors that are analogous to the main color. You can refer to the color wheel to select a hue for the light and another for the shadows.

To give shadow to a blue object, instead of using black, choose a purplish hue. For adding a touch of light to the same blue object, choose a color from the other side of the color wheel.

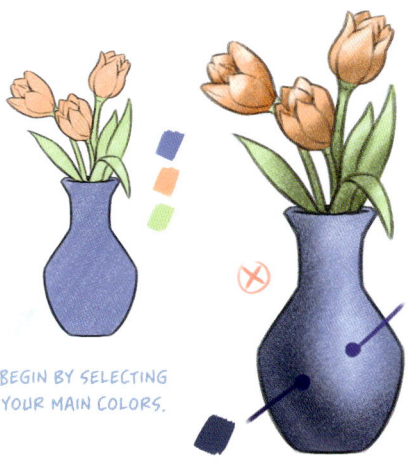

BEGIN BY SELECTING YOUR MAIN COLORS.

USING BLACK AND WHITE TO CREATE SHADING WILL GIVE YOU A DULL DRAWING.

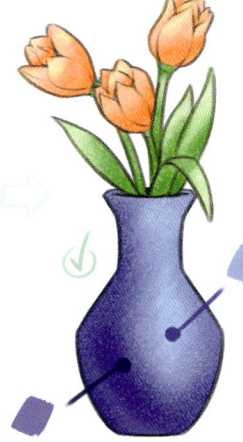

CHOOSING ANALOGOUS COLORS GIVES YOU A LIVELIER DRAWING.

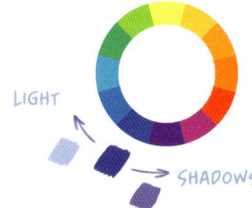

LIGHT

SHADOWS

Adjusting the Value, Saturation, and Hue

To create beautiful colored shadows, it's crucial to adjust these three parameters of your base color—here, orange. For the light, choose the adjacent hue—yellow—and go for a lighter, less saturated nuance. For the shadows, pick the color on the other side of the base color—here, red.

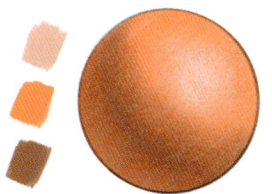

IF YOU ONLY MODIFY THE VALUE OF THE COLOR, YOU WILL HAVE A DULL DRAWING.

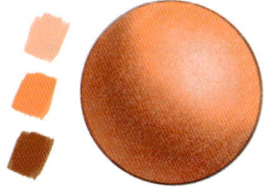

IF YOU MODIFY THE VALUE AND THE SATURATION, YOU WILL ALREADY HAVE A MORE ACCOMPLISHED DRAWING.

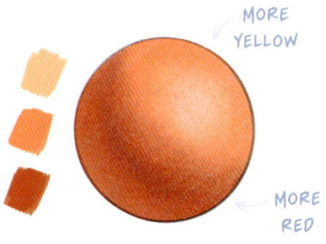

MORE YELLOW

MORE RED

BY ADJUSTING THE HUE AS WELL, YOU WILL CREATE A NATURAL AND VIVID DRAWING.

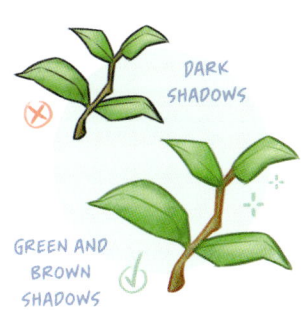

DARK SHADOWS

GREEN AND BROWN SHADOWS

Colored Lines

To intensify the colorful and vivid effect of a sketch, replace your drawing pencil with a colored pencil. Choose a pencil with a shade that is close to the main color of your drawing, but more saturated and slightly darker! For a plant, a dark green pencil is ideal.

🍃 IN THE KNOW

Preparing your color palette ahead of time will help you to identify the hue of the colored pencil you'll use to work on shading. To shade this yellow flower, rather than pressing harder on the yellow colored pencil, use an orange pencil for a more realistic drawing.

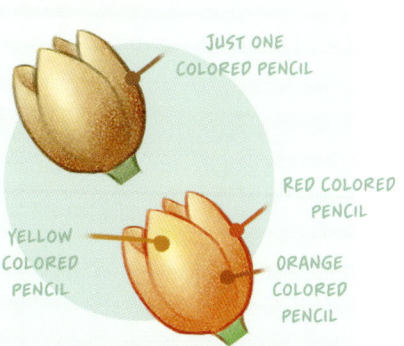

JUST ONE COLORED PENCIL

RED COLORED PENCIL

YELLOW COLORED PENCIL

ORANGE COLORED PENCIL

EXAMPLE

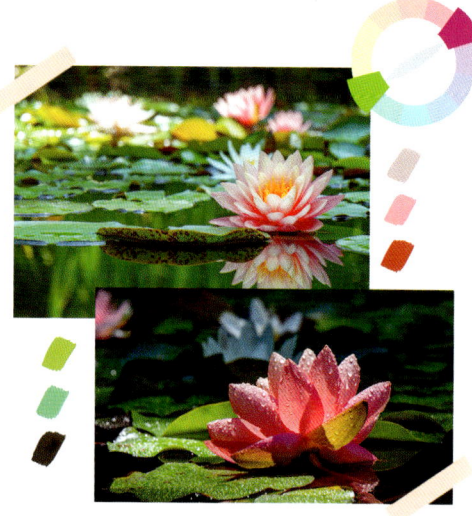

1

Analyze the colors.

To use colors in a realistic way, look for photos to inspire you. Analyze the colors in the photos, studying the harmony of hues. Here, for example, we find complementary colors: pink for the flower and green for the lily pads.

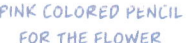

PINK COLORED PENCIL
FOR THE FLOWER

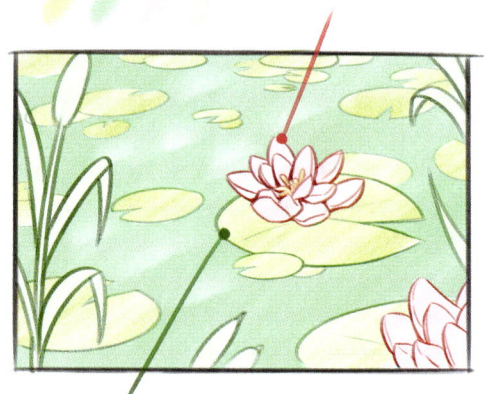

A DARK GREEN PENCIL
FOR THE VEGETATION

2

Begin with light colors.

Select colored pencils that match the hues in the photo. For the lighter, nuanced areas, keep your hand very light: these colors represent the light. Then, leave some empty spaces in the water to create a natural effect.

To make the task easier, you can first create a light sketch with a 2H pencil. Go over this with the colored pencils to create your colored foundation.

③ Increase the saturation.

Now, we can decide where to situate the light source. Here, we position it to the top left of the flower. Next, go over the colors you have already placed with the same colored pencils to intensify them, avoiding areas where you see more live or attenuated light.

KEEP THE CONTOURS BLURRY TO CREATE SHADING.

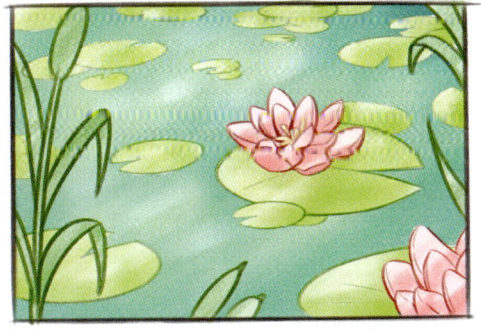

INCREASE YOUR PENCIL PRESSURE TO BLEND BETTER.

CREATE GRADIENTS TO CONNECT THE SHADOWS TO THE MAIN COLOR.

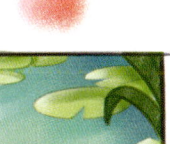

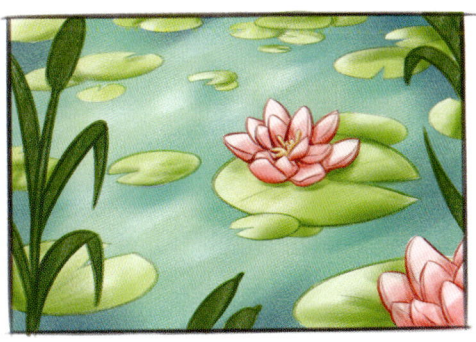

④ Add the shadows.

Add the new hues to create the shadows. For the center of the flower, pick a darker, more saturated pink, close to red. To shade the lily pads and water, choose a saturated green, closer to blue.

⑤ Give intensity to the dark shadow.

We finish with the darkest touches of the drawing: the deep shadow. To enhance the contrast, we will introduce shades of darker colors to showcase the light. We can apply our valuable knowledge about the nature of shadows to create colored shadows in our drawing.

DARKEN UNDER THE ELEMENTS.

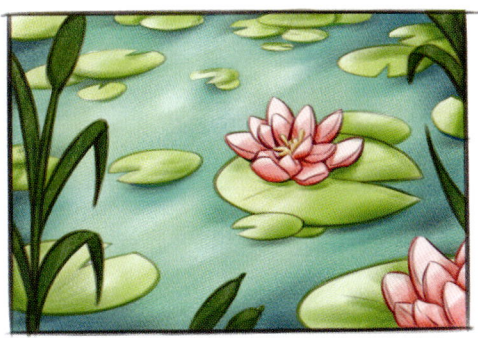

Color a Drawing

To add color to a drawing, it's important to begin with simple objects that offer very basic volumes. The main goal is to practice choosing appropriate colors—both for the object itself and for its shadows.

You will need :

* Your sketchbook or a sheet of paper
* Colored pencils
* 1 drawing pencil
* 1 eraser

Analyze the Model

The nuances of color in a photo are always interesting to observe—and to create a livelier drawing, we must adapt them. Here, we see the pumpkin has a lot of orange color tone. We can simplify this by using only three colored pencils: one orange for the main color, an orangish red for the shadows, and a yellowish orange for the light.

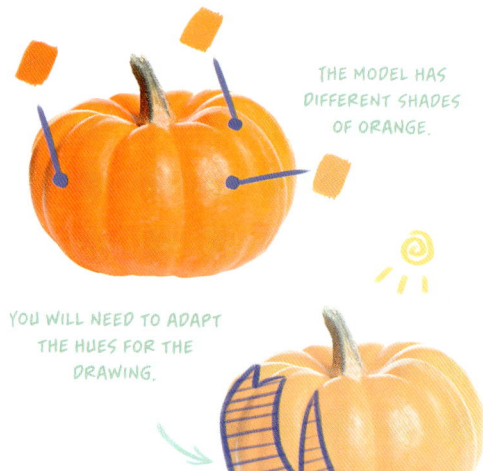

THE MODEL HAS DIFFERENT SHADES OF ORANGE.

YOU WILL NEED TO ADAPT THE HUES FOR THE DRAWING.

MARK THE SHADOW ZONE AND THE LIGHT ZONE.

As you apply what you have learned about shadows and light, focus on the two distinct zones to more easily shade with color.

The Drawing Step by Step

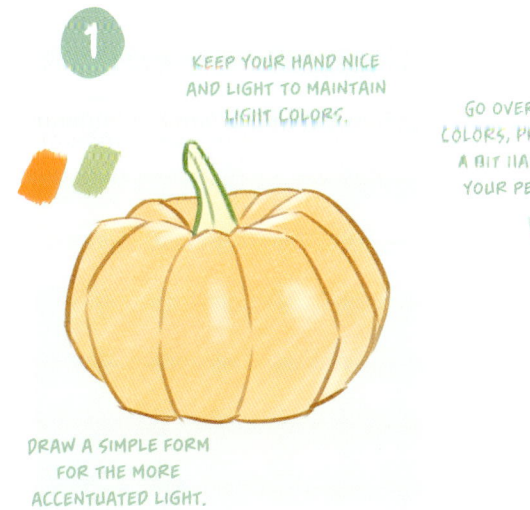

1

KEEP YOUR HAND NICE AND LIGHT TO MAINTAIN LIGHT COLORS.

DRAW A SIMPLE FORM FOR THE MORE ACCENTUATED LIGHT.

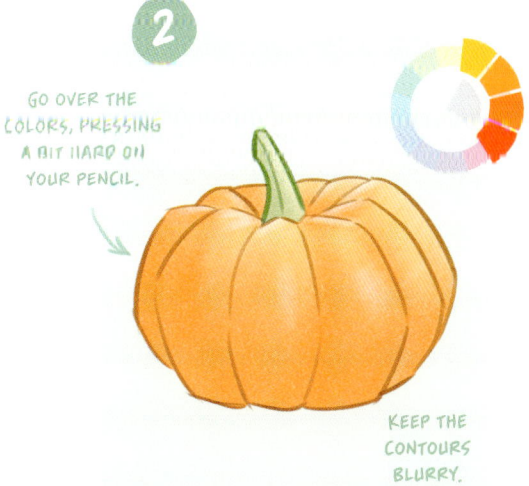

2

GO OVER THE COLORS, PRESSING A BIT HARD ON YOUR PENCIL.

KEEP THE CONTOURS BLURRY.

To begin, apply two areas of color, using the chosen hues for light (yellowish). Keep an empty space for the more accentuated light.

Intensify the colors using the colored pencils you selected while analyzing: orange for the pumpkin and green for the stem.

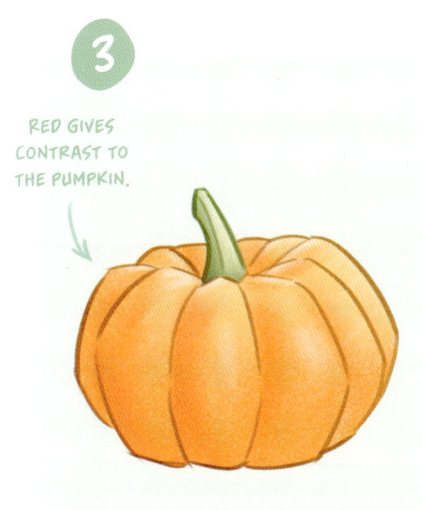

3

RED GIVES CONTRAST TO THE PUMPKIN.

Finally, use the darker, more saturated colors to add nuance to the shaded part of the pumpkin. Push harder on the pencil to blend the shading.

12

CREATIVITY

32 DRAWING FROM YOUR IMAGINATION

Drawing from your imagination will boost your creativity and encourage you to invent your own world. However, drawing from imagination does not mean creating from nothing.

How to Have Original Ideas

Ideas that are original are born from a combination of preexisting elements that offers something unique. Let's take the example of an ordinary object: a bag. By associating it with a new object, like an acorn, we have a more original concept, born from a fusion of two everyday objects.

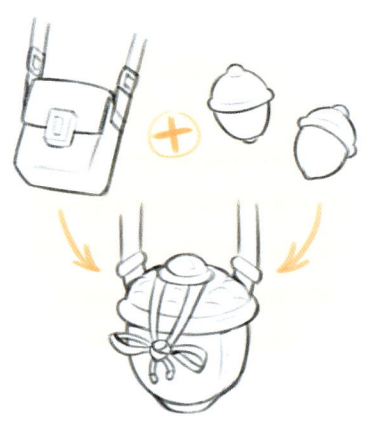

Subjects

Subjects are the main element we wish to draw, whether they be an object, animal, portrait, and so on. We always begin by choosing a subject that appeals to our interest.

SIMPLE OBJECT

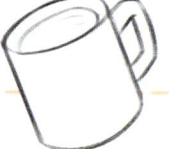

Themes

Next, we integrate a theme to personalize the drawing even more. This might mean adding fantasy, science fiction, or an underwater theme, for example.

MEDIEVAL THEME

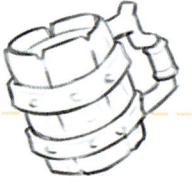

Relying on References

In reality, drawing an object directly from your imagination can be counterproductive. It's difficult to achieve an adequate level of detail, and there's the risk of leaving important elements out. For example, drawing a shoe from memory, we can get the global form of the shoe, but it will lack realism. By observing a model and analyzing its forms and volumes, we understand what a shoe is really made of, and we can thus better represent it.

Drawing based on a model enriches our visual library. We can grasp the function of the object and better recall its forms, allowing us to more easily draw from memory over time.

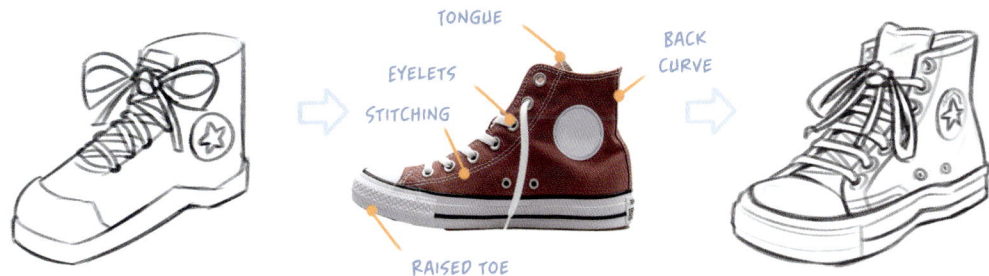

TONGUE

EYELETS

STITCHING

BACK CURVE

RAISED TOE

DRAWING FROM MEMORY MAKES IT NEARLY IMPOSSIBLE TO GET A REALISTIC DESIGN.

IT IS THEREFORE PREFERABLE TO ANALYZE A MODEL TO DECONSTRUCT THE OBJECT.

WE REDRAW THE SHOE FROM A CHOSEN ANGLE, ADDING IN THE CORRECT ELEMENTS.

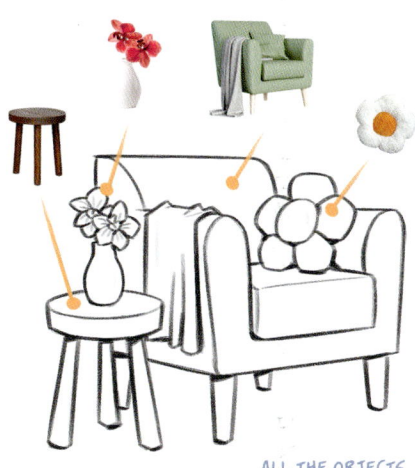

ALL THE OBJECTS TOGETHER CREATE A UNIQUE DRAWING.

Patchwork Effect

Drawing from imagination helps you develop your creativity using elements that already exist around you. To begin, the strategy is to compose a drawing using different references. In other words, rather than using and copying just one object, we assemble several. This is the principle of patchwork. This approach lets us gradually move away from a simple drawing of observation.

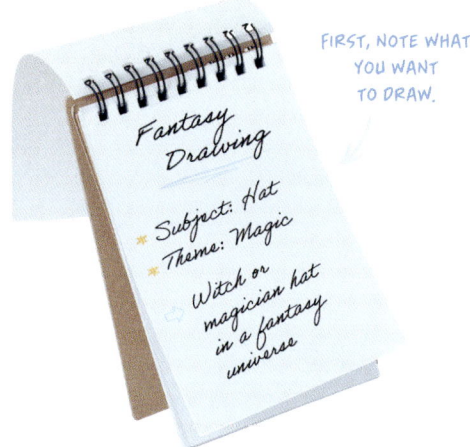

EXAMPLE

1

Choose a subject.

For an original drawing, it's important to reflect ahead of time. Begin by selecting your main subject—here, a witch's hat. Next, come up with a theme to give the object a story and personalize it.

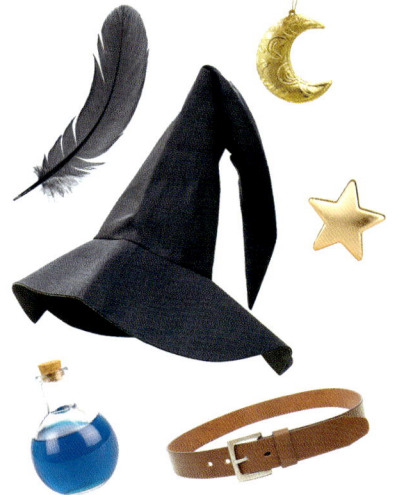

2

Analyze the models.

Before jumping in, gather your models to draw them with more ease. The goal is to create one drawing from several preexisting elements. Choose elements that go well with a "witchy" theme: a feather, stars, a potion, and the like.

Draw the main subject.

First, sketch the main subject by applying the principles you have learned. Define the proportions and forms, then add some volume. Here, rather than just replicating what we see, we can reinterpret it to our liking. In this case, we enlarge the form of the hat.

CRIMP THE END
OF THE HAT
TO MAKE IT MORE
INTERESTING.

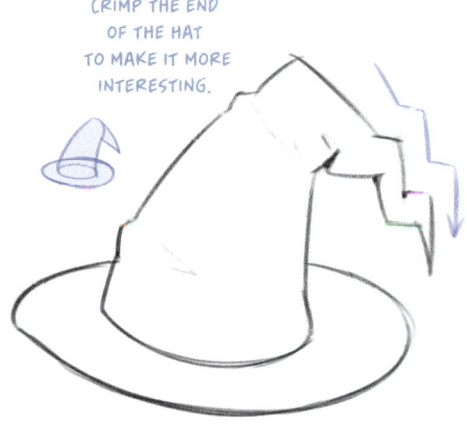

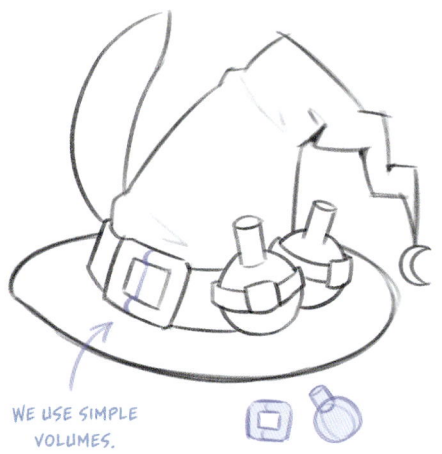

WE USE SIMPLE
VOLUMES.

4

Add a personal touch.

Once the structure is established, determine the position of the chosen elements on the hat. Encircle the hat with a belt, onto which we will place the potions. Place a moon pendant at the end of the hat to justify the twisted part.

5

Add the final details.

To finish the drawing, apply some detail with smaller elements, such as texture. Pay particular attention to the hierarchy of line thicknesses, adding black areas to emphasize the depth of the drawing.

ADD STARS FOR A
MAGICAL TOUCH.

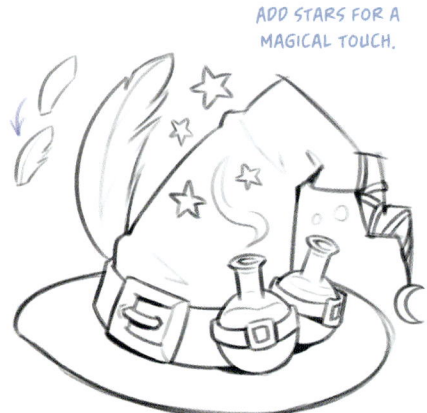

Creating Your First Original Drawing

To inspire your creativity, gather various models to create your first original drawing. Begin by selecting a subject and theme that will give a story and interest to the drawing.

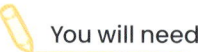

You will need :

* Your sketchbook or a sheet of paper
* 4 drawing pencils (2H, HB, 2B, and 4B)
* 1 eraser

Choose the Models

For this exercise, you will draw a book with a seaside theme. Choose models that you will add to your drawing. There's no limit to the choice of models! The goal is to use the patchwork technique to create an original drawing, combining different sources of inspiration.

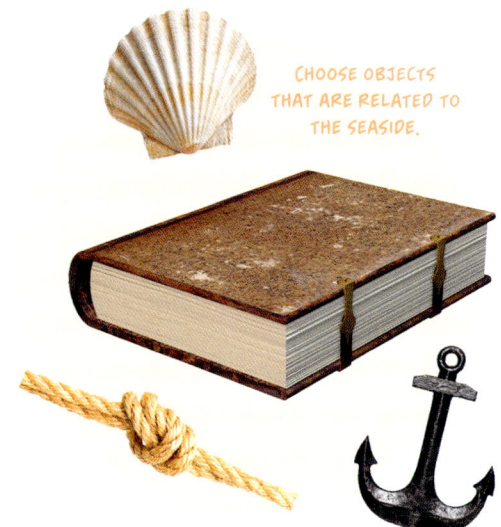

CHOOSE OBJECTS THAT ARE RELATED TO THE SEASIDE.

It's like shopping: You gather the elements you wish to incorporate into your design.

The Drawing Step by Step

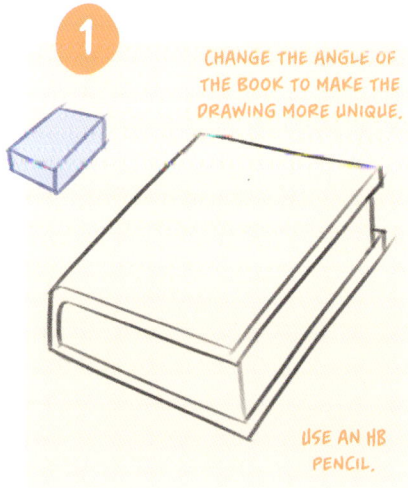

1 CHANGE THE ANGLE OF THE BOOK TO MAKE THE DRAWING MORE UNIQUE.

USE AN HB PENCIL.

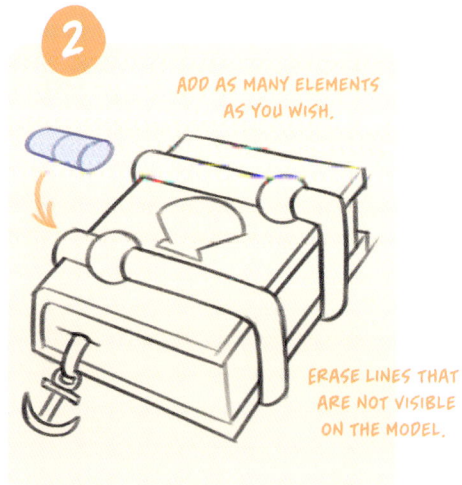

2 ADD AS MANY ELEMENTS AS YOU WISH.

ERASE LINES THAT ARE NOT VISIBLE ON THE MODEL.

Sketch the covers of the book, focusing on perspective. Add thickness to the cover to add volume and depth.

With the same pencil, add elements to personalize the book using basic volumes. For example, the straps surrounding the book can be simplified into a cylindric volume.

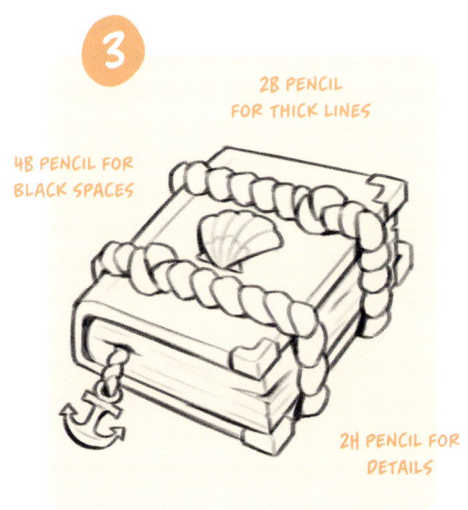

3 2B PENCIL FOR THICK LINES

4B PENCIL FOR BLACK SPACES

2H PENCIL FOR DETAILS

Lightly erase your sketch and go over it using detail techniques. Take care to break up the contours to create relief. Add texture and black spaces to create depth.

33 DRAWING STYLE

Style is the distinctive way we draw, which is individual for each artist. It carries your identity, reflecting your personality and tastes. Developing your style is also a way to develop your creativity and uniqueness.

Finding your Style

The definition of style depends on two essential aspects: your ability to draw and your personality and preferences. The combination of these helps to strengthen your unique style.

Competency

Competency encapsulates all the techniques you've acquired in drawing. Bringing these fundamental principles of drawing with you, you'll have a solid foundation.

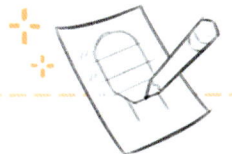

Personality

Personality is manifested through your preferences, that is, what you love to draw and the ambiances you love creating. This is what attracts you naturally, and often this is the reason you have begun to draw!

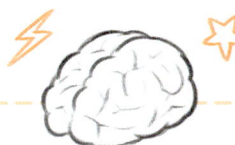

Exploring Different Drawing Styles

There are many drawing styles, such as manga or comic strips, so the first step is to determine the style that attracts you the most and the type of drawing you wish to create. Will it be cartoon characters? Realistic landscapes?

In reality, there are just as many styles as there are artists. Your tastes and experiences will play an essential role in your artistic development. Your creative journey will be unique.

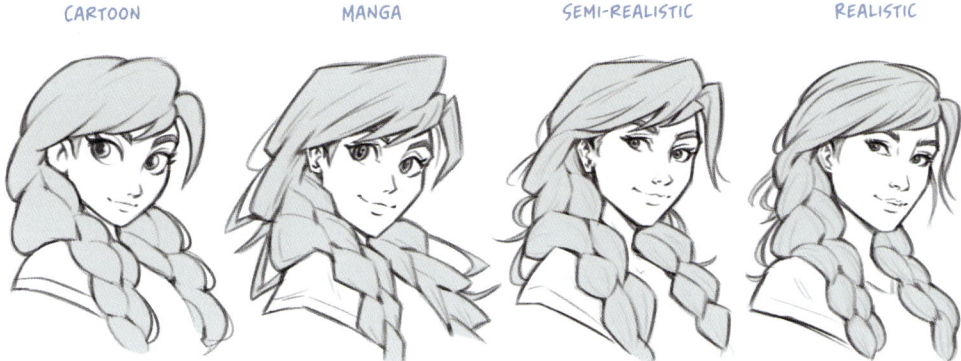

CARTOON   MANGA   SEMI-REALISTIC   REALISTIC

Artists as References

To better understand your preferences and define your style, it's best to begin by researching artists who inspire you and whose work you'd like to imitate.

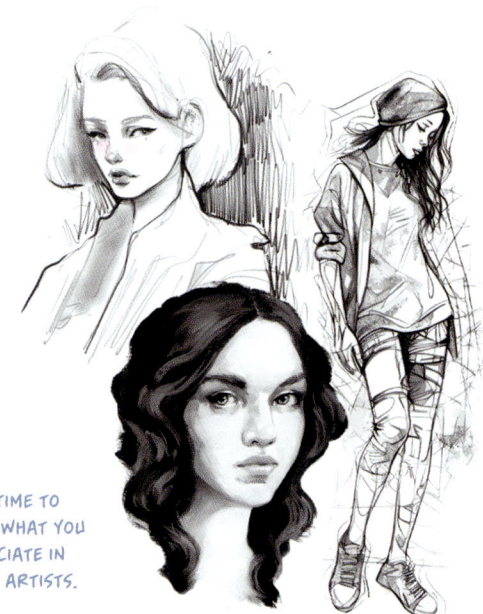

TAKE TIME TO ANALYZE WHAT YOU APPRECIATE IN CERTAIN ARTISTS.

CONCLUSION

THE FINAL PROJECT

To go over all the principles discussed in this book, let's make a complete drawing following the steps we have studied—from observation to the placement of color. As you have discovered, our method consists in drawing in layers. You layer these in your sketch, applying one concept at a time, focusing on each aspect of the drawing before going to the next step.

Observation

To improve your drawing, prioritize drawing from photos of real models. We have chosen the photo of a lion; animals are excellent models to practice with. Refer to the photo at each step to analyze the proportions, perspective, details, and so on. It is necessary to do this several times to possess all the information you need, right when you need it.

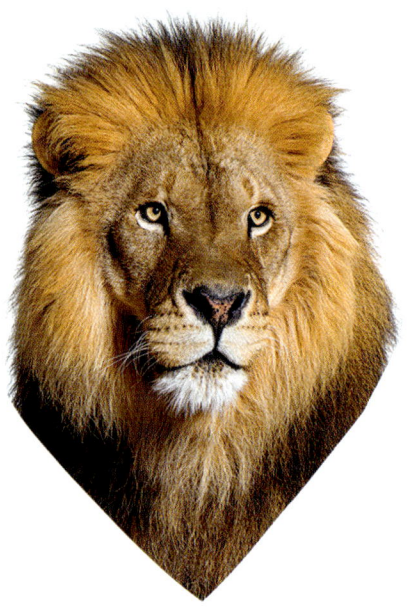

Lines

Draw a silhouette, applying your line skills (see p. 24 and 25) to create a clean silhouette. Use lines that are lightly curved to best deconstruct the angles of the head and muzzle. Begin again several times, if necessary, until you are satisfied with the overall shape of the lion.

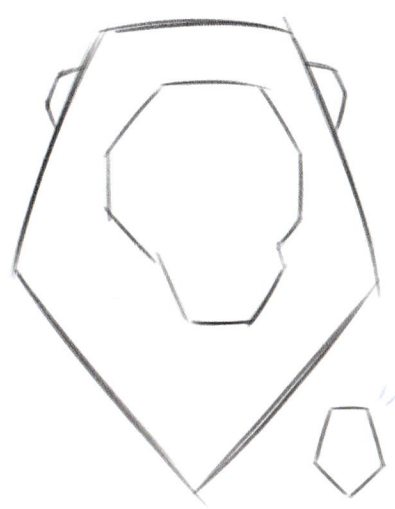

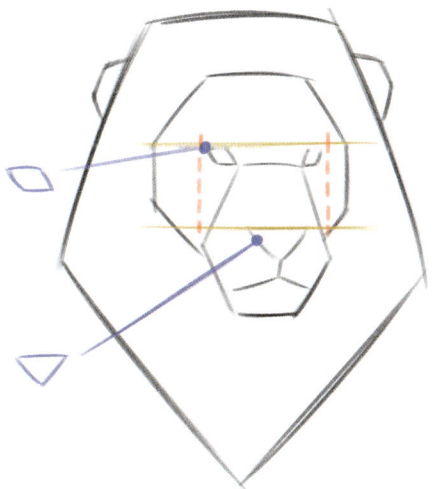

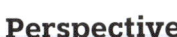

Proportions

Detail the silhouette using the principles of basic shapes and proportions (see p. 32 and 42). Simplify the eyes into a trapezoid and the muzzle into a triangle. Observe the points and check the spacing and rations of each element: for example, the corner of the eye is aligned with the jaw. Take time to correct the drawing until it closely resembles the animal.

Perspective

At this stage, the goal is to understand the orientation of the head and to gradually move to a 3D drawing using the principle of grid lines (see p. 54). Draw a fine line through the center of the lion's head. As we see three-quarters of the head, lightly move the line to the right. This line will allow you to control the placement of the elements and check that they are centered.

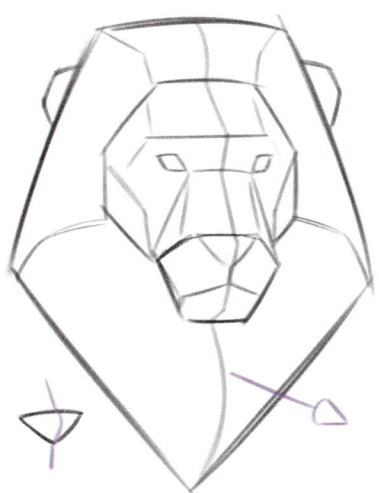

THE FINAL PROJECT

Construction

Using the principles of volumes and construction (see p. 60 and 96), rework the sketch, defining the secondary volumes this time. Divide the fur into three parts to represent its thickness. Refine the muzzle shape with a lightly curved block. Add volume to the thick lips, rounding them more.

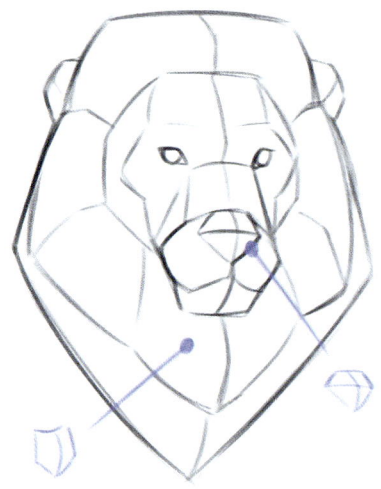

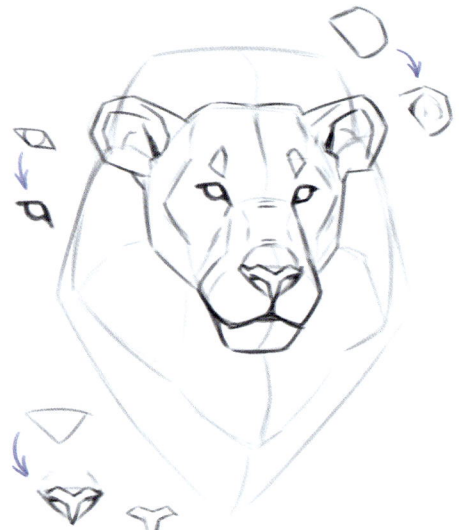

Anatomy

Following the layered approach, lightly erase your sketch to work on the anatomy. Focus here on the face, detailing each element one by one, referring to photos for more correctness. Draw the nostrils with straight lines without too much detail. Darken the corners of the eyes to accentuate their shape. Add triangular shapes just above the eyes to give expression to the lion.

7

Details

Move on to the textures as you have learned to do in the fur example (see p. 120). Use triangular shapes to create puffs of fur and break the contours of the silhouette. Bring more contrast by varying the thickness of lines and adding black spaces (see p. 119). Think about using different grades of pencils to add depth to your drawing.

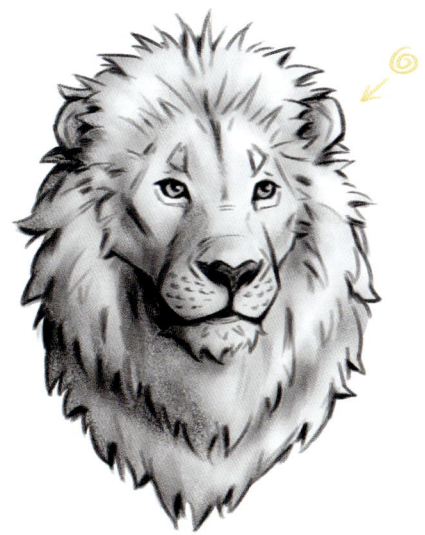

8

Shadows

You can create two types of final drawings: either a shaded drawing with pencil or a colored one with colored pencils. For the first, choose the position of the light source to determine the placement of shadows. Then, apply the eight types of shadows and light (see p. 152) to achieve contrasted and realistic shadows.

9

Color

For the colored version, erase your sketch and go over the contours with a dark brown colored pencil. Next, add shading with the colored pencils (see p. 168). To give more life to the lion, accentuate the saturation of the warm colors. Use red hues for shadows and yellow hues for light to create depth in your colors.

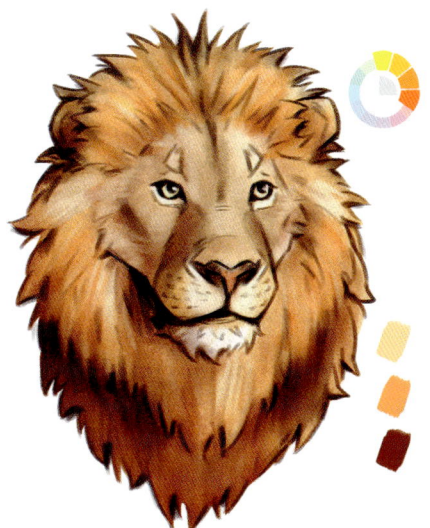

TAKING IT FURTHER

You have studied the fundamental principles of drawing—all that you need to know and master to draw well. Bravo! To go further, it's essential to practice some techniques to become fully independent.

Before a Drawing Session

Now that you have learned the essential categories of drawing, choose just one to work on. Do you want to improve your competency in proportions, perspective, or shadows? It's important to define one specific goal for drawing: tackling everything at one time would be too difficult. You can then select models tailored for this goal.

Don't forget to dedicate time to warming up before your drawing session. This frees the arm and makes a nice transition into your session, improving your concentration and your results.

1

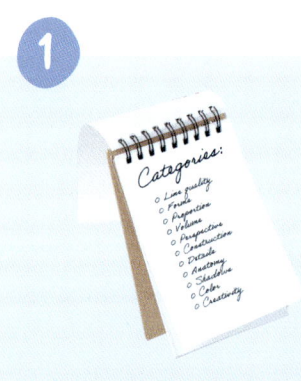

CHOOSE THE CATEGORY YOU WISH TO WORK ON. ONE DRAWING = ONE GOAL.

2

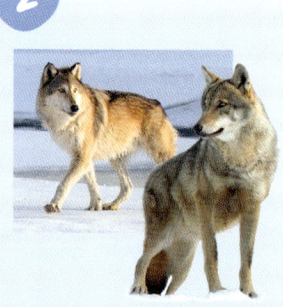

NEXT, DEFINE THE SUBJECT YOU WANT TO DRAW, TAKING CARE TO CHOOSE GOOD, QUALITY MODELS, WITH CLEARLY VISIBLE SHAPES.

3

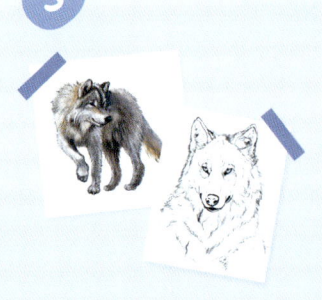

FINALLY, CHOOSE DRAWINGS FROM OTHER ARTISTS. THESE WILL LET YOU STUDY THEIR WAY OF DRAWING AND ALLOW YOU TO OPTIMIZE YOUR SKETCH.

During a Drawing Session

It's crucial to redo your sketch several times to get a satisfying version. It is not a big deal to take your time, erase, and begin again. Redoing a sketch allows you to improve your results. The first sketch is typically not the best one. At times, it's not until the fourth or fifth try that you get the desired result.

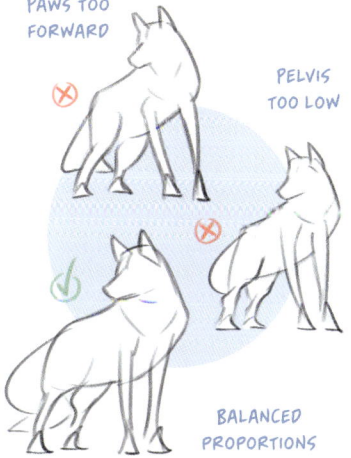

PAWS TOO FORWARD

PELVIS TOO LOW

BALANCED PROPORTIONS

You must constantly look at the model and at your drawing, alternating between the two. Observation is key.

After a Drawing Session

Once the drawing is finished, analyze it in a constructive way. Rather than focusing on the errors right away, look for at least three positive aspects. In this way, you'll change the look you want to give to your drawing and be more objective. Next, note three elements to improve for the next drawing. Thanks to this approach, you will get the best out of your drawings, your motivation will stay strong, and your progress will be visible.

Three Successful Elements

✓ Varying thickness of lines

✓ Simplified texture

✓ Clean, clear silhouette

THINK ABOUT USING THIS POST-DRAWING ROUTINE FOR YOUR FUTURE DRAWINGS.

Three Elements to Improve Upon

✗ The anatomy of the animal

✗ The finesse of lines

✗ The realism of fur

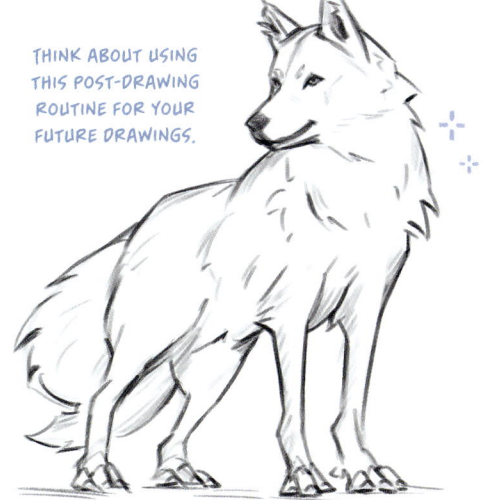

Publication director
Isabelle Jeuge-Maynart et Ghislaine Stora

Editorial director
Émilie Franc et Julie Martin

Editor
Agathe Bourachot

Proofreading
Élise Lejeune

Copy-editing
Laurence Alvado

Art direction
Géraldine Lamy

Design and layout
Valentine Antenni

Cover design
Paul Godot

Manufacturing
Laetitia Messadene

Quarto.com

First Published in USA in 2026 by Quarry Books, an imprint of The Quarto Group,
100 Cummings Center, Suite 265-D, Beverly, MA 01915, USA.
T (978) 282-9590 F (978) 283-2742

EEA Representation, WTS Tax d.o.o., Žanova ulica 3, 4000 Kranj, Slovenia. www.wts-tax.si

Quarry Books titles are also available at discount for retail, wholesale, promotional, and bulk purchase. For details, contact the Special Sales Manager by email at specialsales@quarto.com or by mail at The Quarto Group, Attn: Special Sales Manager, 100 Cummings Center, Suite 265-D, Beverly, MA 01915, USA.

10 9 8 7 6 5 4 3 2 1

ISBN: 978-0-7603-9778-7

Digital edition published in 2026
eISBN: 978-0-7603-9779-4

Credits for this edtion of *Learn to Draw Anything* are as follows:
Cover Design and Page Layout Translation: John Hall Design Group
Photography: All images are from Shutterstock.
English Translation: Domenica Newell-Amato

Printed in Guangdong, China TT 062025